KNOCKUPWORTH

KNOCKUPWORTH

The story of a family

JOHN BAINBRIDGE

First published in 2019
by Kentigern Press

British Library Cataloguing-in-Publication data
A catalogue record for this book is available from the British Library

ISBN: 978-1-9162944-0-0

Designed and typeset by
Carnegie Scotforth Book Production

Printed and bound by Severn

Contents

In memory of
Phyllis Anna Bainbridge
of her brother
Richard Sewell Graham
and of her niece
Ann Isabel Thomlinson

Preface

The Graham family, once the owners of Knockupworth Hall, near Carlisle, were my maternal ancestors. The title 'hall' is applied to a range of dwellings of varying sizes and degrees of distinction. Knockupworth Hall is not a huge mansion but it is an elegant house, suggesting that its owners were rather grander than many of their neighbours in the local agricultural community. In their day the Grahams were well-to-do farmers. Many of them are buried in Grinsdale churchyard, by the banks of the River Eden.

My mother was always interested in our family history but the information she held was from stories passed down to her by word of mouth. She had little opportunity to carry out in-depth research and there were gaps and a few inaccuracies in her knowledge. Sadly, I was unable to seriously begin my own research until after her death. This is the book I would have liked her to read.

I also hope that it may inspire others to research their own family histories, for all families are interesting in their own way.

Heredity

I am the family face;
Flesh perishes, I live on,
Projecting trait and trace
Through time to times anon,
And leaping from place to place
Over oblivion.

The years-heired feature that can
In curve and voice and eye
Despise the human span
Of durance – that is I;
The eternal thing in man,
That heeds no call to die.

Thomas Hardy

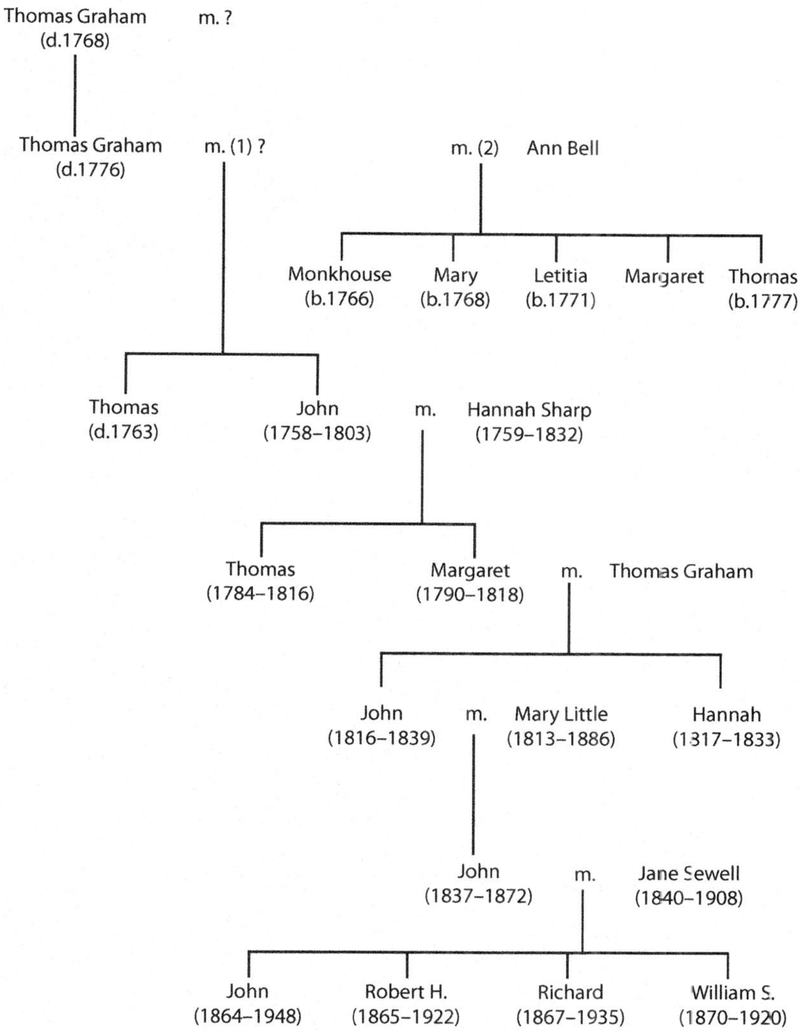

THE GRAHAMS OF
KNOCKUPWORTH

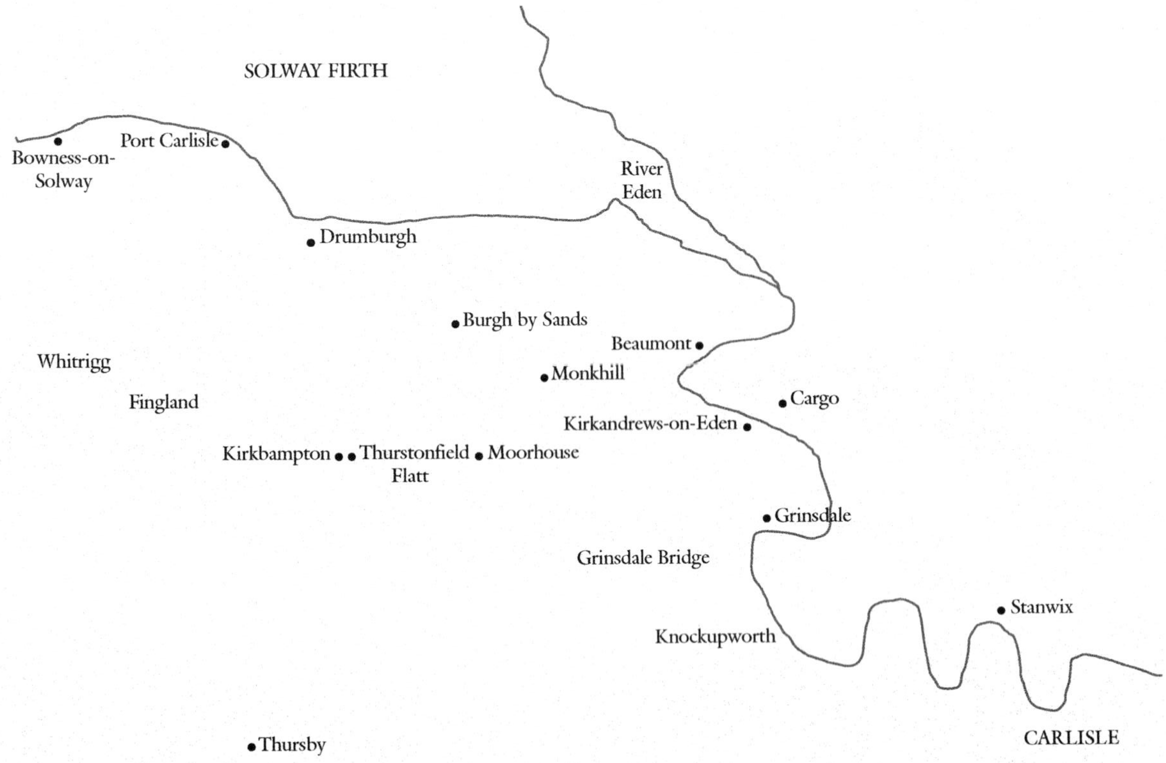

LOCATIONS AROUND RIVER EDEN AND SOLWAY FIRTH (Not to scale)

Note on Text

The place names, Kirkandrews-on-Eden and Bowness-on-Solway, are usually hyphenated, and I have followed this convention. Burgh by Sands, although it is sometimes hyphenated, more frequently appears without hyphens. This is the form I have adopted, except when quoting from contemporary sources in which hyphens have been used.

Introduction

The people of Great Britain went to bed on the night of Wednesday September 2nd 1752. They awoke on Thursday 14th September. This loss of eleven days was brought about by parliament's decision to replace the Julian calendar with the Gregorian system that had been in place in Catholic Europe since the sixteenth century. To those members of a rural community, whose lives were governed by the seasons of the year and by the rising and setting of the sun, time as measured by clocks and calendars was perhaps not greatly significant but this historic event very nearly coincides with the start of this story. Less than twelve months later the Graham family was to take over the ownership of a piece of fertile land on the banks of the River Eden, about two miles to the west of the city of Carlisle.

In 1753, when the Grahams became owners of the land at Knockupworth, in the parish of Grinsdale[1], George II had been king for twenty-six years. Just eight years earlier Charles Edward Stuart had failed in his attempt to overthrow the Hanoverian monarchy and restore his own family to the throne. A contingent of his army had crossed the River Eden between Cargo and Grinsdale on its way to seize Carlisle. The city had briefly fallen into the hands of the Young Pretender and had subsequently been the scene of the executions of a number of Jacobites. Another local consequence of the 1745 uprising was the building of the so-called Military Road, roughly following the course of Hadrian's Wall, to enable troops to be moved more quickly between east and west.

The Graham family's ownership of Knockupworth would last until the nineteen twenties. It saw the reigns of seven monarchs including, until our present queen, the two longest reigns in British history. During its tenure Britain fought wars against America, France, China, Afghanistan and Russia, with the Zulus and the Boers in South Africa, and, of course, with Germany. It saw the expansion of the Empire, the abolition of slavery and, by the time it was over, all British men and forty per cent of women had the right to vote.

Over a period on one hundred and seventy years, seven generations of the Graham family lived their lives against this backdrop of history. Many of these events may have had little direct bearing on them – occurrences in far away places, only to be read about in newspapers. Others had a profound impact on their lives. As farmers they were especially subject to the economic effects of major international conflicts. Sometimes the effects of history would be deeply personal.

Agricultural communities were always subject to the caprice of the weather. There was little respite from the harshness of the climate. They may have lived in an age of great scientific discovery but these advances had not yet extended to making life anything like what we would today regard as comfortable. Medical progress was still relatively primitive. Lives were often short.

Successive generations of the Graham family adapted to the changing world with varying degrees of success. In the end, the struggle to preserve the family's inheritance became too much. But, almost a century after the Hall and its farm ceased to belong to the Grahams, Knockupworth remains at the heart of their history.

Notes

1 It is said that the name of the village may be derived from a Norse farmer who farmed in the dale, or may simply be a corruption of 'Greendale'. (compiled by Revd. G.N. Dobson, *Grinsdale Parish Church; the history of one of Cumbria's smallest parishes* (1981))

CHAPTER ONE

Grinsdale

On 19th February 2001 a routine inspection at an abattoir in Essex found signs of foot and mouth disease in twenty-seven pigs. This was over three hundred miles from Carlisle but the source of the outbreak was traced to a farm in neighbouring Northumberland. As the disease spread, millions of animals were slaughtered and Cumbria, an agricultural county heavily dependent on animal husbandry, was the worst affected area. The epidemic was headline news for months and a personal tragedy for many farmers. Among the more hidden events arising from this catastrophe was one that will conclude our story: it sounded the death-knell for Grinsdale Church.

In one sense Grinsdale, less than four miles from the centre of Carlisle, can hardly be described as remote. The fringes of the city are visible from the village and the eastern boundaries of its former parish merge into industrial estates and urban housing. But most villages, no matter how remote, have a road passing through them that leads somewhere else. Grinsdale has no through traffic. It does, however, have a historical importance that predates its brief involvement in the Jacobite uprising by over a thousand years. The Vallum, the great Roman ditch that was dug to the south of Hadrian's Wall, passes across its land.

The road from Carlisle, that leads west to Burgh by Sands and then heads over Burgh Marsh to reach the Solway coast, turns sharply to cross Grinsdale Bridge. Below is the course of the long vanished railway line to Silloth. From here there is little sign of the village that lies down the 'no through road' on the right. Only a few distant houses are visible among the trees.

Grinsdale is not a big place but when you reach it you find that there is more to it than appears from a distant view. The buildings, including farms, are strung along the road. In my childhood memories the road showed much evidence of herds of cows being walked across it for daily milking. There are more houses now but the shape of Grinsdale has hardly changed. Clusters of new buildings fill in old farmyards and other small spaces. They have not spread out into the surrounding fields nor crept up the road towards Grinsdale Bridge.

Passing through the village we reach the end of this cul-de-sac and come to an ordinary farm gate and an inconspicuous wooden sign directing us to the church. The church itself is still not visible. And here is the reason why religious services were suspended during the foot and mouth epidemic of 2001: for to reach the church we have to walk across a considerable length of open pasture. Worshippers might easily have brought contamination to the grazing cattle.

On my childhood visits we walked among the cattle, avoiding the cowpats. Now the walk is fenced off from the fields but it is still a walk through grass. There is nothing resembling a track. To our right is a steep bank down to the River Eden. The water moves sluggishly from right to left. There was once an island here, large enough for cattle to be grazed, but natural forces and human intervention have combined to change the course of the river and the island has long since disappeared. The church is located above a bend in the river as it sweeps majestically towards the Solway Firth. That it remains invisible until we are close is largely because of the massive copper beech that stands inside the churchyard wall.

Grinsdale is a drowsy place, secluded from the world by having no through traffic. Its church is secluded even from the village. The churchyard has, for centuries, been a place of beauty and tranquillity. Even the new relief road that bridges the River Eden further upstream has maintained a respectful distance. Hidden a little further downstream on the other side of the river is the village of Cargo[1]. My mother recalled, nearly a century ago, playing with the Grinsdale children on the bank of the Eden; they and the Cargo children shouted insults to each other across the water. As there was no bridge for miles, these would have been two entirely separate communities. The Cargo children must have seemed like beings from a different world.

After nearly a year, foot and mouth had been eradicated but services at Grinsdale Church remained suspended. The church was declared closed and eventually deconsecrated. There were five other churches in nearby villages under the stewardship of the same vicar. The Church of England needed to rationalise its resources. Grinsdale church, with its dwindling congregation, was considered superfluous to its needs.

My mother bemoaned the fact that the incomers to the village did not attend services. If they had, she maintained, the church might have been kept open. Perhaps of greater significance was its very remoteness. Attending most churches does not require a long walk over fields. If, in the interests of economy, any of the neighbouring churches had to be sacrificed, Grinsdale's inconvenient location made it the one most likely to have to go.

St. Kentigern's, Grinsdale, has, at the time of writing, still the appearance of a church. A neo-classical building with rendered walls and a small bell-tower, it is well proportioned and unobtrusive. It seems as if it has found a quiet corner and wants to hide away. A huge sandstone memorial on the outside of the south chancel wall stands out like an ostentatious tattoo it wishes it had never had. Stripped of many of its inner adornments, St Kentigern's awaits conversion into a dwelling; for the church authorities have decided that this ancient monument, deemed unsuitable for worship, is suitable for habitation. And, despite having no access road, it requires parking space for cars. For this, several gravestones have to be moved, the graves themselves paved over. In the world of secular finance religion, history and tranquillity give way to economic reality.

Among the gravestones to be relocated are two belonging to the Graham family who once owned Knockupworth Hall, a large distinctive Georgian house, now close to the outskirts of the city. Next to the Hall is a rather older but less distinguished looking farmhouse, which was also a home of the Grahams.

The gravestones stand together on the right hand side as you approach the southern side of the church, between the path and the riverbank. In about 1985 my mother, a descendant of the Grahams, copied down the inscriptions. She did so fairly accurately but the stone was already weathered and I have found that she has made two or three errors. Below, I reproduce transcriptions made more recently by Bridget Casson, a well-known researcher into Cumbrian tombstones. I believe them to be complete and accurate. The first tombstone reads:

> In Memory of John Graham of Knockupworth who died
>
> September 13th 1803 aged 45 years.
>
> Also of Hannah his wife who died June 13th 1832 aged 72 years.
>
> Also of Thomas their son who died June 16th 1816 aged 31 years.

Also Margaret their daughter who died July 28th 1818 aged 27 years.

Also of Hannah who died Sept 6th 1833 aged 16 years.

The inscription of the second reads:

In Memory of John Graham of Knockupworth who died

Novr 23rd 1839 aged 23 years.

The days of my youth hast thou shortened, among thine elect may I be numbered, Oh Lord.

(Below this inscription there has been left a space for his wife's name to be added.)

Also of John their son who died at Whitrigg July 24th 1872 aged 35 years.

Also of Jane his wife who died at Knockupworth Hall February 10th 1908 aged 68 years.

Also their second son Robert Hodgson solicitor Carlisle born 12th Aug 1865 died at Knockupworth 10th March 1922 aged 56 years.

On the reverse of the second gravestone is an inscription to John and Jane's eldest son, John, who died in 1948. Their other sons, Richard (died 1935) and William Sharp (1920) are buried in separate graves nearby.

Ever since my mother made her own copies of the inscriptions I have shared her fascination with our Graham ancestors. As well as a general desire to learn more about our family history there were some specific mysteries thrown up by these memorials:

1. Was Thomas, the last named male on the first headstone, the father of John whose name appears at the top of the second?
2. Could he also have been the father of the mysterious sixteen-year-old Hannah – the gravestone giving no clue as to her identity. This seemed unlikely, as he died some time before her birth – though just possibly not before her conception. Evidence from a newspaper announcement of Hannah's death showed that her father *was* called Thomas Graham but this seemed to be a living Thomas Graham – so if not the Thomas in the grave, who could he be?
3. A space was left on the second headstone for the name of John's widow but it was never added to the stone. My mother

believed that she had remarried and may have gone to live in Liverpool. It was not unlikely that a young woman, widowed in her twenties, would have remarried – and yet the space was left for her name when her son died over thirty years later. Surely then, there must still have been an expectation that she would be buried in the family grave? Who was this 'missing lady'? There seemed to be no clues about her identity.

4. Two of the sons of John and Jane Graham had middle names – Robert Hodgson and William Sharp. Hodgson was easy to explain – it was the family name of their maternal grandmother. For Sharp there was no known explanation. And yet the name would not have been plucked out of thin air. Somewhere there must be a family connection to someone with the surname Sharp.

Recently a fifth mystery has emerged. A story appeared on the Internet about the history of Ayton Hall in North Yorkshire. A nineteenth century occupant of the Hall was said to have been Thomas Graham, son of Thomas and Ann Graham of Knockupworth House near Carlisle. According to the article Thomas had an older brother called Monkhouse Graham, a Liverpool merchant, who died at a young age making bequests to his mother and various siblings in his will.[2] If this story was authentic it revealed a branch of the family of which I had never heard. And I was sure that my mother, from whom all my existing knowledge of her family came, must never have heard of them either. Were these hitherto unknown Grahams really connected to our family?

My mother, born Phyllis Anna Graham in 1916, was a rich source of anecdotal information and she had in her own small way attempted to solve some of the mysteries. But she did not have the advantages of information technology and, unfortunately, I was unable to get very far with my own research before her death in 2013. Her stories inspired my investigations, in which I set out to fill in the gaps in her knowledge and answer the questions we pondered together.

I acquired a good deal of information through Internet research into census records and newspaper archives but none of the above questions had been answered. Going back to the time before the first census in 1841 required more diligent investigation. My cousin, Ann, and I spent several days in the Cumbria Archives in Carlisle, looking at parish records and wills of Graham family members. Since then I have made some fortuitous email contacts that have provided further information. We have uncovered some fascinating stories and, I think, solved most of the mysteries. Some of the answers have been totally unexpected.

Notes

1 Cargo; the unusual name of the village is believed to be derived from 'Carig Howe', meaning 'the rocky eminence'. (T. Bulmer & Co, *History Topography and Directory of Cumberland,* 1901 Edition)

2 Alice Barrigan: North Yorkshire History, northyorkshirehistory.blogspot.uk, 23rd June 2014

CHAPTER TWO

The Mill Builder

Next to the Graham family graves in Grinsdale churchyard is a memorial dedicated, in 1790, to James Robson of Knockupwards and subsequently to other members of his family. This gravestone predates the oldest of the Graham memorials by a little over a decade. James Robson was a neighbour of the Grahams; he may possibly have been a tenant or an employee of theirs, though the size and style of the headstone suggest that he was not without status and that his family was not poor. Although he lies close to the Grahams in death there may be little to connect him to them in life.

Today, when we think of Knockupworth we think of the Hall, of its adjacent farmhouse and of the land that the Grahams once farmed. But this may not always have been the case.

A book of place names, published in 1849, defines 'knock' or 'cnoc' as a Celtic word for a low hill and gives as an example: 'Knockupworth, *cnoc-up-weorth*, a village in Cumberland.'[1] It is difficult to think of Knockupworth as anything so substantial as a village but it may well have been a settlement – a few scattered farms, perhaps – that was once an outpost of Grinsdale parish. The hill or 'cnoc' is also referred to in the report of an archaeological survey conducted in 2011. The site of the survey is described as being 'located on the top of a small hill, overlooking the River Eden.' Referring to a volume of *The Place Names of Cumberland,* published in 1943, it states:

> Knockupworth may have been recorded as early as 1290 as *cnochubert,* and could derive from the old Irish *cnocc*, meaning hillock, and the Germanic personal name of Hubert. The topographical nature of the area, which features a very conspicuous rise, is certainly consistent with *cnocc* as a descriptive term.[2]

This is undoubtedly an appropriate description for the site of the archaeological dig but it hardly applies to the location of Knockupworth

Hall, which lies a short distance to the south-east and where the land is quite flat. If there was a settlement known as Cnochubert or Cnoc-up-weorth, and later as Knockupworth, the heart of this community is likely to have been around the hill itself rather than the place where the Grahams built their home.

It is difficult to ascertain for how long this community existed and how much of it remained by the start of our story. Census records from 1841 and 1851 suggest that by the time the earlier book of place names was published the name 'Knockupworth' was almost entirely limited to buildings connected with the Graham family's farm. But, for the first few years at least, they may have had neighbours, such as the Robsons, who lived in nearby dwellings that were said to be located in a place that was loosely identified as 'Knockupworth'. They would not necessarily be living on land owned by the Grahams, nor have a direct connection with the family. In the early years of the twentieth century there was a field on the Grahams' land that was still known as Bessie's Croft. The name suggests that this may have once been a farmstead rather than simply a field. Had its land been absorbed into the Knockupworth Hall estate and its buildings disappeared? And might other local dwellings have disappeared in the same way?

It seems certain that the name Knockupworth, or Knockupward, or Knockupwards, or Knockupboard, or Knockupert, or Nacupath, did not merely refer to the Hall and the farm but that they took their names from an established location.

The various spellings of the name – appearing as 'Knockupwards' on the Robson gravestone, 'Knockupward' in an early family will, and with other variations elsewhere – may also indicate inconsistencies in the way the word was spoken. It appears as 'Knockupboard' in a death announcement in a local newspaper and 'Knockupert' in a Quaker register. When read aloud these latter two spellings sound very similar, and are also remarkably similar to 'cnochubert', the supposed origin of the name. This leads me to think that this may be close to the way the word was spoken by ordinary people at the time and that the conventional spelling with the 'worth' ending was an attempt to gentrify the name.

An eighteenth century country parish would have many farms and other dwellings scattered within its boundaries. While the inhabitants of the place known as Knockupworth may have lived a little upstream from Grinsdale village, they were part of the same parish.

A church guidebook, published in 1981, records that: 'In 1747 the parish had about 22 families, 1 Quaker, 1 Presbyterian: in 1750, it consisted of 18 houses.'[3]

Three years after this second count was recorded, and less than a decade after the Jacobite uprising, the Graham family became part of this community. A document in the Cumbria Archives, dated 11th August 1753, details the 'surrender and admittance' of a parcel of land 'situate, lying and being in a place called Knockupworth' from Joseph Dacre Esq. to Thomas Graham, his 'heirs and assigns'.[4] The document refers to an annual rent of 15s 9p, but makes no mention of any other payment.

Who was the Thomas Graham to whom Joseph Dacre surrendered this 'parcel of land'?

During the years that followed two adults with this name were described in records as being 'of Knockupworth'. One died as the year 1767 was coming to an end. He was buried at St Mary's in Carlisle and is recorded in the burial register of that parish:

> St. Mary's Parish Register: 2nd January 1768, Thomas Graham of Knockupworth, buried.[5]

We must suppose this to be the father of the second Thomas Graham, who died in 1776. The estate may have passed from father to son on the death of the first Thomas. However we have found no surviving will to confirm this.

It is also plausible that it was the son who was actually the first owner. We know that he was already living there in the late 1750s; it was there that most of his children were born. He may have been the recipient of this parcel of Dacre's land and his father may have moved in with him to spend his final years at Knockupworth.

That the father's body was taken the short distance from Knockupworth to a grave in Carlisle suggests that the family had previously lived in the city. At this time the nave of the cathedral served as St. Mary's parish church and there was a burial ground for parishioners on the north side of the building. This continued until 1870 when a new church was built to serve the parish.

Regardless of whether he was the first Graham to own the land or had inherited it from his father, the second of these Thomas Grahams was one of its first occupants. We know that he was a millwright. At the time it was common for sons to learn their fathers' crafts and for family businesses to be passed on from generation to generation; if the son was a millwright it is not unlikely that the father was too. But we have no information about the older Thomas, excepting the record of his burial.

One of these Thomas Grahams obtained the land at Knockupworth from Joseph Dacre, perhaps in payment for services rendered. The Dacres were one of the predominant landowning families in the area and would have cause to employ the services of a millwright. Windmills and watermills were crucial to the economy and craftsmen with a high level of engineering skill were much sought after and well rewarded. Thomas Graham undoubtedly became a man of some substance. While not abandoning his trade, he made, with the acquisition of the land at Knockupworth, a transition from craftsman to gentleman farmer.

It would seem that the house that the Grahams built as their first residence on their newly acquired land – the building that may once have been known as Knockupworth House – was almost certainly what I now refer to as the farmhouse. I am advised that this could have been built at any time in the second half of the eighteenth century and could therefore date from the Grahams' arrival in the 1750s. The style of the Hall suggests that it is a later building, probably constructed no earlier than around 1780.

A photograph of the farmhouse, taken in the early years of the twentieth century, probably shows it little changed from when it was built. In many respects its design resembles the pictures that generations of children have produced when asked to draw a house: a two-story building with two windows on either side of a central door. Chimneystacks rise from either end of a slate roof. In the photograph the sash windows are still glazed with small Georgian panes. There is a simple stone door surround. The walls are rendered and painted white. Although it is less elegant than the Hall it is a sufficiently fine building to have conferred a sense of status and gentility on the family. That it was nonetheless a working farmhouse is made clear by the long, windowless agricultural building that adjoins it on the right hand side of the front elevation. The roof height of this building is a little lower than that of the house.

When the younger Thomas moved to Knockupworth he already had one son, also called Thomas. In 1758 a second son was born. John was baptised in Grinsdale Church:

> Grinsdale Parish Register: October 1st 1758, John, son of Thomas Graham of Knockupworth, baptised.[6]

This is the John whose death over four decades later was to be recorded on the first of the Graham family gravestones.

Thomas Graham's arrival in his new home with its attached new business venture did not bring him unqualified happiness. His early years at Knockupworth were to be marred by personal tragedy. Within a short time of the birth of his second son Thomas became a widower. We do not know the identity of the woman who bore Thomas Graham's first two sons. Her death must have occurred between John's birth in September 1758 and Thomas's remarriage in 1764. Life was fragile; childbirth was precarious. It is possible that she may even have died giving birth to John. We do not know her name or the exact date of her death. We have not found her grave.

There was to be further sadness for Thomas. His first son died in 1763. The boy was buried in Grinsdale churchyard. There is no surviving memorial to mark his grave, but his may have been the first burial in the family grave. It would be another forty years before another burial occasioned the erection of a headstone. Thomas's burial is recorded in the parish register:

> Grinsdale Parish Register: May 2nd 1763, Thomas, son of Thomas Graham of Knockupworth, buried.[7]

John must have been very young when his mother died. He would not be last member of his family to lose a parent at a very early age. The twelve-month period beginning with his brother's death in May 1763 was to be an eventful time in young John's life. Though he may not have been aware of its significance he was now his father's heir. He may have suffered a period of illness. If his brother died of one of the many contagious diseases that were endemic in the eighteenth century it is not unlikely that John was also afflicted.

Then, in January 1764, John acquired a stepmother. Thomas married Ann Bell from Tarraby in St Michael's Church, Stanwix. The marriage register describes Thomas as a 'bachelor', a term that has in the past been commonly used to denote a man who is single at the time, rather than, as today, one who has never previously been married.

> Stanwix Parish Register: Thomas Graham of the parish of Grinsdale, Batchelor [sic] and Ann Bell of this parish, singlewoman, twenty first day of January in the year one thousand seven hundred and sixty four.[8]

Ann signed the register with her mark.

Four months after his father's marriage John began his schooling. Still not yet six years old, he was enrolled at Carlisle Grammar School in May 1764:

> 1764. Graham, John (adm. May 14) only son of Thomas Graham of Knock-upward, Greensdale (Grinsdale), co. Cumberland, *molarum fabricatoris*[9].

Molarum Fabricatoris translates as mill builder. John was at this time Thomas's only living son. The term 'grammar school' derives from the original purpose of such schools of teaching Latin grammar. A classical education might not seem particularly useful for the son of a rustic craftsman and yeoman but it reflected his father's status and ambition. Thomas might have an illiterate wife but he intended to have an educated son.

John did not remain an only child for long. Over the next few years his stepmother bore four more children. The first, a son named Monkhouse, was born in 1766:

> Grinsdale Parish Register : Sept ? (date is illegible) 1766, Monkhouse, son of Thomas Graham of Knockupworth, baptised.[10]

The boy's unusual name suggests a link between one of his parents and a family with that surname. While this seems the most likely explanation I have not found any other evidence of this connection.

Three daughters followed; the baptisms of the first two are recorded in the Grinsdale register:

> Grinsdale Parish Register : April 11th 1769, Mary, daughter of Thomas Graham of Knockupworth, baptised.

> Grinsdale Parish Register : June 17th 1771, Letitia, daughter of Thomas Graham of Knockupworth, baptised.[11]

It is perhaps no great mystery that the baptism of their youngest daughter, Margaret, does not appear in the Grinsdale register. At a time of high infant mortality baptisms were often performed with some urgency. If Ann gave birth while she was not at Knockupworth the child may have been taken to another church. But of Margaret's existence there is no doubt; her name appears in the wills of her father, her mother and her brother, Monkhouse.

With Thomas's growing family, the house that had been more than adequate when first built must now have seemed of much less generous size.

We may wonder how John adapted to life with his stepmother and half siblings. We do not know if he learned the skills of his father's craft or if he was destined solely to be a gentleman farmer. Nor do we know for how long he continued his education at Carlisle Grammar School. At the age of sixteen he benefited from the will of one of Thomas's fellow millwrights; in 1774 Peter Barwis of Aikton bequeathed him the sum of five pounds.[12] The will does not make clear if Barwis was related to the Grahams.

Our study of Grinsdale Parish Register confirms the existence of this hitherto unknown branch of the Graham family: the children of Thomas's marriage to Ann Bell. We have not yet established a link with another supposed sibling, the Thomas Graham who later inhabited Ayton Hall in North Yorkshire but we will hear more of him later.

When Thomas Graham enrolled his son at Carlisle Grammar School he was described in the school records as a mill builder. A decade may have passed since he began farming the land at Knockupworth but Thomas was still identified by his craft.

That the story of the Knockupworth Grahams began with the farm in the hands of a man who was not truly a farmer provides symmetry to this narrative. It would end in the same way.

Notes

1 W.A. Williamson. *Local etymology, or names of places in the British Isles and in other parts of the World, 1849.*

2 Oxford Archaelogy North, 2011, *Knockupworth Farm, Burgh by Sands, Cumbria Archaeological evaluation report, unpul rep.* With reference to A.M. Armstrong, A. Mawer, F.M. Stenton and B. Dickins, *The Place Names of Cumberland, Part 1 Eskdale, Cumberland and Leath Wards.* (1943) Cambridge University Press

3 compiled by Revd. G.N. Dobson, *Grinsdale Parish Church; the history of one of Cumbria's smallest parishes* (1981)

4 Cumbria Archive Service

5 Cumbria Archive Service

6 Cumbria Archive Service

7 Cumbria Archive Service

8 Cumbria Archive Service

9 *Carlisle Grammar School Memorial Register* (1924)

10 Cumbria Archive Service

11 Cumbria Archive Service

12 Cumbria Archive Service

CHAPTER THREE

Life and Death in Georgian Cumberland

The story of the Grahams of Knockupworth takes us back over two hundred and fifty years. It hardly needs saying that this was a very different world from the one we know today. Watt had still not perfected his steam engine, nor had Cartwright invented his loom. The great mills of Arkwright and others that would soon dominate much of the northern landscape were still waiting to be built. The Industrial Revolution was on the horizon but it had not yet revolutionised the British economy nor transformed its society. Britain still depended on a rural economy and farms were labour intensive. Goods were manufactured by small-scale cottage industries and the bulk of the population still lived in the countryside.

The inventions that were to pave the way for Britain's industrialisation began to take place during the lifetime of the millwright Thomas Graham. His son, John, would see the revolution gather pace. Although, as farmers, the Grahams were not at the centre of this transformation, living only about two miles from the edge of Carlisle they would not be unaffected by it, for the city was to become a centre of textile manufacture. Its growth from a market town of about 4,000 inhabitants in the middle of the eighteenth century to an industrial city of over 9,500 by the end of that century had advantages for the farmers in the nearby countryside. The increased population needed to be fed. However, as we shall see, the building of large city factories would eventually cost the Grahams their own cottage industry.

Developments in agricultural methods enabled farmers to increase food production to meet the needs of the expanding population. Experiments with crops, and livestock breeding programmes led to better yields and bigger animals. New fodder crops, especially turnips and clover, enabled more land to be put into arable use while maintaining a healthy population of animals. We know that by the fourth decade of the nineteenth century Knockupworth was predominantly a dairy farm and this may well have been true from the beginning. We also have reason to believe that the land was a good deal more wooded than it is today and that a proportion of the ground may have been used to grow flax.

Transport was difficult and, for many, largely unnecessary since most had little reason to travel. Vehicles were, of course, horse-drawn along mainly un-surfaced roads, although the Turnpike Acts led to improvements on major routes. Journeys could be made on navigable rivers and by boats along the coastline but few of the canals that would, for a short time, become so important to our industry had yet been built. And several generations of Grahams had lived at Knockupworth before a railway line was laid across its land.

Thomas Graham died before Britain's transformation had really begun. His children and grandchildren witnessed the early stages of industrial development. Today anyone who has the least acquaintance with period drama, let alone knowledge of history, will be aware of how different eighteenth and early nineteenth century society was from our own. And yet some of the changes are less obvious and may be worth reflecting on.

During the winter of 1776, the year of Thomas Graham's death, the River Thames froze over. This event was less remarkable than we might suppose. It had happened twenty-six years earlier and would happen twice more before the end of the century.

When we reflect on how different life was for our eighteenth and early nineteenth century ancestors we should not overlook the fact that they lived in a different climate. After a relatively warm period during the middle ages, the world was, from sometime around the sixteenth century, plunged into what is now regarded as a little ice age. Though by no means comparable to the great prehistoric Ice Age whose glaciers sculpted our landscape, it was a period of exceptionally cold winters. It lasted until the middle of the nineteenth century. Our romanticised view of snow at Christmas, an event that now hardly ever occurs, is a collective memory from an earlier time. It is a memory awoken by Charles Dickens, who, in his depiction of snowy Christmas scenes, was recalling his own childhood when such events were commonplace.

Though the seeds of future climate change were being sown by the coal-fired industrialisation that was beginning to take place, the so-called little ice age had nothing to do with man's activity. Low solar radiation and frequent volcanic activity are usually blamed for the conditions. The winters were not uniformly cold; there were fluctuations in temperature during this period. But many of those around the 1770s and 80s are among the coldest that have ever been recorded.

The people of the time, having known nothing else, would have regarded such harsh conditions as normal. As farmers, the Grahams would have felt the impact of the severe weather. We do not know to what extent they personally worked on the farm. It is likely that from the beginning they were able to afford an adequate workforce. But even if they did not personally plough the land and herd the cattle – and it is possible that they did some of the work themselves – their livelihoods would have been largely determined by the weather. Harsh winters posed problems for animal husbandry; cold springs stunted the growth of new crops; wet summers could ruin the harvest.

The adverse climatic conditions were not confined to the winter months. The years between 1751 and 1760 saw ten successive wet summers. Several wet summers were also recorded during the following decade. Extreme rainfall at any time of year can have catastrophic consequences, especially in wetland areas. Records and reports of climatic conditions in eighteenth century Cumberland are fairly sparse but there is one event in particular that has gone down in history. This was the overflowing of Solway Moss, an area of bog between Longtown and Gretna, in the winter of 1771.

Bill Shannon, of the Cumberland and Westmorland Antiquarian and Archaeological Society, writes:

> On the night of 16 December 1771, after what was said to have been the heaviest deluge for at least 200 years, Solway Moss burst. A slow-motion mud avalanche spread over some 400 acres of the surrounding area, overwhelming about a dozen farmsteads.[1]

The slow advance of the mudslide enabled property to be evacuated and there was no loss of life. What seems to have made this event so remarkable was the source rather than the scale of the devastation. This was not typical flooding that might be expected from the overflowing of a swollen river. The surge came from within the Moss itself. Shannon writes: 'at times of exceptionally wet weather the sodden peat could swell and swell until it burst.'

The events at Solway Moss in 1771 were not unique but they were unusual and they were 'the first to attract scientific enquiry – and media interest.' Such was the attention given to this occurrence that it inspired the poet George Crabbe, a Suffolk clergyman with no Cumbrian connection, to refer to it in a poem that was not published until nearly forty years after the event:

> As Solway-Moss (a barren mass and cold,
> Death to the Seed and poison to the Fold,)
> The smiling Plain and fertile Vale o'erlaid,
> Choked the green Sod, and killed the springing Blade.[2]

The severe winters continued, culminating in the exceptionally cold season in 1776. The early 1780s brought a short respite from summer rain but now there were periods when the weather was unfavourably dry.

During the warm summer of 1783 a volcanic eruption in Iceland led to reports of a blue haze and dry fog across Europe, resulting in damage to vegetation and respiratory problems in people. It was followed by two successive severe winters. In 1784 snow began to fall in October and lasted until April. The 1780s are reported to have been one of the coldest decades on record. During the long winter of 1788–89, frost lasted from November to early January and a frost fair was held on the frozen River Thames.[3]

While these records do not specifically refer to the Cumberland area we must suppose that conditions in the county were comparable to those in other regions. Being on the west side of the country the climate tends to be a little milder and wetter but it is also a good deal further north than London. If the Thames froze over then it is likely that there would also have been ice on the River Eden. On many occasions during the nineteenth century the Cumberland newspapers recorded the effects of harsh winters and summer storms. But we will return to these at a more appropriate time.

We may conclude that the early owners of Knockupworth, and their employees and neighbours, endured a climate that was much more severe than the one we know today – and that they endured it without the advantages of modern heating and insulation. Today Knockupworth Hall must be a very comfortable house, as indeed it would have been, by the standards of the time, when it was newly built. But, heated only by open fires, it cannot have been so comfortable during the harsh eighteenth century winters. Of course, they would never have known anything else. They may have grumbled about the weather just as we do today but they must have accepted the conditions as normal. It had been the same for generations of their ancestors.

Did their exposure to an adverse climate leave them more susceptible to illnesses? We can imagine them struggling to keep warm during the long winters and getting soaked by snow or icy rain. We can picture damp clothes drying in front of open fires and think of Jane Austen's heroines falling victim to life threatening chills. Even the inhabitants of comfortable houses needed to venture out into the winter cold.

They may have been hardy people, not too many generations removed from border reivers, but their health must have been tested by the climate in which they lived.

It does not surprise us that life expectancy was then much shorter; this must have had a profound effect on people's awareness of mortality and attitudes to death. Today we regard the death of a young person not only as a tragedy but also as an act that seems unreasonably unfair. To our ancestors such deaths may have been just as deeply mourned but they were so commonplace they could never have been truly unexpected. Nancy Mayer on her *Regency Researcher* website says:

> Mourning was a regular part of life in the 18th and 19th Centuries. It was rare to find a family that hadn't experienced death. All families with any pretensions of gentility always had to have the proper clothes on hand for a funeral.[4]

We must think of the Grahams as a family that had such pretensions and one that had as much occasion as most to wear mourning dress. For, while the records suggest that most of the Grahams survived the constant threat of infant mortality, few escaped being cut down in their prime and hardly any reached old age.

For people living before the medical advances of the twentieth century every illness must have been a cause for trepidation. Social conditions promoted the spread of infections; the treatments that today would effectively control them did not yet exist. The poor, living in overcrowded, unhygienic conditions in the growing cities, were most vulnerable to disease. The Grahams – relatively well-off country farmers – may have been less exposed to disease than their contemporary townspeople but infections did not respect social class. The *Carlisle Patriot* on Saturday 3rd May 1817 reported that the Duke of Newcastle had recovered after being dangerously ill with typhus at Clumber Park. And yet this was a disease closely identified with the deprivation of the urban working class.

We have no record of the causes of the untimely deaths of members of the Graham family in the eighteenth and early nineteenth centuries. Death certificates were not introduced until 1837 and, although newspaper announcements of the time sometimes state the cause of death, those of the Grahams are not very helpful. We might make the assumption that our ancestors were largely ignorant of the causes of their afflictions but, while it is true that the term 'fever' may have covered a number of different conditions, by the early nineteenth century a good deal of scientific knowledge had already been acquired and steps were being taken to combat some of the most serious diseases.

Smallpox, a disease transmitted directly from person to person or indirectly by contaminated bedding or clothing, had haunted mankind for centuries and was a leading cause of deaths in the eighteenth century. Edward Jenner's discovery, in 1798, that protection against the disease could be obtained by inoculation with the cowpox virus, brought only a measure of control, for it was not until the latter part of the nineteenth century that there was the necessary legislation and documentation to ensure that most infants were inoculated. Deadly and disfiguring though it was, smallpox did at least have one consolation – even before Jenner's time it had been observed that those who recovered were never re-infected.

The late eighteenth and early nineteenth centuries saw a significant rise in the British population. The death rate fell by a third between 1780 and 1820. Yet, despite medical advances, the building of hospitals and the availability of more fresh food, in some respects public health was declining. The urbanization of much of the population during the Industrial Revolution created an environment in which infectious diseases could flourish. When large numbers of people began living in overcrowded conditions with poor sanitation, epidemics that had been relatively isolated during much of the eighteenth century became widespread.

Typhus had been known as gaol fever. In 1759 it was estimated that a quarter of prisoners died each year from the condition. During the decades that followed an increasing proportion of the nation's poor would find itself living in similar squalor to that of the prison population.

Typhus is caused by bacteria transmitted by lice, fleas, mites or ticks. These can be carried from person to person or brought to humans by rodents, cattle or other animals. Symptoms appear about ten days after being bitten – starting with headaches, loss of appetite, general malaise and a rapid rise in temperature. Though the condition was by no means always fatal, complications could include loss of circulation, leading to gangrene. Pneumonia and kidney failure were also common, while cardiac failure was likely to be the immediate cause of death.

Reports from the early years of the nineteenth century refer to fevers of typhoid type, apparently including typhus. There appears to have been no clear definition of typhoid fever as a distinct disease. Though it has similar symptoms to typhus, typhoid fever has an altogether different cause. Also known by several other names, including remittent fever and gastric fever, it is a bacterial infection transmitted by the ingestion of food or water that has been contaminated by the faeces of an infected person. The resulting fever reaches its peak between seven and ten days after the onset of the disease and continues for up to two weeks, often showing a slight remission during the morning hours. A rash appears during the second week and ulcers may form on the wall of the intestine, sometimes leading to haemorrhaging. Other complications might include heart failure, pneumonia and meningitis leading to mental confusion and delirium. By the end of the third week the victim was likely to be emaciated with marked abdominal symptoms and mental disturbance. If they survived until the fourth week the fever would be beginning to decline.[5]

The Grahams, living in a spacious country house, may have been less exposed to typhus, typhoid and other similarly transmitted diseases than were the inhabitants of the city. Most epidemics of typhoid fever were caused by pollution of the public water supply. Water at Knockupworth was drawn from a well at the rear of the house. We do not know how secure this was from contamination, but food could also become infected by carriers of the disease, by being washed in contaminated water or from soil fertilised by sewage. The Grahams and their servants must have spent time in the city from where they might have brought infection back to the farm. And it is easy to see how typhus, carried by ticks and fleas, would be transmitted to people living and working close to animals.

Other diseases such as scarlet fever, diphtheria, measles and whooping cough caused widespread fatalities especially among the young. Frequent outbreaks of influenza and dysentery added to the high mortality rate. Women were vulnerable to conditions associated with childbirth and the reproductive process in general. In *Perdita*, her biography of Mary Robinson, Paula Byrne speculates that an infection arising from a miscarriage may have brought on the rheumatic fever that afflicted the eighteenth century actress, writer and royal mistress.[6]

The outcomes of diseases were rarely predictable and there often seemed to be little explanation why some people recovered from a fever while others would succumb. It was generally true that the very old and the very young were most vulnerable but most of the Grahams died at ages when they might have been supposed to be at their most robust. In fact the Report of the Carlisle Dispensary for the year 1818 stated that the outbreaks of typhus had in general been 'more violent and fatal with adults than with children and young persons, and with the stout and strong rather than the slender and the weak.'[7] Nevertheless, for most illnesses a person's general health must have been a factor in their hopes of recovery.

Conditions such as allergies and mineral deficiencies were, at the time, little understood and, with little protection against unwholesome food and drink, there was a high incidence of food poisoning. Raw milk was a frequent source of disease.

We do not know if any of the Graham family fell victim to the many epidemics that exacted a heavy toll on the population. It is impossible to think that they would have entirely escaped such infections but there is no record of any of the early fatalities being attributable to these causes. There was, however, one disease that hung heavily over our ancestors and which was not brought under control until relatively recent times – a disease that affected all social classes and which we know to have caused the early death of at least one member of the family.

The term 'consumption' was once commonly used to describe the wasting away of the body from pulmonary tuberculosis. It has claimed the lives of many victims throughout history and reached epidemic proportions during the eighteenth and nineteenth centuries, causing as many as one quarter of the deaths in Europe. It was particularly prevalent in young adults between the ages of eighteen and thirty-five. Free from class restrictions, it caused the deaths of several of our most distinguished artistic figures, including John Keats and at least two of the Brontë sisters. Consumption, which was characterised by a loss of body weight, skin pallor, a persistent cough, breathlessness and extreme fatigue, was at the time considered to have constitutional causes and to be expected in delicate people. And yet, as early as 1720, the English physician Benjamin Marten had conjectured that tuberculosis might be caused by minute living creatures being spread by contact with an infected person.

Tuberculosis is a bacterial infection that is not usually caught through casual contact. Its contraction requires close interaction with an infected person over a lengthy period of time. It was, therefore, a disease that was likely to spread among family members living together in the same household and would persist within a family for several generations.

In announcing the death at Moorthwaite in January 1819 of Ann, widow of Thomas Bowman, aged twenty-one, the *Carlisle Patriot* reported that, 'this is the fourth fatal instance of pulmonary consumption in this family which in seven months has carried off a husband and wife, an uncle and a cousin.'[8]

As Nancy Mayer states, families always needed their mourning clothes at hand.

When people knew that diseases were likely to strike at any time, when their outcomes were unpredictable and their causes little understood, it is little wonder that there was a market for the many so-called remedies that were commercially available. Between 1818 and 1820 the *Carlisle Journal* carried advertisements for Ramsay's Pectorial Balsam, 'so justly celebrated for the relief and care of coughs, colds, asthmas and other pulmonary complaints.'

The claims for Ramsay's cure were modest compared to those for Belton's Genuine British Oil:

> A medicine which stands unequalled for the cure of internal and external Bruises, Lameness, Contusions, Green and other Wounds, Burns, Scalds, Contractions of the Nerves, Scorbutic, Rheumatic, and Leprous Disorders; and taken internally Numbers afflicted with Coughs, Inflammations on the Lungs, and Consumptions have been snatched from the brink of the Grave by the timely use of it.[9]

There was, of course, another power in which people placed their faith – one that, even if it did not save them from mortality at least gave them hope beyond the grave.

Notes

1 Bill Shannon, *John Ainslie's Plan of Solway Moss – Recording a lost landscape. Picturing Places* © British Library; 2016
2 George Crabbe, 'Letter 4, Religious Sects' *The Borough,* 1810
3 Much of the above information about the British climate in the eighteenth century is taken from 'Climate History in the British Isles' – meteorology @ West Moor (www.booty.org.uk.weather/climate/histclimate.htm) and 'British Weather from 1700–1849' (www.pascalbonenfant.com/18c/weather.html)
4 Nancy Mayer, www.regencyresearcher.com
5 Encyclopaedia Britannica
6 Paula Byrne, *Perdita, The Life of Mary Robinson,* 2004
7 *Carlisle Journal,* Saturday 13th February 1819
8 *Carlisle Patriot*, Saturday 2nd January 1819
9 *Carlisle Journal,* Saturday 7th May 1814

CHAPTER FOUR

God, Grinsdale and the Grahams

In his great work *English Social History*, published in 1944, G.M. Trevelyan states that it is a common error to regard the eighteenth century as irreligious. What had changed, he says, from the previous century was not that people had become less religious but that they had 'ceased to fight with the sword' over rival doctrines and had become more tolerant of differences of opinion.[1]

Earlier generations had experienced religious persecution on a ferocious scale. Two hundred years before our story of Knockupworth begins Queen Mary had been burning Protestants. Catholics had subsequently been treated with equal savagery. During and after the Civil War the Puritans tried to impose a rigid adherence to a narrow faith. And a king (James II) was overthrown because of his religion.

Trevelyan argues that becoming more open-minded had not made society any less religious. In *Church and State in Modern Britain 1770–1850,* Richard Brown defines how public attitudes were largely determined by religion. Its symbolism, rituals and traditions were integral to social continuity and it still exerted a considerable influence on politics.[2]

The increasing tolerance towards different faiths does not disguise the fact that the Church of England was the established religion and its dominance was felt in ways that would today be regarded as blatant inequality. Roman Catholics and Dissenters alike were excluded from high office. University places were reserved for members of the established church. But at least people could now be open about their faith; membership of other churches no longer carried the threat of state persecution. The Test and Corporation Acts ensured the dominance of the established church but these laws could be bent. Dissenters who occasionally took communion in the Church of England could be said to be conforming to the law even if they normally worshipped in their own chapels and churches. The Anglican Church's monopoly of political power was thereby weakened.[3]

Public attitudes did not always keep pace with the more tolerant approach of government. In 1780 legislation to remove restrictions on Catholics provoked violence in London that became known as the Gordon Riots and resulted in many deaths.

Catholicism does not appear to have had a significant presence in Grinsdale. Reported in 1747 to have one Quaker family and another Presbyterian, we may infer that the other twenty families were steadfastly Church of England.

One of the most significant effects of the more tolerant climate was the rise of more diversified thinking within the Anglican Church. The ideas of various protestant thinkers from the seventeenth century were able to gain influence within a more enlightened established church. The Calvinists, who believed that salvation was predestined, struggled for dominance with the Arminians, who avowed that with God's help people could achieve salvation through their own free will.

Meanwhile the more broad-minded approach of Latitudinarianism was gaining influence. For the Latitudinarians the moral certainty of Christian doctrine depended more on reason than tradition. Such clerics, while believing that the acceptance of certain doctrine was essential, allowed for latitude on a range of other teachings. The church needed to become reconciled to an age of more rational thought and scientific advance.

How far did this enlightened thinking extend into the rural area of the lower Eden Valley? There is no reason to think that this rustic community was more backward or steeped in tradition than anywhere else. Indeed, the local clergymen may have been influenced by one of the great Latitudinarian theologians of the late eighteenth century.

William Paley, who spent many years in the Carlisle diocese, expounded the view of 'natural theology', applying analytical reasoning to issues of theology. If the workings of the universe were more complex than those of a watch, Paley argued, surely there must be a 'watchmaker' behind creation. Under the influence of men like Paley the church was becoming less preoccupied with doctrine and sacrament and more concerned with issues of social justice. From within this compass were emerging clerics and politicians who were prepared to confront the social evils of the day.

The greatest evil of all would soon become a burning issue in Parliament; but when Thomas Graham took over the land at

Knockupworth the abolition of the slave trade was still over half a century away and slavery itself would not disappear from the British Empire for another eighty years.

In 1776, the year of Thomas Graham's death, Paley was appointed vicar of Dalston, a parish only a few miles from Grinsdale. He would later become vicar of Stanwix, which is even closer. In 1782 he became an archdeacon and in 1785 he was appointed Chancellor of the Carlisle diocese. Such an important theologian, holding high office in the diocese, may have had influence on the local clergy. However, the appointment of priests was often in the hands of the landed gentry rather than the church itself.

Formerly served by the monks of Lanercost Priory, St Kentigern's Church in Grinsdale had from the dissolution of the monasteries been in the patronage of the Dacre family. King Edward VI had granted Sir Thomas Dacre the right to appoint the clergy. No services appear to have been held there after the reformation and the church fell into disrepair but Dacre's descendants continued to appoint a curate with an annual salary of forty shillings.[4] By the late seventeenth century this sinecure seems to have fallen into abeyance.

When John Stamper was appointed curate in 1738 he remarked that the church was in ruins and there had not been a priest for over sixty years or a churchwarden for over forty.[5] There was no register nor anything belonging to the church except for one old Common Prayer book printed in the reign of Charles I. Joseph Dacre, the patron who appointed Stamper, clearly did not intend to let this state of affairs continue, and the following year he began the task of building a new church. At the same time a wall was built below the churchyard – one of a number of attempts to prevent the burial ground from being washed away by the River Eden.

The new church was built on the foundations of the original building. It was completed around 1740, the first service being held in the following year. Soon after his appointment Stamper began to compile a parish register and he offered and dedicated a new Bible and a Book of Common Prayer.

Grinsdale was more fortunate than its neighbouring parish of Kirkandrews-on-Eden where the church had also fallen into ruin but was never rebuilt and of it nothing now remains except for the graveyard.

When Thomas Graham arrived at Knockupworth the new church was little more than a decade old. Having obtained his land from

Joseph Dacre we might suppose that Thomas felt an obligation to support his church. Certainly most of his children were baptised there and a young son was buried in its soil.

In embarking on the rebuilding project Dacre showed his concern for the spiritual wellbeing of the people of Grinsdale. Stamper, his new curate, seems to have shared his interest. Such enthusiasm was not universal among eighteenth century clergy. Trevelyan describes the rising status of clergymen during the early years of George III's reign and paints a colourful picture of highbrow parsons boring their rustic parishioners with lofty sermons while the squire slept in the high pew.[6] The incompetence of many parish priests was hardly surprising in view of the total absence of professional training.[7]

Land belonging to the church was let out to local farmers and workers and provided parsons with their source of income. Often they did little to earn it. Concerns about the laxity of the clergy – some of which did not even live in the parish and rarely held services – was one reason for the growth of dissenting groups. In addition to the old denominations, the evangelism of preachers like John Wesley presented a serious challenge to the established order.[8]

It is hardly surprising that many people of faith questioned the example set by the Church of England. And its place as part of the establishment made it a target for the growing number of people who, for various reasons, wanted to challenge the authority of the state. Christianity may have remained a dominant force but the established church, identified with the 'old order' and with the traditional ruling classes striving to maintain control of society, was at odds with the spirit of social and political change.

The early years of the Knockupworth story coincide with John Wesley's growing influence but throughout his lifetime Wesley remained within the Church of England; the formal establishment of a separate Methodist Church not coming until 1795, four years after his death.

Methodism may still have been a movement within the Anglican Church but other groups of dissenters were well established outside it.

George Fox had formed the Society of Friends in the 1650s. The Quakers believed that priests and rituals were an unnecessary obstruction between the believer and God. Fox believed that there was something of God in every person and objected to the hierarchical structure of churches. The Quakers were at first seen as a threat to social order – not least because of their refusal to pay tithes – and were persecuted by Parliamentarians and Monarchy alike. But, in the century that had passed, they had become respectable. Many were noted for their financial acumen and became successful businessmen; and, as the Methodists too were later to discover, people who, for reasons of faith, espouse a simple lifestyle tend to accrue wealth.

Cumberland became something of a stronghold for the Quakers. In 1733 a meeting house with its own graveyard was built at Moorhouse, only a few miles from Grinsdale. This Quaker influence would later play an important part in the history of the Grahams.

The last decade of the eighteenth century saw an even more radical threat to the established church. Writers such as Tom Paine were questioning the very truth of religious thought. While Anglicanism was being challenged by dissenting voices within the Christian fold, the Faith itself was being attacked by atheistic voices from outside. And yet the evangelicals who urged a more rigorous Christian faith and the atheists who sought to destroy it shared much common ground on social issues, such as the abolition of slavery.

The picture of decaying churches and sinecure priests suggests that, if the eighteenth century was not irreligious, the established Church was hardly robust. With the two nearest church buildings in ruins we might wonder where the Grinsdale people went to express their faith before Joseph Dacre's beneficence in 1739. We might conclude that they probably did not. The church was strictly necessary to them for one thing only – the burial of the dead. Neither Grinsdale nor Kirkandrews may have had usable churches but they both had graveyards. Not until the Marriage Act of 1753 did churches become essential for weddings. Parish registers record dates of baptisms but as Grinsdale church did not have a surviving register before John Stamper's time we do not know if the villagers were meticulous about having their children baptised.

Until 1753, marriages did not have to be conducted in churches. In theory they were supposed to be conducted by Anglican priests but even those that were not, were still considered valid. However, the less formal and more secretive the ceremony, the more likely it was that its legality might later be disputed. For poor people this may not have greatly mattered but for the better off, where property was involved, the legitimacy of children was an important issue. The Marriage Act was designed to prevent clandestine and sometimes bigamous marriages. It declared that, to be legally binding, all marriage ceremonies must be conducted by a minister in a parish church or a Church of

England chapel. People under the age of twenty-one could not marry without their parents' consent. Jews and Quakers were specifically excluded from the Marriage Act but non-conformists and Catholics were required to marry in Anglican churches.

The rebuilding of Grinsdale Church and the restoration of a parish register were beneficial to the people of the village; they were also invaluable to those of us who wish to trace our family histories. We do not know how religious the early inhabitants of Knockupworth were, or how often they attended church. Indeed, it seems that, even after the church was rebuilt, services may not have been held frequently. But at least we have a record of when they walked down the aisle to be married, when they carried their children to the font and, after their lives had ended, when they were taken to their graves.

In 1761 William Baty replaced John Stamper as curate of Grinsdale. Following Baty's death in 1777 Thomas Pattinson began a long incumbency, while simultaneously holding livings at Kirkoswald, Kirklinton and Stapleton. In 1814 Walter Fletcher, one of Paley's successors as Chancellor of the Diocese began his Diocesan Book in which he recorded his primary visits to the parish churches, regularly updating his notes. In 1814 he visited Grinsdale, and found that the church was in good repair and was able to accommodate about eighty people. However he reported that the churchyard was shamefully dirty and ordered it to be better kept. He does not specify the cause of its condition but, if the enclosing wall had not yet been built, there would be nothing to stop animals from entering the graveyard. He commented that there were no communion vessels in the church. The sacrament was held three times a year – at Easter, Michaelmas and Christmas – but there were few communicants and no collection was made.

Fletcher ordered that the church should obtain a communion cloth and cup, and a bier cloth, that the pulpit cushion should be covered, the Bible rebound and that the pulpit stairs and door should be repaired. When he revisited in 1818 he found the churchyard to be in rather better state and all except for the communion cloth to have been obtained. He was promised that one would be ordered immediately and a surplice next year. He ordered that the church and chancel should be whitewashed.[9]

We have some evidence of the religious influences that may have played a part in the lives of the Grahams who first inhabited

Knockupworth. How significant a part this was we cannot tell. There are no surviving memoirs, diaries or letters that would give us insights into their characters. We know who they were and when and where they lived. We can surmise certain things from their actions but much of our impressions rely on imagination and guesswork. We cannot really know their personalities.

There is one tantalising piece of information in Walter Fletcher's record of his visits to Grinsdale. He reports that there is no parish clerk but that 'a parishioner officiates who is a constant attendant at Church and an excellent Reader and Singer. The name of this useful yeoman is John Graham.'

If this were one of the Knockupworth Grahams it would be a unique revelation but frustratingly it is not. At that time the only member of the family bearing that name would have been merely an infant. John Graham is an extremely common name in Cumberland and there was at least one other Graham family in Grinsdale.

There was to be a long line of John Grahams in the Knockupworth dynasty but this was not one of them. It is likely, however, that St Kentigern's useful yeoman was not unconnected to the Knockupworth Grahams and would one day play a small part in their story.

Notes

1 G.M. Trevelyan, *English Social History* (1944) p.353
2 Richard Brown, *Church and State in Modern Britain 1770–1850* (1991) p.92
3 Richard Brown, p.109
4 T. Bulmer & Co, *History Topography and Directory of Cumberland, 1901 Edition*, p.201
5 Revd. G.N. Dobson, *Grinsdale Parish Church; the History of One of Cumbria's Smallest Parishes* (1981)
6 G.M. Trevelyan, p.358
7 Richard Brown, p.428
8 Jonathan Downs, *The Industrial Revolution; Britain, 1770–1810* (2010) p.16
9 *The 'Diocesan Book' of Chancellor Walter Fletcher, relating to parish visitations*, Cumbria Archive Centre, Carlisle.

CHAPTER FIVE

Weaver John and the Sharp Connection

By the middle years of the 1770s the Grahams had owned the land at Knockupworth for over two decades. The millwright, Thomas, was now also a farmer. He lived in the farmhouse with his wife, Ann, their son Monkhouse, who was not yet ten, and their three young daughters: Mary, Letitia and Margaret. John, his son by his first marriage, was now in his late teens. Thomas had achieved prosperity and a degree of status. But by July 1776 Thomas Graham was close to death. It was time for him to put his affairs in order and on the 13th of that month he made his will.

His death came at a momentous time in British history. Nine days before his will was signed the American Congress approved the Declaration of Independence. The news did not reach London until 10th August, by which time Thomas may already have been dead. The legal process of proving the will was completed on 20th August. Seven days later the American forces suffered a major defeat at the Battle of Long Island – the first and biggest battle of the War of Independence.

Meanwhile, on 12th July, James Cook had begun his final, fateful voyage.

The dates on Thomas Graham's will tell us that he must have died during July or in early August. We cannot be more precise because we have found no record of his burial. Although he must have been living at Knockupworth for around two decades he was not buried with his son in Grinsdale churchyard. It may be that he and his first wife lie together in the parish where they had lived before they became inhabitants of Knockupworth. Thomas's father had been buried in St. Mary's churchyard in Carlisle. It would have fitted neatly into the story if Thomas and his wife had been taken to the same family grave. But the facts do not bear this out. We have found no records of their burials in either the Grinsdale or the St. Mary's registers.

In his will Thomas left his estate, which was principally the property at Knockupworth, to his son, John, and made John responsible for distributing legacies to his siblings when they came of age. John would be about eighteen at the time of his father's death. As with all other wills I have written a rough transcription, abstracting the key information, simplifying legal language and transposing the text into the third person.

Will of Thomas Graham:

> Thomas Graham of Knockupward in the county of Cumberland, yeoman:
>
> - leaves to his son, John Graham and to his heirs and assigns all property within the precincts of Knockupward,
> - John, his heirs etc. to pay to his son Monkhouse Graham £25 at the age of 21,
> - And to pay eldest daughter Mary Graham £20 at the age of 21,
> - And to pay second daughter Letitia Graham £20 at the age of 21,
> - And to pay third daughter Margaret Graham £20 at the age of 21.
> - John is also to be responsible for any just debts.
> - If he fails to pay any legatees or creditors within three months they have the right to sell as much of the property to discharge what is due to them.
> - All goods, chattels, cattle and personal estate are bequeathed to John Graham.
> - John Graham is made sole executor.
>
> Will dated 13th July 1776. Witnessed by John Hodgson, Thomas Mather and William Nixon. Proved August 30th 1776.[1]

Two people are conspicuously absent from Thomas's will. The first is his widow. His second wife, Ann, was still alive. She is mentioned in her son Monkhouse's will in 1805 and she did not die until 1813. However Thomas's will makes no formal provision for his widow.

Thomas provided for all of his known living children but the will does not mention Thomas, the second of his sons to bear this name and the future occupant of Ayton Hall in North Yorkshire. Again it is a legacy left to him in Monkhouse's will that provides evidence of the boy's existence. Nineteenth century census records for Great Ayton suggest that this Thomas Graham was not born until 1777 – some months after his father's death. He was to become what was a rarity for the Grahams, an exceptionally long-lived male member of the family. In the 1861 census the landed proprietor of Ayton Hall gives his age as eighty-four and his birthplace as Grinsdale, Cumberland.

Though he was meticulous in providing legacies for all his living children the millwright farmer of Knockupworth does not seem to have considered the possiblilty that Ann might have been pregnant at the time of his death. Her son may have been born at Grinsdale, though he does not appear to have been baptised there. Ann moved back to Tarraby. Unsurprisingly she named this child after his late father.

After John inherited Knockupworth we must assume that he honoured his father's bequests to his siblings but we found no further record of any contact between him and the rest of his family. He left nothing to them in his own will and, although John predeceased his brother by two years, Monkhouse does not mention John's children in his. There appears to have been a parting of the ways between the son of Thomas's first wife and the children of his second.

The lives of Thomas Graham's second family are outlined in Alice Barrigan's online North Yorkshire History article about Ayton Hall. Monkhouse became a successful Liverpool merchant, dying in 1805 at the age of thirty-eight. Alice Barrigan states that:

> he left neither wife nor child. His beneficiaries were his mother Ann and his siblings Thomas, Letitia, Mary and Margaret. They shared the money he had made as a merchant in Liverpool and the property he had bought in the parish of Stanwix, just north of Carlisle.[2]

The amounts he left were considerable and included £3,000 to pay yearly interest to his mother for the rest of her life. Ann may have been omitted from her husband's will but her son left her well provided for. The interest from smaller, but still substantial, sums was set aside to provide for each of his four full-siblings and their offspring. There were also bequests to other members of his family and several among his circle of friends. But Monkhouse was not only a man of considerable wealth, he was also, it appeared, a man who showed benevolence to the needy. He left money to two Liverpool hospitals, to the Liverpool

Blind School and £100 in trust for the distribution of bread to the poor of Stanwix parish.

But I have discovered another, darker, story. Monkhouse may have been childless at the time of his death but a son, James, had been baptised at Stanwix on 11th May 1800. The boy had lived for little over a year. The record of his baptism identifies his mother by a single word: 'African'.[3] And this is a clue to the source of this rich Liverpool merchant's wealth: Monkhouse Graham was a slave trader.[4]

Two of Monkhouse's sisters were married to Newcastle men: Mary to John Spotswood and Letitia to Joseph Taylor. Margaret married Antrim cattle dealer James Maguire. When she died in 1813, Ann left everything, including her gold watch and chain to Margaret's children.[5]

The youngest sibling, Thomas, who became the occupant of Ayton Hall, was the main long-term beneficiary of Monkhouse's fortune. In 1854, towards the end of a long and seemingly colourful life, Thomas was to take as his second wife a young Carlisle woman who was almost fifty years his junior.

But the lives of Ann's children took them away from Knockupworth and they play no further part in its story. It was John, the millwright's eldest son, who inherited the farm. And it is with John that we take up the story.

John married in 1783. His wedding took place in Grinsdale church and is recorded in the parish register:

> Grinsdale Parish Register: John Graham of this parish, bachelor, aged 25, to Hannah Sharp of the parish of Burgh by Sands, single woman, aged 24, were married in this church by licence this 20th day of January 1783.[6]

This gives us our connection between the Graham and Sharp families and provides a partial explanation for John's descendant being given the middle name Sharp almost ninety years later.

His bride, Hannah, was the only daughter of a Quaker family who lived at Flatt, a settlement close to the villages of Kirkbampton and Thurstonfield and about five miles from Grinsdale. Hannah's parents, John Sharp and Hannah (or Hana) Jackson had married on 30th May 1754. The family attended the Quaker meeting house at Moorhouse, where Hannah's birth was recorded in 1759. Her name on her birth record is spelt 'Hana'. This is the spelling used for all girls with this name written on the pages of the register around that time:

> The birth of Hana the daughter of John Sharp of Flat was on 3rd day of 7th month called July 1759.[7]

It would seem from this that at the time of her marriage Hannah would actually have been a few months short of her twenty-fourth birthday. It would seem too that she had already moved out of the family home, for although Flatt is only a short distance from Burgh by Sands it was not in the same parish. That the marriage was by license rather than the longer and more usual process of calling banns did not necessarily indicate that there was any urgency about the proceedings. Those who could afford to pay for them and did not want the rest of the parish knowing their business often regarded a marriage by license as a status symbol. And it would be nearly two years before the marriage produced a living child.

Hannah had two older brothers: John, born in 1755 and William, in 1757. Almost exactly three years after Hannah was born, her mother gave birth to twin boys – Joseph and Jonathan. By the time Hannah married John Graham in 1783 two of her brothers were already dead – Joseph died in 1771 and John in 1778.

Late January might seem a risky time of year to hold a wedding, considering the climate of the time, but it appears that this particular winter may have been less severe than most. The couple may actually have hoped for snow. According to eighteenth century superstition snowfall on your wedding day portended wealth and fertility. They married on a Monday, a day that was also believed to bring wealth. Months later the Icelandic volcano would spread its blue haze across Europe and the next two winters would be especially harsh.

Marrying outside her faith, in an Anglican church, would have led to Hannah being disowned by the Society of Friends. This seems largely to have been a technicality; many 'disowned' Quakers continued to attend meetings and remained on good terms with their families.

John and Hannah had two children. Their baptisms are recorded in the Grinsdale parish register:

> Grinsdale Parish Register: November 6th 1784, Thomas, son of John Graham (weaver) and Hannah his wife of Grinsdale, baptised.
>
> 27th ? [month is illegible] 1790, Margaret, daughter of John Graham of Grinsdale (weaver), and Hannah, his wife, baptised.[8]

When we saw these entries we did not at first believe that they referred to our family. Surely the Knockupworth Grahams were yeomen? A weaver was someone who slaved in the Carlisle cotton mills, or on a cottage loom. And yet the names matched those of John and Hannah's children engraved on the Grinsdale gravestone and the dates of their baptisms also seemed correct. Was it possible that, only eight years after inheriting Knockupworth, John Graham was being employed as a loom worker in Grinsdale village? If so, this would indicate a sudden and substantial decline in the family's fortunes and one that, though temporary, must have lasted for at least six years between the births of his two children. What could have caused such misfortune and what happened to the farm during his absence? Or is there another explanation? Could the information in these baptismal records not quite be what it seems?

The booklet *Grinsdale Parish Church, the history of one of Cumbria's smallest parishes*, compiled by Revd. G.N. Dobson in 1981 contains the following passage:

> In the eighteenth and early nineteenth centuries there was a linen industry in the village. From the deeds we learn that certain farmers had the right to bleach and in the church records we find that many people termed themselves weavers. This was a cottage industry and it was bound to fade away as large industrial towns grew.

From this I see another possible way of reading these entries in the parish register. Might, in this case, the term 'weaver' have indicated a farmer who was involved in the production of linen rather than someone who personally worked at a loom? Today someone may be described as a builder even if they do not physically construct the houses with their own hands; the owner of a bakery business may employ others to make the loaves and yet still be known as a baker. Might not someone who owned looms and employed people to work on them have described themselves as a weaver? This seems a more satisfactory explanation. It is perhaps odd that John and Hannah are described as being 'of Grinsdale' rather than of Knockupworth but, since Knockupworth was in Grinsdale parish, this does not necessarily mean that they were not living at the farm.

If John Graham owned a linen business at Knockupworth the fact that he referred to himself as a weaver rather than as a yeoman or as a farmer may indicate that this was the major part of his commercial enterprise. While production would have been small-scale compared to that in the emerging industrial cotton mills it may have been the most profitable part of his business. It may also have been a title that carried some prestige since it indicated that this was a farmer who had bleaching rights.

Although in later times much of the flax used in linen manufacture was imported, it seems certain that this was a cottage industry that grew out of the farm's agricultural activities. Grinsdale was certainly not the only Cumbrian village to number linen weavers among its inhabitants. Flax must have been a profitable crop, especially if the farmer could add value by processing it on his own premises, but Knockupworth would almost certainly have been a mixed farm with a dairy herd supported by the rich pasture that flourishes in the damp conditions of the fertile Eden valley.

We do not know if John was responsible for introducing linen production to the farm or if it was an enterprise that he had inherited from his father. Nor do we know for how many generations it continued. It certainly seems to have disappeared from the farm by 1836, which is the year that Carlisle's most famous cotton manufacturers – Dixons – opened their iconic Shaddon Mill, but the Grahams' cottage industry may have declined long before then. The growing popularity of cotton had led to the decline of linen as a fabric for fine clothing though there was still a demand for flax in the production of twine, rope and canvas. And crime reports in the Cumberland newspapers suggest that linen was still a sufficiently valuable product to be a frequent target for theft.

On Saturday 8th March 1817 the *Carlisle Patriot* published a feature advertising a new machine for use in the processing of flax. It was addressed 'to the Landed Interest and Agriculturalists of Great Britain and Ireland' – an indication, perhaps, that linen production was, at that time, still largely a cottage industry practised by the farming community. Though this was several years after John Graham's death the article gives a useful insight into what must have been involved in the handling of this crop during John's tenure at Knockupworth.

The article promotes: 'A new method of breaking and preparing FLAX and HEMP without Dew-Retting, in the best and most expeditious Manner, by HILL and BUNDY's Patent Machines.'

It describes at length the process of dew retting, which was common practice at the time. This involved steeping the flax while in the stem in water and then exposing it to the air for three to four months, which caused the outer coat to decay and separate and the glutinous matter that enveloped the fibre to dissolve.

It goes on to say:

> The fibre is so extremely injured by this exposure to the weather, and so excessive a waste of material is the consequence, that only one ton of Flax is produced from eleven tons of stem, and the expense of working each ton obtained by this method is upwards of twenty eight pounds. It besides fixes a deep grey stain upon the Flax which can only be removed by a long expensive process of bleaching aided by chemical preparations and acids, which, unless very judiciously used, are always detrimental to the strength and durability of the linen.

The method of dew retting, including the bleaching necessary to remove the stain, occupied five or six months. The article points out that another disadvantage was that it rendered the crop useless as a form of manure – a major drawback in an era when farmers relied on natural waste products to fertilise the land. As well as speeding up the process and producing better quality fibre, Hill and Bundy's machines would, it was claimed, preserve the straw 'in a state of freshness, and being full of oily particles, is not only a nutritious food for Cattle, but is in itself an excellent manure.'

It is not clear how effective the new machines turned out to be, nor if they succeeded in transforming England into a country 'as celebrated for the exportation of those articles [flax and linen] as she now is for her woollen trade.' If the machines ever became popular it seems likely that their success was short-lived for history tells us that the English linen industry did not have a great future.

If the occupants of Knockupworth were still weaving linen in 1817 it is possible that they may have taken advantage of this new technology. Back in 1784 and 1790 when John and Hannah were taking their children for baptism in Grinsdale church their business must have relied on traditional methods. Though it may have been an expensive process, the returns from this cottage industry must have contributed to what seems to have been a profitable period for the farm.

Economic conditions after 1815 put pressure on manufacturing industries and competition from factories eventually destroyed small-scale enterprises in villages such as Grinsdale. In the 1841 census, four Grinsdale people describe themselves as weavers. It would be wrong to assume from this that linen production continued to flourish in the village until this date, because the four weavers recorded in the next census are specifically described as 'hand loom weavers (cotton)'. While the type of fibre may have changed this does suggest that, despite the development of power looms and the expansion of city factories, village weaving had not yet died out. And it would suit the telling of this story to believe that some weaving may have continued at Knockupworth for at least the first three decades of the nineteenth century.

Although I have found no records to date the building of Knockupworth Hall I am advised that its architectural style, particularly as it is situated in this northern location, makes it unlikely to have been before around 1780. This makes it likely that it was John who commissioned its construction.

The construction of such an elegant house indicates that this must have been a time of great prosperity for the Grahams and if John was indeed responsible it should dispel any idea that he may ever have been employed as a humble weaver. The Hall was built only a few yards to the east of the existing farm buildings. In this setting, rural yet close to the city, the family would own a house grand enough to reflect its status; and though, at that time, they may not have been the only land-owning family living within the confines of the place then known as Knockupworth, it was *their* home that was considered sufficiently important to be known as 'Knockupworth Hall'.

Knockupworth Hall is an imposing building but its grandeur lies in its style rather than its scale.

The Hall was built as a symmetrical Georgian house. Its Grade II listing by English Heritage describes it as being of 'painted stucco on chamfered plinth with raised V-jointed quoins, graduated greenslate roof, rendered end chimney stacks. 2 storeys, 3 bays.'[9] Its central and most distinguished feature is its neoclassical porch – a moulded architrave supported by Doric columns. Flanking the porch are double sash windows with stone mullions on each floor, the small glass panes supported by glazing bars. Above the porch is a single sash window. The regular stone blocks, or quoins, rising up the corners of the walls add visual as well as functional strength to the plain stucco walls. Otherwise, apart from the porch, the Grahams' house was of simple design and unadorned.

What brought about the increased prosperity that enabled the Grahams to move into this stylish new abode? The farm was obviously prospering. Its proximity to the city made it ideally placed to supply food to the growing population. A flourishing linen industry would also have boosted the family's income.

It is also likely that its fortunes were enhanced by momentous world events.

Notes

1 Cumbria Archive Service, Carlisle
2 Alice Barrigan: northyorkshirehistory.blogspot.uk
3 Cumbria Archive Service
4 Stephen D. Behrendt, *The British Slave Trade, 1785–1807,* University of Wisconsin-Madison (1993)
5 Will of Ann Graham, widow of Tarraby, Cumbria Archive Service
6 Cumbria Archive Service
7 England & Wales, Society of Friends [Quaker] Births
8 Cumbria Archive Service
9 https:historicengland.org.uk/listing/the-list/list-entry/1087519

CHAPTER SIX

In Times of War

When John Graham inherited Knockupworth Britain was about to lose its American colonies. When he died the country was in the middle of a longer war, fought closer to home – a war that would have a profound effect on its people.

Many British people had welcomed the fall of the Bastille in July 1789. It was thought that the overthrow of the autocratic Bourbon monarchy would propel France towards a parliamentary system similar to our own. George III was directly involved in the appointment of governments and liable to interfere in the implementation of their policies in ways that would be considered unacceptable today but he was subject to a constitution that ensured that at least some of the people had political representation. He was not the despotic ruler that the French king, Louis XVI, had been. Liberal politicians, poets and a wide section of the general public greeted the Revolution with enthusiasm. We do not know what John Graham, yeoman weaver of Knockupworth, or his Quaker wife thought of it but members of the Society of Friends tended to have liberal political views.

But, within three years, the revolutionary French government had declared war on Austria, Prussia and Piedmont, and in January 1793 it executed its king. These events had a profound impact on British public opinion. The French had declared their intention of turning countries that they conquered into republics. The citizens of Britain may have been sympathetic to their continental neighbours' desire for greater freedom but republicanism seemed a step too far. George III was at times subject to mob demonstrations and to occasional assassination attempts but, recovered from his insanity, he was, on the whole, a popular king. And, while it may have been an era of religious tolerance and dissenting voices, the atheism of the revolutionaries was anything but tolerant. By now the Revolution was descending into a bloodbath – a demonstration of the havoc that could ensue when the established order was overthrown. And on February 1st 1793 the French declared war on Britain.

Apart from a brief interruption, war was to last for over two decades. It was fought, not only on the continent and the seas around our shores, but in West Indian colonies, North Africa and the Mediterranean Sea. It involved shifting alliances and treaties made and broken. Danger came not only from France but from the west too, where the Irish saw an opportunity to shake off centuries of brutal British oppression.

Attitudes to the war were not universally patriotic. There was much discontent. It was a time of high food prices and low wages. A Corn Law, introduced in 1791 to protect farmers, prohibited the import of grain when prices fell below fifty shillings a quarter. The effects of war combined with the harsh climate to further drive up the price of corn. There were food shortages and riots to which troops often responded with extreme violence. In 1794 the government suspended habeas corpus. There were trials for treason, sometimes leading to executions. To many it seemed that the British authorities were as repressive as those they were fighting in France.

And yet there were attempts, albeit unsuccessful ones, to introduce liberal reforms. In 1793 Grey's motion on Parliamentary Reform was heavily defeated and, despite support from such leading politicians as William Wilberforce, William Pitt and Charles James Fox, Parliament refused to abolish the slave trade.

As farmers, the Grahams may have profited from the high prices. But, for the poor it was a time of extreme hardship. Prime Minister Pitt encouraged the development of the Speenhamland scheme, under which designated labourers received poor relief in relation to the price of bread. Wages could be supplemented from the rates. While these measures may have alleviated the worst examples of poverty they doubled the poor rate and lowered morale. The scheme was not applied across whole country, for in parts of the north competition from mines and factories tended to keep rural wages relatively high.[1] The climate continued to play its part in the hardship. In 1795 a terrible winter was followed by a summer drought.

Meanwhile, after a number of reverses, Pitt introduced a wide range of taxes to pay for military expenditure. The hair powder tax, introduced in 1795, may seem frivolous compared to many but it hastened the decline of the fashion for wearing wigs. We have no portraits to tell us if John Graham ever wore one.

By the end of 1796 people were longing for the war to end. The costs had been great and there had been little military gain.[2]

In February 1797 the threat of invasion prompted a financial crisis. Bank of England reserves were running dangerously low. The banks suspended cash payments, and the issue of new notes without the promise of being backed by gold led to inflation.

As the century drew to a close more bad winters and poor harvests continued to drive up the price of food. Pitt, desperately trying to finance the war effort, introduced income tax in January 1799. Despite the threat of invasion and the precarious state of the economy, taxation was a controversial issue. On 16th January 1802 the *Carlisle Journal* reported:

> Rumours of the new taxes already circulate. Among others it is said that, by way of a hedge for the hair-powder tax, persons wearing wigs, or false hair will be obliged to take out a licence at five guineas per annum, unless they can prove baldness, which will exempt from the duty. Grey hairs will obtain no indulgence.

Income tax was particularly despised and regarded as a short-term measure forced upon the government by the need to finance the war. In March 1802, when the Treaty of Amiens seemed to have brought peace, the abolition of this tax was seen as a priority. Only days later, the Chancellor of the Exchequer announced that he hoped shortly to repeal the income tax law, stating that 'as he had ever seen it as a War measure, he was no advocate for its continuance in times of peace.'[3]

To a nation that had become used to struggling with the hardships of war and with the fear of being overcome by a hostile foe this brief period of peace was to be a time of relief and hope. In June 'A General Thanksgiving for the restoration of Peace took place throughout the United Kingdom.'[4] Several high profile visitors journeyed to France, some even meeting its leader, Napoleon Bonaparte. And in January 1803 the *Carlisle Journal* reported that: 'Madame Buonaparte held her first Grand Drawing-room at St. Cloud, when the Duchess of Dorset and several other English females of distinction were presented.'[5]

But the peace was fragile and the optimism it generated was short-lived. By mid-May Britain and France were again at war.

We have no record of any of the Grahams who lived prior to the late nineteenth century having had a military history and no reason to think that any of them fought in this particular war. But military involvement was not exclusively about fighting on the battlefields. As well as the regular soldiers and yeomanry, the defence force was supplemented by large numbers of militia and volunteers. Each county raised the militia units through a ballot system. Those who were chosen in the ballots had to serve unless they could afford to pay for a substitute. The main tasks of the militia were defending against invasion, guarding prisoners of war and keeping public order.[6] Volunteers served largely at their own expense. Both militia and volunteers were mainly involved in duties in their own areas. After the resumption of hostilities following the short-lived Treaty of Amiens, an 'Army of Reserve' was established.

John had been about thirty-five when the war broke out. We have no evidence of his participation in any of the military groups. His Quaker in-laws would be neither willing nor required to enlist. Did Hannah by her Anglican marriage leave behind the pacifist views of the faith into which she was born or did her husband share these views? Long before the hostilities were over their son, Thomas, would have been old enough to serve. The Napoleonic War Records list a Thomas Graham called into the Army of Reserve in Cumberland in 1803.[7] There must have been many other Thomas Grahams living in the county at this time and there is no particular reason to think that this was the heir to Knockupworth. Whether or not any of the Grahams were directly involved in military service, the Grinsdale community is unlikely to have been left untouched by it. Recruitment and balloting resulted in around one fifth of families being in some way involved in the war effort.[8]

The inhabitants of Knockupworth Farm may have viewed life with mixed emotions. As producers of food and linen they must have profited from the high prices resulting from shortages caused by war and weather. But they would be heavily taxed and may not have been unaffected by the banking crisis. Nevertheless there is reason to think that John left the farm in a healthy state.

John died on 13th September 1803 at the age of forty-five and was buried two days later, becoming the first of the Knockupworth Grahams to be recorded on a surviving gravestone in Grinsdale churchyard:

> Grinsdale Parish Register: September 15th 1803. John Graham of Knockupworth, householder, aged 45, buried.[9]

His wife, Hannah, was to outlive him by nearly thirty years. Married women of the time were heavily dependent on their husbands and their rights, especially in financial matters, were restricted. Nevertheless it is perhaps not too surprising to discover that Hannah figured prominently in her husband's will, both as a beneficiary and as an executor. Although Quaker views on women did not amount to total equality their attitude was generally more progressive than elsewhere in society. We might suppose that, for her time, Miss Sharp may have been quite an independently-minded young woman with a degree of self-reliance that her husband admired and encouraged. And in middle age he trusted her to have a major share of responsibility for the handling of his estate. When John died their son, Thomas, was about twenty years of age. Unusually for the Grahams, John made his will a full two years before his death. He may then have been in robust health and expecting Thomas to be a good deal older when he came to inherit the farm.

John divided his estate between his wife, Hannah, and his son, Thomas, making Thomas responsible for the payment of legacies to his daughter, Margaret.

Will of John Graham 1804:

Mr John Graham of Knockupworth,

- debts, legacies, funeral expenses, legal fees etc. to be fully paid,
- bequeaths his daughter, Margaret Graham, be paid £300 by his son Thomas in the following manner: £100 at the age of 21, £200 at the age of 28 – or as much sooner as Thomas thinks fit,
- if she dies before £300 has been paid the remaining unpaid to be paid to any lawful issue,
- his son to pay interest at an annual rate of £4 per hundred pounds until the whole of the legacy has been paid.
- All remaining money, securities for money, goods, furniture, chattels and credits to be divided equally between his wife, Hannah Graham, and his son, Thomas Graham.
- They are to be joint executrix and executor of the will.
- Will dated 20th September 1801, witnessed by Mary Norman, Eleanor Norman, John Norman.
- Proved 14th March 1804.[10]

It is noticeable that the sums bestowed on Margaret are considerably greater than those that John's father had left to his own children nearly thirty years earlier. While it is true that the value of money had fallen, even allowing for inflation, the total Thomas had bequeathed to his second son and his three daughters was less than half of Margaret's legacy. This would seem to confirm that the farm had prospered during the decade of war. Today Margaret's inheritance would be valued at nearly £30,000.[11]

John died at a time of great fear and uncertainty. The shadow of war hung over the whole country. Fears of invasion were supplemented by threats of insurrection from within. Poverty was driving many towards sympathy with republicanism. And there were those who, tired of the war, would have sought peace at any price.

The shadow of death hung over Knockupworth Hall. Less than six months after John Graham's death, his mother-in-law died there too. After forty years of marriage, Hannah Sharp had been widowed in 1794. It may be that she went to live at Knockupworth when her husband died or she may have joined her daughter there after John Graham's death. Her burial in the Moorhouse cemetery is recorded in the Quaker records:

> The burial of Hannah Sharp of Knockupert formerly of thrustinfield was on 24th day of 2nd month 1804.[12]

The resumption of war had put an end to hopes of abolishing income tax but this still caused great resentment. In December 1803 it had been reported that:

> A Grumbler against the Income Tax was lately answered with much propriety, in this way: – "The Minister, it is true takes *Five per Cent* of your profits. Should Buonaparte succeed, you will be happy if he does not reverse the matter – by leaving you only *Five per Cent.*[13]

But as the war continued and the military situation grew more desperate, further taxation was deemed necessary. Early in 1805 there was a Parliamentary debate on a Bill for raising 'an additional Duty on Salt.' Proposing an amendment to the Bill, Lord W. Russell considered the idea 'oppressive upon the people, especially those of the lower orders, who could scarcely sustain the burdens already imposed on them.' Mr Fox agreed that 'the proposed tax was oppressive', but the Lord Chancellor contended that 'this tax was by no means burdensome to the poorer classes of society, who in proportion to their condition were not so much taxed as those of superior rank' and Lord Russell's amendment was defeated.[14]

Seven months later Nelson's defeat of the French fleet at Trafalgar saw an upturn in Britain's fortunes but the shadow of war would hang over the country for many years to come. In *In These Times*, her account of social life during these years, Jenny Uglow describes the wars as being 'like permanent bad weather.'[15]

When John Graham died his widow, Hannah, now in her forties, was left with her son Thomas, not yet twenty, and daughter Margaret, barely in her teens. But we know that, at some time, her brother, Jonathan, went to live at Knockupworth. Jonathan remained a Quaker all his life and, as we have found no record of him having married within the Society of Friends, we may suppose he was unmarried. Hannah may have married outside her faith but she clearly remained on good terms with her family.

When the Bastille had fallen Hannah's son, Thomas, had been five years old. His sister, Margaret, was not yet born. For almost the whole of their lives Britain had been at war. And, despite the triumph of Trafalgar in 1805, hostilities continued for another decade.

There were other dramatic events not directly connected to the war. The law banning the slave trade was finally passed in 1807, though slavery itself continued. In 1810, shortly after his Golden Jubilee, George III fell into his final bout of insanity. Early the following year his son, the unpopular and extravagant Prince of Wales, became Prince Regent. In May 1812 the Prime Minister, Spencer Perceval, was assassinated in the lobby of the House of Commons. After a relatively benign period in the 1790s, Britain was again gripped by severe weather. The winter of 1813–14 was the last time that a frost fair was held on the River Thames.

Jenny Uglow points out that there was a sense in which the wars had a unifying effect upon the nation. The threat of invasion, the shared tribulations, the propaganda and the celebrations of victories had promoted a new sense of being 'British'.[16]

Wellington's victory at Waterloo brought an end to over two decades of military conflict. A month later the *Carlisle Journal* was congratulating the city's inhabitants for their efforts in raising funds for the dependants of soldiers killed and injured in the battle:

> The subscriptions in this city for the benefit of those brave men who have shed their blood at Waterloo already amount to nearly £900; and if the immense city of London can boast its thousands and tens of

> thousands, we can sit down and reckon that the pecuniary sacrifice of Carlisle, considering its extent, has been at least in equal proportion – We trust – we confidently anticipate that every town and village in the county will press forward, and, stretching out the hand of beneficence, endeavour to dry up the tears of the distressed.[17]

A year after the battle the *Journal*'s rival newspaper, the *Carlisle Patriot*, reflected the mood of celebration and patriotism:

> The anniversary of the glorious conflict of Waterloo on Tuesday week will be celebrated in Carlisle by Public Dinners at all the principal Inns. The recollection of such a day, in which Britain humbled her proudest foe, and in a manner more honourable to herself than all of her former victories, must inspire every bosom with enthusiasm and just pride. Such celebrations are calculated to keep alive that national spirit which is our glory and our strength, and which is the surest foundation of future victories.[18]

However, Britain could not afford to wallow in its newly found 'national spirit'. Unrest at home, fuelled by high prices, low wages and the hated Corn Laws, was growing. There was machine breaking in factories and riots in streets. And Grinsdale, a small Cumbrian village a few miles from Carlisle, would not escape this anger.

Notes

1 G.M Trevelyan, *English Social History,* p.469
2 Jenny Uglow, *In These Times* (2014), p.163
3 *Carlisle Journal,* 3rd April 1802
4 *Carlisle Journal,* 15th January 1803
5 *Carlisle Journal,* 22nd January 1803
6 Roger Knight, *Britain against Napoleon: the organisation of victory 1793–1815* (2013) p.538
7 ©Barbara Chambers, Napoleonic War Records
8 Jenny Uglow, *In These Times* (2014), p.1
9 Cumbria Archive Service
10 Cumbria Archive Service
11 bankofengland.co.uk/monetary-policy/inflation
12 England & Wales, Society of Friends [Quaker] Deaths
13 *Carlisle Journal,* 3rd December 1803
14 *Carlisle Journal,* 9th March 1805
15 Jenny Uglow, p.2
16 Jenny Uglow, p.638
17 *Carlisle Journal,* 22nd July 1815
18 *Carlisle Patriot,* 15th June 1816

CHAPTER SEVEN

Margaret Graham Keeps her Name but May Lose her Fortune

Thomas was about twenty when he inherited Knockupworth Hall and Farm. The end of the war was still over a decade away. The need for home-grown produce may have ensured the farm's prosperity during the hostilities.

After the Grahams moved into the Hall the level of their involvement in the management of the farm is uncertain. John, twice recorded in the Grinsdale register as a weaver, was at the time of his burial described in the same register as a householder. At the time of his death he may have regarded himself as a landowner rather than as a farmer. His son, Thomas, referred to in his own will as a yeoman, may have taken a more active role on the farm. However it may be a mistake to read too much into labels given to people in official documents.

The Grahams still owned the farmhouse. In later years it was to be occupied at various times by tenant farmers, by farm managers and by agricultural labourers but there is little information about its occupancy during the early years of the nineteenth century. Even if Thomas was directly involved in managing the farm he would have employed an ample workforce and may have had little involvement in physical farm work.

We have little knowledge of the details of Thomas's life or of his character. There seems to be no clear evidence that he joined the volunteers during the war. We do not know at what age his health began to deteriorate. We might suppose him to be of a religious and philanthropic nature. His mother had been brought up as a Quaker, and he is listed in the *Carlisle Patriot* of Saturday 15th January 1814 as having donated 10s 6d to the British and Foreign Bible society. This society, which was formed to fund the translation and distribution of the Bible, both in Britain and overseas, counted William

Wilberforce among its founder members. When Thomas Graham made his donation the organisation had been in existence for barely a decade. He was, therefore, one of its earliest subscribers. A donation today, equivalent to Thomas's 10s 6d would be approaching £40.[1]

In November 1814, seven months before Napoleon was finally defeated at the Battle of Waterloo, Thomas's sister, Margaret, married. She was then twenty-four so would have received the first instalment of her inheritance. Thomas may well have thought fit that this was the occasion to advance her the rest of their father's legacy.

The man Margaret married was a spirit merchant from Carlisle. He had the same name as her brother: Thomas Graham. It was only by the coincidence of her marrying a man with the same surname that the family name has remained Graham, for it is through Margaret that the line was to be continued.

> Grinsdale Parish Register: 13th November 1814. Thomas Graham of St. Mary's Parish, Carlisle and Margaret Graham, spinster of Grinsdale.[2]

The marriage was announced in the *Cumberland Pacquet, and Ware's Whitehaven Advertiser*:

> Sunday se'ennight at Grinsdale Mr Thomas Graham, of Carlisle spirit merchant, to Miss Margaret Graham, only daughter of the late Mr John Graham of Knockupworth.[3]

We might wonder what Hannah and the Sharp side of the family, with its Quaker values, thought of Margaret's marriage to a spirit merchant.

After their wedding Thomas and Margaret lived in Carlisle. Their son was baptised in St. Mary's parish on New Year's Day in 1816.

> St. Mary's, Carlisle, parish register: 1st January 1816, John Graham, son of Thomas and Margaret Graham, Scotch Street, Spirit Merchant. Baptised.[4]

The choice of the boy's Christian name is interesting and would have long-term significance. His father was called Thomas – a name shared with Margaret's brother. This was the name that had traditionally been given to eldest sons in the Graham family. But Margaret named her son after her own father, whom she had lost when she was about thirteen years old. And for the next three generations John became the name given to first-born sons. The name Thomas was to disappear entirely from the family line.

1816 is known as 'the year without a summer'. In April of 1815 a volcanic eruption of Mount Tambora on the island of Sumbara in the East Indies – modern Indonesia – had poured enormous amounts of dust and sulphur dioxide into the stratosphere, filtering out the sunlight, polluting the air and leading to a distortion of wind patterns. This caused a global climate catastrophe. Continuous rain and low temperatures led to total crop failures across much of Western Europe, as well as in other parts of the world. It was notably cold in June and remained so until September. There were still snowdrifts on Helvellyn in late July.

The poets Byron and Shelley, and Shelley's soon-to-be wife Mary, spent much of that summer with friends by Lake Geneva. Forced by the disappointingly cold, wet weather to stay indoors, they amused themselves by writing ghost stories. One was to become one of the most famous stories in the English language. But by the time the resurrection of Frankenstein's creature took shape in Mary Shelley's mind, the life of Margaret Graham's brother, Thomas, was ebbing away.

When Thomas, made his will in May 1816 he surely knew that he was dying, for he does not make provision for any future possibility of him having a wife and children. He died, unmarried, at the age of thirty-one on 16th June and was buried two days later.

> Grinsdale Parish Register: Thomas Graham, of Knockupworth, buried 18th June 1816, 31 years.[5]

We do not know if the conditions of that unseasonal summer hastened or even caused his death but when Thomas departed this life the prospects for that year's harvest must have been very bleak.

Thomas left his estate to his mother, Hannah, for the duration of her life, then to his sister, Margaret, then to Margaret's children. Thomas seemed to betray some anxiety about his sister's situation and tried to make provision for her financial future. Should she die without living issue various uncles and cousins would inherit. The will shows the Grahams' continued involvement with the Sharp family.

> Will of Thomas Graham 1817
>
> Thomas Graham of Knockupworth in the Parish of Grinsdale, yeoman, appoints his uncle William Sharp and his cousins Edward Nixon of Grinsdale (son of John Nixon) and William Nixon, now of

Maryport, their heirs and assigns to raise money to pay his debts and expenses and to:

- permit his mother, Hannah Graham, to enjoy his estate during her life and to receive rents and profits,
- after her death into the hands of his sister, Margaret, wife of Thomas Graham, 'for her separate use and so as not to be liable to the power, control, debts or engagements of her present or future husband.'
- After the deaths of his mother and sister to be in trust for Margaret's child or children or their descendant or descendants in equal shares.
- If his sister has no child or other descendants living at her death then in trust for his uncles William Sharp and Jonathan Sharp for their lives and the life of the longer liver of them,
- And then in trust for his cousin George Graham of Wetheral, yeoman, his heirs and assigns forever.
- The trustees are to retain from rents and profits enough to reimburse themselves for all reasonable charges and expenses.
- He bequeaths to his mother Hannah Graham all his goods, chattels and personal estate for her own use and appoints her sole executrix of his will.

Will dated 13th May 1816.

Witnessed by Thomas Wilson, Bush Inn, Carlisle; James Wilson, Knockupworth; Jacob Stordy, Carlisle.

Proved by Hannah Graham, 12th January 1817.[6]

Thomas's will provides us with some useful information but it also throws up some intriguing questions. We can identify his uncles William and Jonathan Sharp easily enough – they are the surviving brothers of his mother, Hannah, members of the long-established Thurstonfield Quaker family. But who are his cousins Edward and William Nixon and George Graham?

Thomas's first cousins would have been the children of siblings of his father, John Graham, or of his mother, Hannah Sharp. Nixon was a common surname in Grinsdale and the surrounding area. Someone called John Nixon witnessed John and Hannah's marriage in 1783.

This may well be the John Nixon of Grinsdale to whom Thomas refers in his will. The 1851 census – the first that records actual birthplaces – reveals a seventy-seven year-old farmer called William Nixon, who was born at Grinsdale, farming at Crosscanonby, which is very close to Maryport. He would have been forty-two at the time of Thomas's death. While these quite probably are the people to whom Thomas refers in his will, this does not establish that they were actually his uncle and cousin. First cousins not called Graham or Sharp would be the children of married sisters of Thomas's parents. Hannah had brothers but no sisters. John's sisters married men called Taylor, Spotswood and Maguire.

Despite their shared surname, George Graham of Wetheral, is no easier to identify. He does not appear to be a son of either of John's half brothers, Monkhouse or Thomas. Indeed, prior to the twentieth century, George is a name that I have not come across anywhere else in the Graham family line.

It is possible, though not particularly likely, that one of 'Weaver' John's half-sisters – Mary, Letitia or Margaret – had an illegitimate son who, by the time of Thomas's death had set himself up as a yeoman at Wetheral. Since it does not appear that Thomas's father maintained a close relationship with his half-siblings it seems an improbable explanation. And it would still leave the Nixons as unexplained cousins.

Today, when we talk of cousins, we do not usually specify that we mean first cousins. It is generally understood that this is what the word 'cousin' means. In the late eighteenth and early nineteenth centuries the word was often more broadly applied to a wider range of relatives. Tracing the family connections of the Nixon and Graham 'cousins' may involve going back to earlier generations. For this period of history we must rely on parish records for information and, as we have seen in the case of Grinsdale Church, the earliest records do not always survive.

The Quakers were more careful. Methodically kept registers of births, marriages and burials held at Moorhouse Meeting House date back to the middle of the seventeenth century. They do not, however, contain any information that would reveal the identities of Thomas's Graham and Nixon cousins.

Any doubts the family had about the wisdom of Margaret's choice of husband may have been well founded. Thomas's carefully worded bequest to his sister *'for her separate use and so as not to be liable to the power, control, debts or engagements of her present or future husband'* may have been a fairly standard legal phrasing to protect the interests of female relatives at a time when married women had few economic rights, but its greater significance is revealed by an announcement in the *Carlisle Patriot* eight days before the will was proved. Notification was given to her husband's creditors to attend a meeting where, among other things, it would be decided if Margaret must lose her £300 legacy from her father in order to pay off the spirit merchant's debts.

> To Thomas Graham's Creditors:
>
> The creditors who have proved their debts under a commission of Bankrupt awarded and issued forth against Thomas Graham of the City of Carlisle in the County of Cumberland, Dealer and Chapman, are desired to meet the Assignees of the said Bankrupt's Estate and Effects on the 16th Day of January next, at the House of Thomas Wilson, sign of the Bush Inn, in Carlisle aforesaid, at Eleven in the Forenoon, to assent or to dissent from the Assignees setting apart, for the use and benefit of Margaret, the Wife of the said Bankrupt, any and what portion of a legacy of Three Hundred Pounds left to her in and by the last will and Testament of her father, John Graham, late of Knockupworth, in the said county of Cumberland, deceased. And also to assent or dissent from the said Assignees commencing, prosecuting, or defending any suit or suits at law or in Equity for the recovery of any part of the said Bankrupts Estate and Effects; or in compounding, submitting to arbitration or otherwise agreeing to any matter or thing relating thereto, and on other special affairs.
>
> R. Lowry, Solicitor.[7]

We might wonder if Margaret knew what she was letting herself in for when she married Thomas Graham. Was Thomas's love for his new bride uncomplicated by financial considerations, or was his ardour enhanced by the three hundred pounds she had inherited from her father and the knowledge that one day she might inherit the Hall and farm of Knockupworth itself?

It is easy, and perhaps unfair, to think of Margaret's husband as a man of dubious character. There was nothing illegal about trading in spirits and we do not know the circumstances of his insolvency. Many have been brought to bankruptcy by misfortune rather than by irresponsibility. The war might be over but its aftermath still cast a shadow over the economy. His motives may have been honourable, his love sincere.

Of all the characters at the centre of this story Thomas Graham, the spirit merchant, is one of those of whom we have least knowledge. The parish record does not give his age on the date of his marriage. He is likely to have been about the same age as Margaret but he may have been older. Without this information we do not know when he was born and therefore tracing the ancestry of someone with such a common name is well nigh impossible. Nor do we know for certain when or where he died. He disappears from the story as mysteriously as he first appeared. And yet his place in the lineage should not be overlooked. He may not have been part of the family that had settled at Knockupworth over half a century earlier but it is because of him that subsequent generations have retained the surname Graham.

As she weathered the storm of her husband's bankruptcy Margaret's life was also turbulent in a more literal sense. The aftermath of the volcanic eruption was still being felt. The inclement summer had turned into a violent winter. The same edition of the *Carlisle Patriot* that announced the meeting of Thomas Graham's creditors gave a graphic report of a storm that had befallen the city a few days after Christmas. It noted that the weather had been changeable and stormy over the past fortnight but 'on Saturday night last we were visited by a violent hurricane. The rain descended in torrents the greater part of the day, and the storm increased in fury soon after dark.' It reported that slates had been blown off roofs, chimneys blown down and that people walking in the street were in serious danger. 'Before the rain began there was much snow on the mountains, the melting of which, assisted by the heavy rains, caused the Eden and Caldew to rise very rapidly and flood their banks.' There had been great losses of sheep and crops and the *Patriot*'s readers were told that 'the water was very high in Rickergate, and as usual, entered many homes.'

It seems that the situation continued to worsen, for on the 11th January the newspaper reported that:

> It appears from observation taken at Low-holm in the parish of Cumwhitton where the Eden is confined by hills within its natural course, that the river has never risen to so great a height, as in the late flood, since the overflowing of Solway Moss in 1771.[8]

Margaret and Thomas, most probably still living in the city, had storm and flood to contend with as well as their impending confrontation with creditors at the Bush Inn. This was not all. To add to her troubles Margaret was by now heavily pregnant with their second child.

We do not know if Margaret was actually required to give up her legacy. Thomas Wilson, at whose house – the Bush Inn – the meeting took place, was also a witness of her brother's will. Hopefully he was sympathetic towards her and influenced the creditors to be generous.

Thomas's severe financial difficulties could have had grave consequences for this was the age of debtors' prisons. Debt, like crime, was seen as something that demanded revenge and retribution. The law made little distinction between those who had behaved recklessly or even fraudulently and those whose debt had been the result of misfortune. Imprisonment was a punishment that might satisfy the creditors' sense of grievance but did nothing to restore their fortunes. And some debtors preferred even a lengthy confinement as an alternative to meeting their liabilities. In the absence of evidence to the contrary, we may hope that Margaret's new husband avoided incarceration. Of course, it may have been his wife's money that saved him from captivity.

In any event, Margaret's long-term prospects were for a more secure future. Her brother had carefully worded his own will to ensure that any property or money he left her would not fall prey to her husband's debts. But for this inheritance she would have to wait until after the death of their mother. Sadly, this was a legacy that Margaret would never receive.

Notes

1 bankofengland.co.uk/monetary-policy/inflation
2 Cumbria Archive Service
3 *Cumberland Pacquet, and Ware's Whitehaven Advertiser,* 22nd November 1814
4 Cumbria Archive Service
5 Cumbria Archive Service
6 Cumbria Archive Service
7 *Carlisle Patriot,* 4th January 1817
8 *Carlisle Patriot,* 11th January 1817

CHAPTER EIGHT

Town and Country

It appears that, sometime after her brother's death, Margaret moved back to Knockupworth with her husband and infant son. Their daughter, Hannah, was baptised in Grinsdale church in April 1817.

> Grinsdale Parish Register: April 6th 1817, baptism, Hannah, daughter of Thomas and Margaret Graham, Knockupworth, yeoman.[1]

The move is likely to have been mutually beneficial. Thomas's financial problems may have made it difficult to continue living in the city. At worst the family may have been made homeless. At Knockupworth they had comfortable accommodation and Thomas had a new line of business. At the same time Margaret would provide company for her mother and, while Thomas may not have been Hannah's ideal son-in-law, he was at least a male presence in the household.

The relationship between Thomas and his mother-in-law may have been perfectly cordial but we may wonder if Hannah approved of her daughter's marriage. She had been brought up as a member of the Society of Friends. The Quakers held strong views about the misuse of alcohol and were also noted for enterprise and good financial management. Thomas was a bankrupt spirit merchant.

Any thoughts we might have of Thomas and his wife forsaking the turmoil of the city for the tranquillity of the Grinsdale countryside should be dispelled by an article published in the *Carlisle Patriot* around the date of Hannah's birth. The civil unrest, largely provoked by low wages, food shortages and the hated Corn Laws, aroused violent disorder among the Carlisle millworkers. This spilled over into the rural community:

> It is, this week, our painful task to detail the particulars of some lawless proceedings nearer home than those which we have lately described in another part of the county.

> On the night of Friday 21st inst. A considerable number of weavers, and others moving in a similar sphere, assembled on Grinsdale common with the avowed intention of proceeding to acts of plunder and destruction; but for reasons not known to us, they dispersed without committing any violence – though, we are informed, a proposal was made to fire some corn stacks near Knockupworth, but which the majority rejected; this fact is ascertained by a person who watched their motions, and heard their deliberations when concealed behind a hedge near the stacks.
>
> About nine o'clock on Monday night last, the same description of persons began to assemble from different parts of the city and suburbs – but, as we have reason to believe, chiefly from Caldewgate – at a row of buildings (the very focus of Reform) known by the name of "Belle Vue" situate at a very small distance from Newtown. Before ten o'clock, upwards of two hundred men and a few women congregated together at this place, and proceeded thence direct to Sandsfield (the port of Carlisle) armed with bludgeons and some firearms.[2]

The report goes on to describe how the gang entered a public house, demanded the keys of various warehouses, which they entered but found little of value. They returned to the public house and 'regaled themselves of the entire stock of ale and spirits.' Then they moved on to raid public houses at Old Sandsfield and Monkhill.

Although most of the participants must have escaped punishment early nineteenth century justice could be extremely severe on those who were caught breaking the law, especially where civil disorder was concerned. Describing the consequences of 'the 1817 food riots, after warehouses at Sandsfield and Monkhill were broken into, when it was suspected that grain was being exported to Liverpool at a time of food shortage,' local historian Sydney Towill says:

> Two weavers, two women and a young girl seen making their way into Carlisle with bags of meal, were arrested, and the constables also fired at another suspect who made his escape. After being tried and sentenced the two weavers were transported, the women sent to the House of Correction for 6 months, and the girl – the eldest of a fatherless family of ten – was imprisoned for a month.[3]

Notwithstanding this outbreak of lawlessness and despite the financial problems that had beset him during the previous year, Thomas Graham may well have spent much of 1817 with a sense of self-satisfaction. His wife had given him a daughter, a sister for his son and heir. They had become occupants of a very fine house. After the lifetime of his mother-in-law his wife would inherit Knockupworth Hall, its land and the working farm that went with it. And one day all this would be passed on to young John. Even if Thomas were not the owner of the property he could certainly consider himself to be well connected.

When Hannah's baptism was recorded in the parish register Thomas felt able to proclaim himself a yeoman. He had reason to feel confident of an upturn in his fortunes. After last year's disastrous summer and stormy winter, the bad weather continued into 1817. However, in Cumberland at least, there must have been a timely improvement. On Saturday 20th September 1817 the *Carlisle Patriot* reported:

> The Harvest in the County is proceeding under the most favourable circumstances; the weather was never finer nor the crops more excellent. A considerable portion of the Wheat and Barley in the county has been cut and on light dry soils, the Rye and Oats are also fit for the sickle: but in the heavy grounds, and on some of the commons, these sorts of grain are rather backward.

However there was a downside. The report goes on to say that 'our markets are now well supplied with new grain, and the prices are rapidly declining.' At least they were protected from the import of cheap foreign grain. The weavers may have cursed the Corn Laws but the farmers had reason to be grateful for them.

If the linen industry was still prospering in Grinsdale we may wonder if Thomas persuaded his mother-in-law to invest in one of Hill and Bundy's patent retting machines and what impact such an innovation may have had on the business. But Knockupworth's cottage industry may have already gone into decline.

If the Knockupworth folk working on that September's harvest had time to read the *Carlisle Patriot* they may have noticed a short article reprinted from the *Tyne Mercury*. Under the title 'The Canal' it read:

> We are happy to state that the preliminary subscription for the canal is now filled up. The committee therefore will be enabled to take the requisite steps for carrying the measure into effect. We should be glad to see a committee formed at Carlisle with a view, at least, to the construction of a canal from Carlisle to the Solway Frith [sic]. This would form a portion of the general line and be productive of incalculable advantage to Carlisle.[4]

This visionary scheme would have a profound effect on the Cumbrian economy and on the landscape of Knockupworth. But it would be two years before the construction of the canal commenced and in that time much would have changed.

Just over a month after the *Carlisle Patriot* was reporting on a bumper harvest and on the genesis of the scheme to build the canal, the nation's press carried more sombre news. Princess Charlotte, daughter of the Prince of Wales and his estranged wife, died at the age of twenty-one, while giving birth to a stillborn child. Her death meant much more than the tragic loss of a young life. Charlotte had been seen as the greatest hope for the future of the monarchy. The ailing king was in the grip of his final bout of insanity. The dissolute Prince of Wales, now also Prince Regent, was widely unpopular. The monarchy may not have been highly regarded but the excesses of the French Revolution had demonstrated what might ensue if the old order were to be overthrown. Had she lived Charlotte would eventually have become queen. Her death not only deprived the royal family of its brightest hope, it left the king without a legitimate living grandchild. This was not the end of royal mourning. A year later, in November 1818, George III's wife, Queen Charlotte died in her bedroom at Kew Palace. But before this event death had also touched the village of Grinsdale.

On 4th January 1818, Lieutenant Thomas Pattinson, the son of Reverend Thomas Pattinson, rector of Kirklinton and curate of Grinsdale, was killed in battle at Serore in the East Indies. His death was not reported in the *Carlisle Patriot* until 13th June. The death of the priest's son may have occurred in a distant land but mortality was never far from the village. While grieving for his own son the Reverend Pattinson may have had the task of burying other inhabitants of his various parishes; among them Margaret Graham.

Margaret's death is recorded on the gravestone as the 28th July 1818. The church records show that this was actually the date of her burial.

> Grinsdale Parish Register: Margaret Graham, of Knockupworth, 28th July 1818, burial, 27 years.[5]

Two announcements of her death appeared in local newspapers on Saturday, 1st August, both stating that she died on the previous Sunday. Her death must, therefore, have occurred on 26th July.

> On Sunday last at Knockupworth, near Carlisle, Margaret, wife of Mr Thomas Graham, in her 27th year; much lamented by all her acquaintance.[6]

> On Sunday morning last at Knockupboard, Mrs Margaret Graham, wife of Mr Thos. Graham, aged 27, much lamented by all her acquaintance.[7]

We may note that the latter announcement is more specific as to the time of day – a small point, perhaps, but it adds another detail to Margaret's story.

The announcements of Margaret Graham's demise do not give any indication of the cause of her death. According to newspaper reports typhus had been prevalent during that year.

On 6th December 1817 the *Carlisle Patriot* noted the observations of former army physician, Dr Roberts of Bishop Stortford that the disease had raged in different parts of the United Kingdom simultaneously. He stated that:

> The lower classes [...] have been for the most part the subjects of the disease. But the fever, although originating in the habitations of penury, is not confined to them but will gradually ascend to the mansions of the wealthy by communication.

Dr Roberts advocated the setting up of 'houses of recovery' in every parish: 'Into which, upon the earliest seizure of the fever, every pauper should be removed without delay.'

The disease might also contaminate the rich but it was clear which section of the community was being blamed for its spread. Only the poor it seemed were to be forcibly isolated by the authorities. Roberts goes on to state:

> Upon his removal or death, the walls of the room in which he lay should be whitewashed, and the bedding and his cloaths [sic] carefully cleansed before they are used again.

Rooms, he says, should be daily fumigated for a couple of hours with nitrous gas. Dwellings of the crowded population should be regularly inspected and cleanliness inculcated. Although Dr Roberts' recommendations may seem to be based on class prejudice, our knowledge that ticks and fleas carry the disease means that they may have had some slight scientific basis. One assumes that the better off attempted to keep themselves clear of such infestations. His final suggestion is therefore unsurprising:

> Vagrants and tramps in general should be discouraged in public-houses, for it has been ascertained that the contagion has been disseminated by them throughout the country.

Concerns about the spread and control of typhus continued to be reflected in newspaper articles throughout 1818. The Report of the Carlisle Dispensary for the year 1818 that appeared in the *Carlisle Journal* of Saturday 13th February 1819 stated that:

> In general, its character was mild, and more uniform than in 1817: the mortality has been the same, the proportion of deaths to recovery been about one in ten.

The length of the illness was said to have varied. Some recovered within one or two weeks, others lasted for over four weeks. The deaths happened at different stages of the disease.

It is possible that Margaret Graham was a victim of one of the outbreaks of typhus that occurred during that year. However there are more likely causes of her death. She had given birth to two children within the past three years. Complications related to childbirth were a frequent cause of death. It is entirely possible that Margaret may have suffered the same fate as the royal princess. But there is a yet more likely cause.

Her brother, Thomas, had died two years earlier. Both were within the age group most likely to die of consumption. It may well be that tuberculosis was slowly spreading among members of the Graham family and that it would cast its shadow over Knockupworth for at least another generation.

When their mother died John was less than three years old, Hannah just over a year. Though it was their grandmother who received the income from Knockupworth, in practice the running of the farm seems to have been in the hands of her son-in-law who had already been describing himself as a yeoman at the time of Hannah's baptism. Whether or not the bankrupt spirit merchant from Carlisle had any agricultural expertise he does appear to have attempted to carry out the business of a farmer. On Saturday 19th April 1820, the following advertisement appeared in the *Carlisle Patriot*:

> Turnip Seed: On sale by Thomas Graham at Knockupworth near Carlisle, a Quantity of Bates's Warranted Globe Turnip Seed of the owner's growth which gives him confidence in recommending it to the public.

But Thomas had other things on his mind besides the management of the farm. In late October of that year he remarried. His new wife was a widow from Pow Bank, near Dalston. Their wedding took place in Dalston Church and was conducted by none other than the Chancellor of the Diocese, Walter Fletcher, who had so meticulously recorded his visits to Grinsdale Church. Fletcher had succeeded Paley, not only as Chancellor, but also as incumbent at Dalston, a position he was to hold for over fifty years:

> Dalston Parish Register: 19th October 1820. Thomas Graham of Grinsdale Parish, widower and Elizabeth Strong, widow of this parish.[8]

The new Mrs Graham signed the register with her mark. This was not unusual at the time. Many attached little importance to female literacy. As with his first marriage to Margaret six years earlier Thomas had his wedding announced in the local press, again using the now archaic word 'se'ennight' for a week.

> On Thursday se'nnight, at Dalston, by Rev. Mr Fletcher A.M, Chancellor of the Diocese, Mr Thomas Graham, of Knockupworth, near Carlisle, to Elizabeth, relict of the late Mr John Strong, of Pow Bank, near Buccabank.[9]

The *Monthly Magazine: Or British Register*[10] also records the marriage of 'Mr T. Graham of Knockupworth to Mrs E. Strong of Powbank.' Two years after losing their mother John and Hannah had acquired a stepmother.

In 1819, two years after the idea had first been discussed, the company set up to build a canal between Carlisle and Fisher's Cross on the Solway Coast was formed. The canal would allow ships of up to 100 tons into the heart of the city. Its purpose was to improve communications and trade, in particular to reduce the cost of transporting cotton from Liverpool to Carlisle's mills. Fisher's Cross was renamed Port Carlisle. Part of the canal was dug across Knockupworth land, a bridge connecting the two parts of the estate. Another was built closer to Grinsdale village to enable the road to Burgh and Bowness to cross the canal.

For the people of Carlisle and the surrounding countryside, Wednesday 12th March 1823 was a historic day. The navvies' work was complete. The canal had been dug and filled. All was set for the grand opening.

We can only imagine what the opening of the Carlisle Navigation Canal meant for the local people. These were people whose only means of transport were travelling on foot or in horse drawn vehicles along often poor roads. They had known nothing else. The opening of the canal must have seemed like the dawning of a new age.

To capture some of the excitement of the day we can turn to the local press. The *Carlisle Patriot* gave a dramatic account of the proceedings:

> The opening of the Carlisle Canal on Wednesday last was one of those events which claim a conspicuous station in local history. It is highly important whether considered with reference to its probable commercial advantages, or an unequivocal testimony to the public spirit of our ancient City.
>
> The day was looked forward to by all classes of people with great anxiety. Much was expected; but we may venture to assert that the imagination of the most sanguine had failed to depict anything equal to the reality. There was nothing wanting to render the gratification complete – the weather was delightful.[11]

The day began at eight o'clock when the committee breakfasted at the Bush, and 'a musical band played a variety of favourite airs in front of the inn.' Then the committee, travelling in carriages, made the five-mile journey to Burgh where eleven sea-going vessels and several smaller craft, all decorated with flags, were waiting. Crowds had already gathered:

> At an early hour a great number of spectators had assembled on this spot from all parts of the surrounding district; many hundreds from Carlisle alone.

Nearly all of the shops had closed for the day and by midday 'immense masses' had congregated around the canal basin and along the banks nearly all the way to Burgh:

> A short time after ten, the Robert Burns, belonging to Messrs J.M. Head and Son, having on board the Committee and a large party of ladies and gentlemen, began to move onwards for Carlisle, and about eleven had passed the locks at Beaumont: the other vessels followed in succession.

We may imagine that among the spectators that lined the banks where the canal cut across Knockupworth land were Thomas Graham, his wife and his two children, seven year-old John, and Hannah, who was not yet six. They may even have stood on the new bridge that linked the two parts of the estate. From here they would be able to look down on the vessels passing beneath them:

> At Knockupworth the vessels were saluted and cheered by a numerous party, with drum and fife and several flags belonging to the City guilds.
>
> As the fleet proceeded, in gay and gallant trim – decked out in all the pride of marine ornament, and crowned with beauty – the masts and rigging completely covered with temporary jack-tars in long coats – guns were fired at intervals on board each of the vessels, and the spectators on shore loudly greeted.

The children's grandmother, Hannah, may have stood with them. She was now in her early sixties – quite an elderly lady, by the standards of the time. Almost exactly forty years earlier Hannah had come to Knockupworth as a new bride. When she had arrived the Grahams had been owners of the land for only thirty years. She had lived in the Hall when it was a new building. Born before the Industrial Revolution had really taken hold, the intrusion of this new waterway across the land that her husband and his father had farmed must have been a symbol of a vastly changing world. For most of her lifetime the rural landscape had hardly changed; she may have viewed this innovation with some apprehension. Her city-bred son-in-law, Thomas Graham, probably had no such reservations and was happy to pocket whatever compensation the company paid out to the landowners whose property was in the path of the canal.

The first vessel, the Robert Burns, entered the basin at about ten minutes to three, preceded by a band in an open boat playing 'Hearts of Oak', 'Rule Britannia' and 'God Save the King' and accompanied by a twenty-one gun salute. It was estimated that at least 26,000 people had witnessed the spectacle. The *Carlisle Patriot*'s commentary continued in the same effusive style: 'The conduct of the populace was particularly orderly and praiseworthy in every respect.' It had been suggested that people were too apathetic: 'that they did not heartily cheer and throw up their caps.'

The *Patriot*'s reporter was not about to let such a suggestion dampen the occasion:

> The fact is, we believe that they were too much gratified to be boisterous. The scene was so new, so unexpected that it astonished. Some could hardly credit the evidence of their senses, when they saw so many sea-going vessels sailing along a track where, till lately they were in the habit of beholding corn in ear or grazing cattle. An old man, ninety-seven years of age, resident in Caldewgate, on hearing that ships had come up to Primrose Bank, declared that nothing but

> seeing them would be sufficient to induce him to believe the fact: and he was on Thursday actually carried by two friends to the Basin, where he was obliged to resign his incredulity to the reality.

This unnamed old man, born in the reign of George I, represents an astonishing bridge between different periods of history. Now he was watching the trading traffic of the industrial age. It is quite possible that he also witnessed the hanging of the Jacobite 'traitors' after Bonnie Prince Charlie's failed uprising in 1745.

The cathedral bells were rung to honour the grand opening – a well-intentioned tribute but, as the *Patriot* reporter commented, 'their melancholy sound would have been quite as appropriate if intended as a knell for the departed city.'

The mayor, in his speech, said he hoped the canal would promote the corn trade: 'If the farmer could only dispose of his produce, the public at large would immediately feel the effects as well as himself.'

So concluded a day of great celebration, great excitement and great hope for the future. But perhaps the cathedral's bell-ringers had a premonition of what was to come. As railway historian, Stephen White, later observed:

> In 1830, one of Stephenson's locomotives, intended for the Liverpool and Manchester Railway, was shipped at the Canal Basin for Liverpool. The boiler, the only part of the locomotive that could be seen, was described as "very small and compact." So the seeds of the canal's destruction were sent slowly south.[12]

Notes

1 Cumbria Archive Service
2 *Carlisle Patriot*, Saturday 29th March 1817
3 Sydney Towill, *Georgian and Victorian Carlisle,* Carnegie Publishing (1996), p.100
4 *Carlisle Patriot*, Saturday 20th September 1817
5 Cumbria Archive Service
6 *Carlisle Journal*, Saturday, 1st August, 1818
7 *Carlisle Patriot*, Saturday 1st August 1818
8 Cumbria Archive Service
9 *Carlisle Patriot,* 4th November 1820
10 The *Monthly Magazine: Or British Register*, Volume 50 (1820)
11 *Carlisle Patriot,* 15th March 1823
12 Stephen White, *Solway Steam*, Carel Press, 1984

CHAPTER NINE

The Wrong Pig by the Lug

The old king had died in January 1820. His long reign began seven years after the Graham family obtained the Knockupworth land. John Graham, a baby at the time of George III's accession, had lived his entire life knowing no other king. The same was true of both his children, though they had also seen some of the Regency years. John's by now elderly widow, Hannah, would live on through the reign of George IV and into that of William IV.

Europe was still in the grip of the so-called little ice age. The winter of 1823–24 was sufficiently cold to freeze the water of the new canal, for on Saturday 24th January the following item appeared in the *Durham County Advertiser*, reprinted from the *Carlisle Patriot*:

> The Hannah, a small fragile coal-vessel, sank in our canal on Thursday near Knockupworth Bridge, in consequence of being cut through by the ice. She was coal-laden and on her passage downwards.

Did the young Graham children walk to the canal bank to see the stricken vessel, little Hannah, perhaps, excitedly remarking that it shared her name?

1830 saw the accession of William IV to the throne following the death of his brother, George IV. It also saw the fall of the Duke of Wellington's Tory government and his successor, the Whig Earl Grey, took the opportunity to instigate parliamentary reform. Among other measures, the Great Reform Act of 1832 broadened property qualifications, giving the vote to small landowners, tenant farmers and shopkeepers. Before the Act, Carlisle's two Members of Parliament had been chosen by the city's 330 freeman. In future they were to be elected by property owners of £10 annual value. But rural Cumberland was less dramatically affected by the reform. The county's electorate had consisted of 40 shilling freeholders and £50 tenants and this would continue with some extensions to include people with an equivalent cash income.[1]

The Reform Act may have made little difference to the electoral status of the Graham family. After her son's death Hannah had been receiving the profits from the farm but regardless of her wealth, as a woman, she had no right to vote. She died within days of the Reform Act receiving its Royal Assent. Her grandson, John, now inherited the estate but in 1832 he was only sixteen years old. John's father, Thomas, described himself as a yeoman and may have claimed voting rights even though he did not officially own the property.

At the time of the Reform Act the Grahams had been living at Knockupworth for nearly eighty years. Children from three generations had been baptised in the font inside Grinsdale Church; two generations had been laid to rest in its graveyard. The family was firmly established in the neighbourhood. What do we know of the community in which they lived?

During the nineteenth century Knockupworth frequently attracted the attention of local newspapers, often with regard to poaching or thefts of animals or farm produce. As I suggested earlier, the community known as Knockupworth may once have included more dwellings than it does today and its inhabitants may not all have been connected with the Graham family and its land. But by the time of the 1841 census it seems that Knockupworth was limited to three dwellings – the Hall, the farmhouse and a cottage occupied by farm workers. It would appear that before the middle of the century most, if not all, of Knockupworth's inhabitants were living on land owned by the Grahams.

The working relationship between the Graham family and the occupants of the farmhouse may have changed over the years depending on the extent to which the occupants of the Hall wished to be involved in the practical running of the farm. After arriving at Knockupworth as Margaret's husband in 1816 or 1817 Thomas Graham assumed the role of yeoman farmer. His efforts to sell home- grown turnip seed suggest that he may at least have made an attempt to engage with farming. It is uncertain if this former spirit merchant had any aptitude for agricultural life and we do not know for how long or how seriously he persisted with his personal involvement. With a new wife to entertain and with his son still years from maturity, leasing out the land and living off the rent may have been a much more attractive proposition. Hannah may well have shared this view. She was probably wise enough to realise that the future of the farm and the interests of her grandchildren would be best served with their livelihood in the hands of a real farmer.

One of the names occurring most frequently in newspaper reports of the 1820s and 30s is that of Thomas Thomlinson. Thomlinson was a farmer who was described as living at Knockupworth, so he may have been a tenant, farming the Grahams' land and living at the farmhouse next to the Hall. If so, it is unclear when he began his tenancy.

We first hear of him in 1827 when reports of 'Outrages at Carlisle' reached the London press and included an account of an attack on a Mr Sibson of Grinsdale, who, after attending a party at Newtown:

> was stopped and assaulted by a gang of fellows whom he met on his road home near Knockupworth. Finding resistance vain, he leaped over a wall in front of Mr Thomlinson's house and called for assistance. Mr Thomlinson had not retired to rest; he therefore speedily sallied forth to his friend's rescue, armed with a loaded fowling piece.; but before he had power to use, even if inclined, the gun was taken from him and broken in pieces before his face. Both Mr Sibson and Mr Thomlinson were severely beaten.'[2]

A few years later, when Mr Thomlinson again made the news, but for very different reasons, he was said to be living at Knockupworth. In 1834 Thomas Thomlinson was appealing against a conviction:

> under a clause of "An act for Watching, Regulating and Improving the City of Carlisle, and Suburbs thereof":- which enacted that no person should scatter dirt or rubbish in the streets after seven o'clock in the morning, and a police officer named Russell swore that some night-soil had been scattered by the defendant in Blackfriars street and remained in the street about nine in the morning.

It might at first seem puzzling why a Grinsdale farmer would want to scatter night-soil in a city street at any hour – before seven o'clock was presumably permissible! However, as the report goes on it becomes clearer. It seems that Mr Thomlinson was transporting human waste to his farm for the purpose of fertilising his land when some may have fallen off his cart:

> James Armstrong, another police officer, corroborated the last witness. The night-soil was taken away by Thomlinson's carts. He had served the summons on Thomlinson who had snapped his fingers and said he did not care for any of them – they had got the wrong pig by the lug.[3]

The appeal court decided that it was difficult to say from which cart the night-soil had fallen and quashed the conviction. Mr Thomlinson may have been fortunate for this was not his first transgression. In 1831 he had been fined five shillings for a similar offence[4] and the same amount in 1833 'for removing night soil at an improper hour.'[5]

Human excrement was a useful asset for local farmers who relied on natural fertilisers and was well worth the effort of transporting it from the city. However, while it may have been beneficial for the growth of crops, it brought the danger of contamination and could lead to deadly diseases being spread from crowded urban areas into the surrounding countryside. By now it was not only typhoid that people had to fear.

Cholera had initially been confined mainly to the Indian sub-continent but with increased travel it was, by the early thirties, spreading across Europe. It reached British shores in the autumn of 1831 when it was recorded in Sunderland. The first deaths in Carlisle were not confirmed until the end of the following June, the Carlisle Patriot of 30th June 1832 stating that the 'disease originated in a low, damp situation called the Bog.'

Cholera, like typhoid, is caused by a bacterium spread by food and water contaminated by human faeces. Like typhoid it is, therefore, mainly the result of poor sanitation. This was not known at the time. The perception that it was caused by bad smells may have shown a glimmer of an understanding of its source but this did not really grasp the nature of the problem. And other public health advice was further off the mark. The Carlisle Patriot announced that the Board of Health was urging people to wear warm clothing – especially woollen stockings and flannel next to the skin. Diet was also considered important:

> Avoid above all things overloading the stomach. Indigestion, however produced, disposes the body to the disease. If in easy circumstances, take for dinner a moderate quantity of roast meat in preference to boiled, with stale bread or good potato, two glasses of wine with water, or an equivalent of weak brandy or whisky, or of sound porter or ale. Eat garden stuff and fruit sparingly and avoid fat, luscious meals.[6]

Parents and nurses were advised to keep ripe fruit out of the reach of children. People were further urged to 'observe great caution eating suppers, for cholera most frequently attacks about midnight or very early in the morning.'

The advice of Board of Health was well meaning but hardly useful. The causes of diseases were still little understood. As Thomas Thomlinson might have said the authorities had again 'got the wrong pig by the lug.'

Notes

1 Sydney Towill: *Church and State in Diocese of Carlisle, A Spiritual and Temporal History 1559–1900* (2000), p.36–37
2 *Public Ledger and Daily Advertiser,* 24th January 1827
3 *Cumberland Pacquet, and Ware's Whitehaven Advertiser,* 15th April 1834
4 *Carlisle Patriot,* 10th September 1831
5 *Carlisle Journal* 9th September 1833
6 *Carlisle Patriot,* 30th June 1832

CHAPTER TEN

The Shortened Days of Youth

Young Hannah Graham can hardly have had any memory of the mother she lost when she was so young. We must suppose that, at first, her grandmother would have played a pivotal role in her care. But, when she was less than four years old, another woman came into her life.

The situation at Knockupworth Hall following Thomas Graham's marriage to Mrs Strong in December 1820 may have been less unusual then than it would be today but it was hardly a typical family relationship, and it was one that was potentially fraught with difficulty. The widowed, Hannah Graham, now in her sixties, had lived at Knockupworth for several decades. She was entitled to think of herself as the matriarch of the family. Having lost her husband and both of her children, she was now living with a son-in-law, about whom she may always have felt uneasy, and the wife who had taken her daughter's place. It was a situation that was likely to generate jealousies and tensions, especially with regard to the upbringing of Hannah's two grandchildren.

Hannah's brother, Jonathan, may have already been living at the Hall. After her husband's death in 1803 Hannah may have felt the need to have a senior male presence in the house. He would have been able to assist his young nephew, Thomas, in managing the farm. However it seems more likely that he did not move into the Hall until after his nephew's death. When Thomas made his will he appointed not Jonathan but his other uncle, William, to take care of his financial affairs. We know that Jonathan died at Knockupworth but we do not know for how long he had lived there. It is tempting to think that he may have moved in with his sister during the 1820s. We may wonder if Hannah felt she needed the support of another member of the Sharp family during the years when she was living with her late daughter's husband and his new wife. If the atmosphere in the house remained cordial it says much for the tolerance of the characters involved.

Whether amicably of not, we may suppose that the two women of the household shared responsibility for the girl's upbringing and that the grandmother played a part in teaching her young namesake the skills and attributes required of a respectable young lady of her day. Skilful embroidery would be high among the proficiencies expected of her. Like many of her contemporaries Hannah worked on a sampler, which she completed in November 1828 at the age of eleven.

Today we may regard these pieces of needlework as a symbol of female subservience; sewing was one of the few skills expected of a woman from a genteel family. But, in another light, we might see them as a worthwhile contribution to girls' education. A sampler involved stitching letters, numbers and, often, whole sections of verse. Practising embroidery may also have contributed to female literacy. And, as many of these samplers still hang on walls today, the girls who made them have truly left something for posterity.

While his sister worked at her needlecraft John was being prepared for his future role as the master of Knockupworth. We do not know the extent of his education nor what practical instruction he had with regard to running a farm. His surviving parent had been a dealer in alcoholic drinks, though that is not to say he may not have had some agricultural background. And we know that John developed friendships with some older local farmers.

Hannah's sampler still survives. Among various floral motifs is a depiction of a house that is surely intended to be a simple representation of Knockupworth Hall. Though drawn from memory rather than observation – the windows are not quite accurate – it captures the essence of what the house must have looked like in her day. Below it, the following words are delicately stitched:

In the glad morn of blooming youth,
Those various threads I drew,
And pleased, beheld the finished piece
Rise glowing to the view.
Though, when bright youth shall charm no more,
And age has chilled my blood,
May I review my life and say
Behold my works were good.

Hannah Graham finished this work Nov AD 1828 aged 11.[1]

It is impossible to read this without reflecting on the poignancy of the words. Hannah could indeed be pleased with her 'finished piece' for it is a fine piece of embroidery. But her blood would never be chilled by age. For Hannah had barely five years left to live.

There are, so far as we know, no surviving diaries or memoirs to give us an intimate insight into the lives of the Grahams who inhabited Knockupworth Hall in the eighteenth and early nineteenth centuries. We can attempt to piece together an impression of what their lives may have been like from contemporary newspaper reports of events that would have influenced them. The Carlisle newspapers, serving a largely rural community, give us several useful accounts of the weather and its effect on agriculture. From these, and from our knowledge of the Knockupworth farm, it may be possible for us, like Hannah, to draw together various threads and create something of a tapestry of daily existence during her short life.

Winters were still exceptionally cold. In a relatively unremarkable year of 1824, the ice was sufficient to sink a collier on the canal. The mid-1820s saw a number of dry summers. On Saturday 29th July 1826, the *Carlisle Patriot* reported a return to dry weather after a brief spell of rain. No rain had fallen since the previous Friday. The newspaper went on to paint a vivid picture of rural activity:

> The late dry weather has brought on a complication of business for the farmers:- Turnip sowing, meadow hay-grass harvest, a close grain harvest without a day's relaxation, and fallow preparing for winter wheat. Labourers are not to be got in the country – all were engaged during the last week around this city. Even unpractised shearers and labourers obtained 2s 6d per day at Carlisle Cross this morning. There is no able and willing person lately out of employment, but may at present obtain 12s per week and meat or 15s without meat.

The routine of a farmer's life was determined by the weather. But this also illustrates the precarious nature of labourers' employment – hired and fired according to seasonal demand. And the weather was, as ever, unpredictable. Almost exactly two years after the above report the newspaper printed very different news:

> Along the banks of the Eden, large quantities of hay and hay-grass have been destroyed ... And in numerous places considerable damage has been done to the wheat and oats by the heavy and long-continued rain. On Wednesday, the Caldew rose very rapidly. Various articles of value passed down the stream, including hay, the body of a cow, and

> a living pig, which perished as soon as it got into the more copious waters of the Eden.[2]

The following year the farmers were desperate for rain. On Saturday 6th June 1829 the *Carlisle Patriot* reported:

> With the change in the moon, on Monday, there was a considerable change in temperature, the wind since that day, having blown rather coldly from W.N.W., atmosphere heavy, the air full of moisture. A few drops of rain fell, indeed in various places: but the thirsty earth yawns for more.

Hannah Graham, formerly Hannah Sharp, born into a Thurstonfield Quaker family in the mid-eighteenth century, died in the summer of 1832. One of the few characters in this story to attain over three score years and ten, she had outlived her husband by nearly thirty years.

> Grinsdale Parish Register: June 13th 1832, Hannah Graham, Knockupworth, burial.[3]

Although this was the year that cholera was, for the first time, taking hold in Britain and the very month that it reached the city of Carlisle there is no reason to believe it to be responsible for Hannah's death.

Like most of the highly infectious diseases that ravaged the country, cholera flourished in the conditions endured by the urban poor. Though it did, in time, reach the countryside – and Thomas Thomlinson's night-soil cart may potentially have brought contamination to the Knockupworth land – Hannah Graham is unlikely to have been one of its early victims. She was in her early seventies – a respectable age for the time. Her death may well be attributed simply to old age.

When their grandmother died, John was sixteen years old, his sister, Hannah, a year younger. Their grandmother had been one of the most significant female family members in their short lives. Though we do not know the details of their relationship we may suppose it to have been a close one and that this was a time of genuine grief. How the children's father, Thomas Graham, was affected by his former mother-in-law's death is harder to imagine but Knockupworth was not free of Sharp family influence because Hannah's brother, Jonathan, continued to live at the Hall.

About two weeks after Hannah's death the citizens of Carlisle were treated to a spectacular entertainment. But, following the family's very recent bereavement, it would perhaps not have been seemly for the two teenage Grahams to have made their way into the city on 28th June to watch Mr Green make his balloon ascent from Mr Gate's timber yard. While there were few paying spectators in the enclosure, thousands lined the streets to view the spectacle for free.

The *Carlisle Patriot* described the 'silken sphere skirting the edge of a cloud, like a chariot traversing the summit ridge of a lofty mountain.'[4]

If the wind had been blowing in the opposite direction the balloon might have flown over Knockupworth but instead it drifted east and then south, landing after an hour's flight in a field near the village of Ainstable.

Saturday 6th April 1833 was sixteen years to the day since young Hannah's baptism. It was the last such anniversary she would live to see. On that day the *Carlisle Patriot* reported that: 'March has been rather more fickle and variable in its character than usual.'

On Saturday 15th June 1833 the same newspaper reported a 'Tremendous Storm' that had occurred during that week:

> On Tuesday last we were visited by one of the most tremendous storms that we have witnessed for some time. The morning was bright and sultry; but about nine o'clock the clouds began to gather, and show every indication of an approaching storm. In about an hour rain came and, in a short time, it poured down in torrents, mixed with large hailstones, or rather large pieces of ice, and vivid and frequent flashes of lightning followed by loud peals of thunder added to the fearfulness of the storm.

The report goes on to describe the flooding of city streets, the rising waters of the Rivers Caldew and Petteril, the damage done to crops in the surrounding meadow lands, while 'The Eden, as became the dignity of its character, was more slow and majestic, and we fear more destructive in its movements.'

Hannah, less than three months away from death, may have listened to the fearful storm from her sick bed. We have no record of the cause of her death but we have no reason to believe it was sudden or unexpected. Her mother had died in her late twenties; her uncle had been little over thirty. This was the age group most likely to succumb to consumption. Hannah's final illness is likely to have been protracted.

Hannah may have had no memories of her mother but it seems likely that Margaret may have left her a deadly legacy.

Hannah's burial is recorded in the parish register:

> Grinsdale Parish Register: Hannah Graham, Knockupworth, burial, September 8th 1833, 16 years.[5]

The following week her death was announced in the *Carlisle Journal*:

> At Knockupworth, near this city on Thursday week, Hannah, Aged 16, daughter of Thomas Graham; much and deservedly regretted.[6]

Hannah's inscription on the family headstone states only her first name, her age and the date of her death. It does not give any indication of her relationship with other members of the Graham family. It does not state that she was Margaret's daughter. Her uncle, who was buried in the grave, and her father who was not, shared the same name – Thomas Graham. To give more information about her would have been complicated and confusing. But it left us with a mystery over Hannah's identity that would puzzle future generations of the family and would not be solved for a hundred and eighty years.

In little over a year John had lost his grandmother and his sister. And three years later he was also to lose his great uncle. Jonathan Sharp died at Knockupworth in August 1836:

> At Knockupworth, near this city on 5th inst. Mr Jonathan Sharp aged 75 years. He was a member of the Society of Friends.[7]

Jonathan was buried on 7th August in the Quaker burial ground at Moorhouse.[8]

By the time of his great uncle's death John was approaching the age of twenty-one. There are signs that the farm he was inheriting – once profitable in the hands of his 'weaver' grandfather, John, and his uncle, Thomas, may have hit difficult times. His predecessors had profited from farming during a long period of war but now there had been two decades of peace. The linen industry had already gone into decline. Perhaps his father's lack of agricultural experience – and possible lack of business acumen and financial wisdom – had put a strain on the farm's fortunes. Thomas Thomlinson may not have been the most reliable tenant. It may be that John was a less than enthusiastic farmer. At any rate, he seems to have wasted no time in looking for alternative ways of making money. Late in 1836 he advertised the whole of Knockupworth – the Hall and the farm – to be let:

> KNOCKUPWORTH FARM
>
> To be let for a Term of Years, with Entry at Candlemas 1837, either Together or in such Parcels as may suit intending Takers, the above named Tithe-free FARM situate on the banks of the CANAL in the Parish of Grinsdale, about One Mile from Carlisle and containing

> an excellent MANSION HOUSE and Garden, a Farm House and Garden, convenient Outbuildings and about 100 Acres of Arable and Meadow Land of superior quality.
>
> The Mansion House and Garden will be Let with or without any part of the Land which is admirably adapted for, and for many years, has been advantageously occupied as a Dairy Farm and, if let in parcels, is equally as well calculated to suit Private Families, Graziers, Butchers, or others keeping one or more Milch cows or other stock.
>
> Proposals in writing will be received by Mr GRAHAM of Knockupworth, until 2nd day of January next, when, if adequate offers have been made, the Tenant or Tenants will be declared at Knockupworth, where, in the meantime, all applications must be made to the said Mr GRAHAM, Knockupworth. (10th Nov. 1836.)[9]

1836 was a time of industrial expansion in Carlisle. It was the year in which Dixons opened their new cotton mill with its iconic chimney in Shaddongate. But if John Graham was experiencing financial difficulties he was not alone. It was a period of great instability in the money market. And Carlisle was about to experience a calamitous event. A few days after the notice for the letting of Knockupworth appeared in the local press one of the city's most respected banks, Messrs Forster and Co, collapsed. If John had delayed placing his advertisement by a week we might have surmised that his situation had been brought about by the loss of assets in this failed institution. As the appearance of the advertisement predated the bank's demise it seems this was not the cause of his predicament. Nevertheless, as first Messrs Connell and Co and then other local banks followed Forsters' into liquidation, it is not unlikely that John's finances were further stretched by the crisis.

The letting of the Knockupworth estate may also have marked the end of an era for Thomas Thomlinson. In January 1837 the whole of his farm stock was advertised for sale by auction. The timing of the sale, just weeks before the letting of the estate at Candlemas[10], is unlikely to have been coincidental and strengthens the case for believing that Thomlinson was the Grahams' tenant farmer.

The property to be sold included twenty-seven head of cattle 'mostly of the Short-horned breed', five workhorses and one colt, ten fat pigs and one sow and eighteen stacks of various types of grain. All of his farming utensils were also up for sale.[11]

We may wonder if Mr Thomlinson had voluntarily decided to give up the farm or if he was forced out, perhaps by a substantial increase in rent. The new tenant appears to have been a Mr John Irving.

Finding a new tenant for the farm may have been a fairly routine matter; vacating Knockupworth Hall, which had been the family home, was a momentous decision. The Grahams would not occupy it again for over fifty years.

The new tenant for the Hall was Mr John Wright, a retired farmer of independent means. Mr Wright was in his early fifties; being retired at such a young age suggests he was a man of some substance. The occupancy of such an imposing house as Knockupworth Hall by himself, his wife Ann and their large family must have been an attractive proposition and no doubt he was prepared to pay a sizeable rent. But they too were soon to suffer the tragic loss of a young daughter:

> At Knockupworth Hall, on Monday last, after a short but severe illness, Miss E. Wright, third daughter of John Wright Esq. in the 21st year of her age. The sudden demise of this young lady, who was in Carlisle on the Wednesday previous in good health and spirits, has caused great affliction to her relatives, and also to a numerous circle of friends by whom she was highly respected.[12]

John may have found a tenant for the Hall but his efforts to raise capital did not end there. He appears to have been responsible for the deforestation of a large area of the estate:

> To be SOLD by auction at KNOCKUPWORTH, in the Parish of Grinsdale, near Carlisle, precisely at One o'Clock, on THURSDAY 23rd day of MARCH instant, a large quantity of excellent WOOD, consisting of 75 fully grown Oak Trees, all numbered; 438 Ash Trees, 68 Plane Do., 137 Alder Do., 5 Saugh *(willow)*Do., 27 Scotch Fir Do. The Ash, Plane Tree, Alder, Saugh and Scotch Fir, are cut and Laid in Lots to suit Purchasers.[13]

The notice also advertised the sale, by private contract, of a large quantity of stakes, rails and firewood and stated that further particulars could be obtained from John Graham of Knockupworth.

This makes it clear that John, now over the age of twenty-one, had taken over responsibility for running the estate. We do not know what further role, if any, his father, Thomas, played in his life but they appear to have remained on good terms.

It is impossible to know if John saw this as a long-term arrangement or how far he had mapped out his future, but letting out the farm and Knockupworth Hall to tenants was not the only important decision he was to make in 1836. By now John Graham's thoughts had turned to marriage.

Notes

1 Reprinted courtesy of Liz Johnson
2 *Carlisle Patriot,* 26th July 1828
3 Cumbria Archive Service
4 *Carlisle Patriot,* 30th June 1832
5 Cumbria Archive Service
6 *Carlisle Journal,* 14th September 1833
7 *Carlisle Journal,* 20th August 1836
8 Quaker burial records
9 *Carlisle Journal,* 12th November 1836
10 Candlemas. 2nd February
11 *Carlisle Journal,* 7th January 1837
12 *Carlisle Journal,* 25th November 1837
13 *Carlisle Journal,* 18th March 1837

CHAPTER ELEVEN

The Missing Lady

Who was John Graham's bride – the woman whose inscription was never added to the family gravestone? Until recently I did not even know her first name. The solving of this mystery has been helped by quite a lot of good fortune.

Her Christian name was Mary, she was born at Bewcastle and she was about two years older than John.

In February 1837 a marriage took place in Grinsdale Church between John Graham and Mary Little:

> Grinsdale Parish Register: 8th February 1837, John Graham and Mary Little, both of this parish, married.[1]

The marriage was also announced in the *Carlisle Journal*:

> At Grinsdale Church on Wednesday last, Mr John Graham to Miss Mary Little.[2]

As well as her surname we can add two other facts about his bride. First, she was already pregnant – their son, John, was born three months after the wedding. Secondly, she was illiterate; Mary Little signed the register with her mark.

There is also a possibility that they were already related – if so, probably on John's father's side. In his will, written in 1839, John made bequests to cousins called Little – one was actually called Mary Little. However Little, like Graham, is a very common name in Cumbria and this may well be coincidental.

In censuses Mary consistently gives her birthplace as Bewcastle, a remote village roughly half way between Hadrian's Wall and the Scottish border. Little was a common surname in Bewcastle. The 1841 census records over a dozen families and several other individuals called Little in a parish that then had just over 1,200 inhabitants. Today it is much smaller; the nearby mines and the limestone workings that helped to sustain the early nineteenth century community are now long gone.

In the Grinsdale parish register Mary Little is described as being 'of this parish'. In other words at the time of her marriage she was already living in Grinsdale. What brought her, when she came and what she was doing there are questions for which we have no conclusive answers. However there is one intriguing possibility. A girl called Mary Little was christened at Bewcastle in July 1813:

> Bewcastle Parish Register: July 4th 1813, Mary daughter of Thomas and Mary Little of Flatt Cottage[3]

Subsequent records of Mary's age, on censuses and at the time of her death, suggest that this would have been the year of Mary's birth. As this was not the only Mary Little born in Bewcastle that year we cannot be certain that this was John Graham's future bride.[4] But this entry in the parish register contains an interesting detail: Thomas Little's occupation is recorded as a weaver. The 1841 census also records a couple called Thomas and Mary Little, both aged sixty, living at Flatt in Bewcastle. Thomas is described as a linen weaver. If Mary was their daughter and she came from a family of linen weavers she may have had skills that were still in demand in Grinsdale when she was a teenage girl seeking work. Did young Mary Little make the journey from Bewcastle to work at Knockupworth where she caught the eye of her young employer?

The marriage took place six days after Candlemas and, with the Wrights moving into the Hall, John and his bride did not remain in Grinsdale for long. They moved to Thursby where they could presumably live more cheaply on the income John was receiving from the letting of Knockupworth. Their son, John, was born at Thursby, as shown later on census returns and in the parish register of Thursby church:

> Thursby Parish Register: June 25th (1837) baptism of John, son of John and Mary Graham of Thursby, late of Knockupworth, statesman.[5]

The word 'statesman' is a term used mainly in Cumbria to describe someone who is able to live on the income from land without farming it himself. This would precisely describe John Graham's situation at the time.

There may be a clue as to why John and Mary went to live in Thursby, a village between Carlisle and Wigton. On 26th June 1837 a political meeting was held in Carlisle to re-establish the Cumberland Reform Society and bring forward candidates for the Eastern Division of the county. The 1832 Act had been a step towards greater democracy but there was growing support for further reform. On 1st July the *Carlisle Journal* published a list of several hundred men who had signed a resolution pledging their support to two radical Whig politicians, Francis Aglionby and William James, as prospective candidates. Among the signatories was John Graham of Knockupworth. Immediately above him on the list is William Sharp of Thursby.

Could this be the older brother of John's late grandmother? We have no proof that William Sharp, once of Flatt near Thurstonfield, ever lived at Thursby but, though he would have been a very old man, there is good reason to believe that he was still alive in 1837. The close conjunction of their names suggests that the two men signed the resolution at the same time and may have attended the meeting together. Having vacated the Hall, it is possible that John and his wife were staying with his elderly great uncle in Thursby.

This political meeting was held exactly a week after eighteen-year-old Victoria had succeeded her uncle, William IV. The young queen's accession heralded a different style of monarchy from that of the two dissolute old men who had preceded her. Hitherto most of the Knockupworth story has taken place during the reign of what had up to then been Britain's longest serving monarch, George III. But now an even longer reign was beginning.

It was not long before John, Mary and their infant son returned to Knockupworth. As John Wright and his family were now occupying the Hall it is almost certain that the Grahams moved into the farmhouse. This would coincide with the sale of John Irving's farm stock at the end of January 1839 – just in time for the termination of his lease at Candlemas.[6] The farmhouse was not so grand as the home in which John had grown up but it was a robust, functional house of ample size. John's father and stepmother may have moved on to pastures new but it is likely that another relative joined them in their new home. John's great uncle, William Sharp, was now over eighty. Having provided them with a home during their short absence from the farm, William may have left Thursby and moved with them to Grinsdale. The evidence for this is circumstantial but it provides a reasoned explanation for some later events.

We may wonder what awaited John and Mary when they returned to Knockupworth early in February. In January 1839 the worst storm in memory sank many vessels at sea with extensive loss of life. The wind also turned its destructive force on the land. About a week after the event the *Carlisle Journal* gave a graphic account of the devastation in the city:

> The morning dawned upon a scene of desolation such as has rarely been witnessed. The streets were strewed in all directions with slates and bricks. Windows innumerable were broken or driven in; the roof of almost every house was more or less injured, – many presenting an appearance as if riddled with shot. Several of the trees which surround the Cathedral were blown down and lay across the street, like temporary barricades against an enemy. And as the tempest had abated none of its fury, slates were still flying from the house tops, whirled about like pieces of paper.[7]

In Carlyle's Lane, Castle Street, an old woman was crushed to death when a tall chimney fell on three or four houses. The only other fatality in the city was a man buried in the rubble of a bakehouse. There are many other accounts of people miraculously surviving being buried in fallen masonry. There was severe damage to churches and factories but there was great relief that Dixon's new chimney at the Shaddongate mill had survived the storm.

The report continued with an assessment of the damage in the countryside:

> In the neighbourhood of the town the storm has been felt with equal fury. Corn and haystacks have been upset and scattered about in all directions. Cattle have been smothered by the falling in of roofs; trees, nay whole plantations, have been torn up in every direction; and the loss of property this way must be immense.

John had, of course, already felled much of the timber on the Knockupworth land. Nevertheless his property is likely to have been badly affected by the storm and any damage must have caused anxiety, inconvenience and expense.

John may have spent the next few months overseeing repair work at Knockupworth but his ability to engage in any such tasks surely diminished as his health failed. He died on November 23rd at the age of just twenty-three:

> Grinsdale Parish Register: November 25th 1839, burial of John Graham of Knockupworth, aged 23 years.[8]

His death was announced in the *Carlisle Journal*:

> At Knockupworth, in the parish of Grinsdale, on the 23rd instant, after a lingering illness, borne with great patience and resignation, Mr John Graham, yeoman, aged 23 years, deeply regretted by all who knew him.[9]

In 1836 the Whig government had introduced the Registration Acts, putting the registration of births, marriages and deaths into the hands of civil officials. Civil registration began on 1st July 1837. This means that John's death, unlike those of his ancestors, is recorded on a death certificate. While there was as yet no requirement for the death to be certified by a doctor there is no reason to doubt the stated cause of his lingering illness. He died of consumption.

We know that tuberculosis ran through families and was a common cause of death among teenagers and young adults. It is more than likely that his sister, Hannah, his mother, Margaret, and his uncle, Thomas, died from the same cause.

John's grandparents, his uncle, his mother and his sister were all buried in the same grave on the south side of Grinsdale church. For John, a new grave was dug alongside, slightly closer to the river, and a new headstone erected.

On the day that the announcement of John's death was published in the *Carlisle Journal* there appeared a notice for all persons having claims or demands on his estate to send particulars to the trustees or to the solicitor, Mr George Sibson, and for persons indebted to the estate to immediately pay their debts.

It appears that John had not only moved back to Knockupworth but that he had also started farming the land, for a month after his death an advertisement appeared for the sale of his stock.

> Farming Stock, Crop &C &C.
>
> For Sale
>
> At Knockupworth, near Carlisle. Mr Kirkup begs to announce that he has received instructions from the Executors of the late Mr John Graham, deceased, to SELL by PUBLIC AUCTION, upon the Premises, at KNOCKUPWORTH, in the Parish of Grinsdale, on Friday the 27th December 1839, the whole of the Superior STOCK of Horses, Cattle, Sheep etc. upon the said Farm, together with the CROP of Grain, Hay and Turnips, and the whole of the Husbandry and Dairy Utensils.
>
> Conditions will be made known at the Opening of the Sale, which

> will commence precisely at 12 o'clock at Noon, and Hand-bills, descriptive of the various Lots, may be had of Mr KIRKUP, and at the office of MR GEORGE SIBSON, Solicitor, Carlisle.
>
> December 17th 1839.[10]

After John's death John Wright's son, David, took over the tenancy of the farm and moved into the farmhouse.

Pregnant with his child, Mary Little had married John Graham in February 1837. Less than three years after their marriage, Mary was, at the age of twenty-five, a widow with a baby son. On that small infant rested the whole future of the line of the Knockupworth Grahams.

Notes

1 Cumbria Archive Service
2 *Carlisle Journal,* 11th February 1837
3 Cumbria Archive Service
4 Also recorded: Mary, daughter of James Little and Peggy his wife, 7th October 1813 (England and Wales Non-Conformist and Non-Parochial Registers, 1567–1970)
5 Cumbria Archive Service
6 *Carlisle Journal,* 26th January 1839
7 *Carlisle Journal,* 12th January 1839
8 Cumbria Archive Service
9 *Carlisle Journal,* 30th November 1839
10 *Carlisle Journal,* Saturday 21st December 1839

CHAPTER TWELVE

Friends and Relations: Mysteries of John Graham's Will

John's long and somewhat rambling will, four pages in length with a half-page codicil added on the same day, was written in June, five months before his death. He would already have been suffering from his 'lingering illness' – the latter stages of tuberculosis. Much of the will is concerned with paying off debts, including what must then have been a sizeable mortgage. As there was no mention of this mortgage in his uncle's will, a little over twenty years earlier, this would seem to have been a fairly recently incurred debt. John may have had to pay for an extension to the Hall in order to accommodate the large family of his new tenant. He had also restocked the farm. It is also possible that his father, with his history of insolvency, may have run up further debts. Along with the other drastic measures John had taken to secure funds, this loan suggests he was a young man who, while he might own valuable property, found himself in a degree of financial difficulty.

John appointed two friends to act as trustees for his estate until his son reached the age of twenty-one. He gave them authority to sell his farming stock and personal estate, which they obviously did with some haste even before the will was proved. He made provision for his wife and he left an annuity for his father. This is the last confirmed record we have of Thomas. John instructed the trustees to make provision for his son's education – perhaps an understandable concern in view of Mary's illiteracy. Unlike his grandmother who was appointed as an executor to the wills of both his grandfather and his uncle, John's wife was not assigned a role in the execution of the will. She was not even given responsibility for the upbringing of their son. While she may have been provided for financially, Mary's long-term role seems to have been left uncertain.

John Graham's Will, 1840

John Graham of Knockupworth, in the parish of Grinsdale, gives, devises and bequeaths to his friends John Graham of Kirkandrews in the parish of Kirkandrews upon Eden, yeoman, and Thomas Sibson of Grinsdale, yeoman, all his freehold and customary estate and premises at Knockupworth (subject and chargeable with a mortgage encumbrance of one thousand nine hundred pounds) together with all his farming stock, crop and husbandry, utensils and personal effects from the day of his death until his infant son, John, or the youngest of his children if more than one, shall attain the age of twenty one years, upon trust.

- That John Graham and Thomas Sibson shall with all convenient speed as they in their discretion think fit sell and dispose of all farming stock and personal estate with the exception of his household furniture which he requests may be allowed to be used by his dear wife so long as she remains his widow but no longer unless his said friends think proper
- either by public sale or private contract for the best prices that can be had to be applied towards the payment of funeral and testamentary expenses and debts and the remainder (if any) to be applied towards the liquidation of the mortgage.
- Upon further trust, his real estate to let or assign the same to such tenant or tenants as they in their discretion shall think proper and to apply the rents and proceeds first towards the liquidation of the interest of the mortgage
- and then towards an annuity of ten pounds per annum to Thomas Graham, his father,
- and the remainder to be paid and applied to the maintenance of his dear wife, Mary,
- and the maintenance, education and support of his infant son, John Graham, and any other child or children he might have living, or his wife might be pregnant with at the time of his decease until his said son or the youngest of his children (if more than one) shall attain the age of twenty one years.
- After his child or children attain the age of twenty-one years he gives him or them all his real estate to share and share alike as tenants in common and not as joint tenants.

- He gives and bequeaths to his father, Thomas Graham, a clear annuity or yearly sum of ten pounds during the term of his natural life to be paid to him in two equal half-yearly payments to commence and be paid at the end of six calendar months next after his decease.
- From and after his children attain the age of twenty-one years he gives his wife an annuity or yearly sum of ten pounds per annum in lieu of her claim of Dower
- He charges the annuities to his father and wife upon the freehold of his customary estate.
- If his child or children should die before attaining the age of twenty-one (without leaving lawful issue) then he gives the freehold and customary estate to his wife for the term of her natural life provided she remains his widow.
- From and after her decease or marriage he gives the same to his father for the term of his natural life and after his decease to be sold and after paying the mortgage to be divided between his following cousins: John Forster, Thomas Forster, William Forster and Mary Dailey, the wife of William Dailey.
- The trustees shall not be liable for any debts incurred in the execution of the trusts and they may retain all the costs, charges and expenses which they may sustain.
- He appoints the said John Graham and Thomas Sibson guardians of his child or children and desires that they will see him or them brought up and educated in a proper manner suited to his condition in life and place him or them with a suitable master or masters to be taught or instructed in respect of some respectable occupation, profession or business and to do such or other acts as may be found necessary for his or their advancement in life.
- He appoints John Graham and Thomas Sibson joint executors of his will.
- Will dated 11th June 1839.
- Witnesses: George Sibson, solicitor, Carlisle; John Graham (Senior), Grinsdale.

He then adds a codicil written on the same day as the will. In it he:
- bequeaths one share of the residue after the death of his father to his relation Joseph Hewson of Maryport and one share to

> his cousins Mary Little, Margaret Little and Thomas Little, the children of Thomas and Margaret Little deceased and declares that the said shares shall be equal with those of John Forster, Thomas Forster, William Forster and Mary Dailey.

Will proved April 16th 1840.

Effects sub £300.[1]

The solicitor, George Sibson – who was a brother of the trustee, Thomas Sibson – was undoubtedly responsible for the wording of the will. Nevertheless it presumably reflected the dying man's intentions. Considering the state of John Graham's health, the provision made for further children was an over-optimistic legal necessity, though one that his great-grandfather might have been wise to consider. Perhaps understandably, in view of his wife's lack of education, John was anxious that his son would be 'brought up and educated in a proper manner that suited his condition in life.' That this was to be the responsibility of the trustees suggests that he did not have faith in Mary's ability to achieve it. The remaining references to the boy's upbringing are also revealing. He was to be placed 'with a suitable master or masters to be taught or instructed in respect of some respectable occupation, profession or business and to do such other acts as to be found necessary for his advancement in life.' Whether this reflected the precarious nature of the Knockupworth finances or John's own lack of interest in farming, it seems that his ambitions for his son lay elsewhere.

The provision that John made for his widow does not seem over-generous and was largely conditional on her remaining a widow, though a small annuity would be preserved even if she remarried. As she was only in her mid-twenties John must have thought that she was unlikely to remain a widow for long.

John's will – like that of his uncle, Thomas, – raises interesting questions about the identities of some of the relatives to whom he makes bequests. The friends that he appoints as trustees, John Graham of Kirkandrews and Thomas Sibson of Grinsdale will play an important role as the story unfolds and we will return to them later. But who are Joseph Hewson, the Forsters, the Daileys and the Littles? All of them are somehow related to John, yet not one is an obvious member of the Knockupworth family of Grahams.

The will refers to three cousins, probably children, with the surname Little. The fact that John's wife, Mary, was from a family called Little may only add to the confusion. Being relatives of his wife would not make them John's cousins. If they were actually his wife's cousins it is surprising that he does not make this clear. As I have said, Little is an extremely common name in Cumbria and this may be a different family altogether.

The will of John's uncle, Thomas Graham, left several unanswered questions. From the information we have it does not seem likely that any of the people Thomas referred to as 'cousins' could be first cousins and their exact relationship remains unclear. With John there is a convenient, though unproven, explanation. The Hewsons, Forsters, Daileys and Littles do not have an obvious place in the Knockupworth line of the Graham family; but they may be related to John's father.

Thomas Graham, one-time Carlisle spirit merchant and more lately self-styled yeoman, is shrouded in mystery and obscurity. He was clearly still alive when his son wrote his will, for John left him an annuity. We do not know when or where he was born. The entry for Thomas and Margaret's marriage in the Grinsdale Parish Register does not give their ages. From the date of her baptism we know that the bride must have been about twenty-four but we do not know the age of her husband. We have insufficient information to have much hope of tracing his life story.

We do not know if Thomas had any siblings. He could have had sisters who married men called Little and Forster. Their children would, therefore, have been John's first cousins. Unfortunately it is too early for there to be any census information that might substantiate this.

This is all speculation but there is one good reason for believing that these various relatives may have belonged to John's father's side of the family: under the terms of the will they were all to obtain their legacies only after Thomas Graham's death.

John Graham died just two years before the 1841 census. This was the first census that retained information about individual households. Even in an age of high mortality it is reasonable to suppose that most of the people who are mentioned in his will outlived him by at least two years and should therefore appear somewhere in the census. Locating them is a different matter! Nearly all have very common names. We do not know their ages. Siblings may be grown up and no longer living in the same household.

The census of 1841, unlike those carried out in later years, does not detail the relationships between family members. However, by looking at their ages, it is usually possible to make an educated guess that the older members of a household are likely to be the parents of younger ones with the same surname. How far does the census take us in trying to locate the recipients of John Graham's bequests?

We will start with the Littles: Mary, Margaret and Thomas – children of Thomas and Margaret Little, deceased. John has added them in a codicil, an afterthought by a sick man whose mind may have been just about sound enough to dictate a will. Perhaps his wife, his father or someone else pointed out to him that these orphaned children should not be overlooked. A search of the 1841 census provides a brief moment of false hope. At Castle Dyke, in the neighbouring parish of Beaumont, lived Margaret, Mary and Thomas Little – aged between twenty and sixteen. But these are not the orphans of Thomas and Margaret Little; they are the children of living farmer David Little and his wife Cathrine.

Joseph Hewson of Maryport is described as a 'relation'. Therefore it would seem that he was less closely related than the Little cousins. Joseph was also added to the will as an afterthought in the codicil. Hewson was not a particularly common name in Cumberland at the time and a search through the Cumberland records of the 1841 census reveals only two Joseph Hewsons who would have been alive at the time that the will was written. One is a thirty year-old bank agent living in Wigton. The other is a fifteen year-old apprentice who is in lodgings with a Mrs Sharp (surely a coincidence) in Market Place, Brigham. Brigham is reasonably close to Maryport, though actually much closer to Cockermouth. If we extend the spelling of the name to 'Howson' or 'Hooson', to allow for variations in the census records, perhaps a couple more possibilities appear. The Brigham apprentice may be the most likely candidate but the true identity of John Graham's relative remains elusive.

From the way John Graham words his bequests to his Forster and Dailey cousins it seems likely that Mary Dailey is the married sister of the three Forster brothers. Forster is another very common surname in the north of England and it occurs many times in the 1841 census. There is, however, one entry in particular that is worth noting. In Lowther Street, Carlisle, there lived a 95 year-old chair maker called John Forster. At the same address is thirty year-old William Forster, probably the old man's grandson. Is this one of John Graham's cousins?

What makes this entry especially interesting is that among several other people at the address are two children called Little: Margaret, aged twelve, and Thomas, aged seven. Could these be two of the missing orphans? There is no Mary listed but Mary, who appears to have been the oldest of the siblings, may have been at least fourteen and, in those days, old enough to start making her own way in the world. The inclusion of Forsters and Littles with the correct Christian names in the same household may be coincidental but it strengthens the case for these being John Graham's relatives.

Mary Dailey, who I take to be a sister of the Forster brothers, and her husband William, are easily identifiable in the census. They live in Houghton, Stanwix, and have a four year-old daughter, Sarah. William is a tailor. By 1851 they had moved to Westgate, Newcastle upon Tyne – William still working as a tailor. Although there are a number of Daileys in the census most are Irish families. Both William and Mary are recorded as having been born in Cumberland.

And so what of John's father, the elusive Thomas Graham? John made provision for him in his will but what became of him after John's death brought an end to the family's occupancy of the Knockupworth farm? We have too little information about him to be able to trace him with any degree of certainty. To even try to locate him in the 1841 census we have to make some assumptions. The first is that he survived his son by at least two years. The second is that he continued to live in Cumberland. The third regards his age; let us assume that he was no more than five years older or five years younger than his late wife, Margaret.

Even with such a common name, this narrows the search down quite considerably. We can narrow it even further if we assume that his second marriage was a good deal longer than his first, and that Elizabeth was still alive and living with him in 1841.

Although we cannot positively identify Thomas in the census there is one likely candidate. A publican called Thomas Graham, was living at Cumwhinton, Wetheral with Elizabeth Graham. Is this the couple who were married at Dalston Church in October 1820? Both are described as fifty-five years old but this census rounds ages to the nearest five years. Although it does not give a precise indication of their ages it suggests that they would have been in their mid thirties at the time of their marriage and Thomas would have been only a few years older than his first wife, Margaret.

The 1841 census did not succeed in recording all the inhabitants of

England who were living at the time and it is not certain that this is the late John Graham's missing father. However it is an interesting thought that this aging former spirit merchant may have ended up once again in the business of trading in alcoholic drinks. Somehow he seems like the sort of person who always managed to land on his feet!

Newspaper reports of deaths may add to our speculation about his final destiny. John's father may possibly have been the 'much esteemed' innkeeper, Thomas Graham, who died at Harrington in June 1843.[2] But with so many Thomas Grahams to choose from and so little concrete information about him, John and Hannah's father disappears into the crowd.

Notes

1 Cumbria Archive Service
2 *Carlisle Journal,* 24th June, 1843

CHAPTER THIRTEEN

His Dear Wife and Son

According to my mother, her grandfather, the infant John, was brought up by trustees who cheated him by using his money to buy stock for their own farms. While it is clear from his father's will that they had responsibility for his upbringing, as well as for his financial affairs, it seems doubtful that the trustees brought him up in a physical sense during his early years. The 1841 census records a Mary Graham, aged twenty-five, living in Grinsdale with a four-year-old John. The boy is around the correct age to be the heir to Knockupworth. On the night of the census John would have been a few days short of his fourth birthday. Mary would actually have been twenty-seven but her age would have been rounded down in that census. They were not at Knockupworth where David Wright, had taken over the running of the farm and was living in the farmhouse. Mary and John were living in Grinsdale village, near to Thomas Sibson, who was one of the trustees, and to Sibson Graham who was brother of the other. Also in the house was a five-year-old girl called Ann Dixon.

Dixon is a common name in the area but it is not a name that was associated with Grinsdale at the time. It does not appear on any of the gravestones in Grinsdale churchyard. Ann's identity remains a mystery but it seems unkind to leave her without a story.

When the announcement of John Graham's death appeared in the *Carlisle Journal* of 30th November 1839 the following notice appeared directly above it: 'At Carleton, on Sunday last, Ann, wife of John Dixon, farmer, aged 29 years.' Carleton is to the south of Carlisle, on the other side of the city from Grinsdale. There is no particular reason to think that the Grahams and the Dixons knew each other.

But four years earlier on 24th October 1835 a girl called Ann Dixon was baptised at St. Cuthbert's Church in Carlisle. Her parents were John and Ann Dixon.[1] The mother may or may not be the same Ann

Dixon who died in the same week as Mary's husband and it is not certain that her daughter is the little girl who appears in the census. But the girl who was baptised in 1835 would, like Mary's guest, have been five years old on the night of the census. We might wonder if Mary Graham and John Dixon, both recently bereaved, became known to each other and if, on the night of 6th June 1841, Mary was looking after John's motherless daughter. The evidence is circumstantial and may simply be a series of coincidences but it does at least give little Ann Dixon a possible story.

Three months before the census was held a death occurred in Grinsdale that may be highly significant in the history of the Graham family. We may recall that John and Mary had spent the early days of their marriage in the village of Thursby and it was here that their son had been born. There is reason to believe that they may have been living with John's great uncle, William Sharp.

On 5th March 1841 a death was recorded by the registrar at Carlisle of a William Sharp, aged 84 years – the same age that Hannah's older brother would be if he lived until this date. If this is the same William Sharp – and his age makes it extremely likely that it is – then he was clearly still alive when John and Mary lived at Thursby and might well have afforded them hospitality during the short period they were away from Knockupworth. His death certificate reveals that William died at Grinsdale. The cause of death is recorded as 'decay of nature', which we may interpret as natural old age and the death was reported to the registrar by Joseph Elliot of Monkhill. The census of that year reveals Joseph Elliot to be a sixteen-year-old joiner's son.

There would seem to be only one likely reason for William Sharp to have been in Grinsdale at the time of his death. There were no Sharp families in the village; there are no Sharp memorials in the churchyard. The only association that the Sharps had with Grinsdale was through their connection with the Grahams. And the only members of the Knockupworth Graham family living in Grinsdale in 1841 were John's widow and her young son.

If John and Mary lived with William Sharp before moving to the Knockupworth farmhouse was Mary now repaying that hospitality? It would seem that William continued to live with Mary after her husband's death and that she looked after him during his final years. If William had lived a few weeks longer he would have been recorded in the census. Without such evidence this remains supposition but it would explain a continued connection between the two families that may help to solve one of our later mysteries.

We have no way of knowing for how long young John remained in his mother's care or how big a part the trustees played in his upbringing. I have been unable to conclusively identify John in the 1851 census and, though there are some anecdotal family stories, I have no positive information about him from this period of his life. Tracing someone with a name as common as John Graham can be very difficult, especially if they give their place of birth as Carlisle or Cumberland rather than the specific village in which they were born.

While John remains elusive, the person most closely connected to him does not. His mother moved to Carlisle where she remarried in 1845. Her second husband was a publican called John Beck, a widower with three sons from his first marriage. Mr Beck, a former butcher, had taken over the tenancy of the Wheat Sheaf in Rickergate from the mother of his first wife.

Almost exactly six years after announcing the death of Mary's first husband the *Carlisle Journal* carried this happier announcement:

> At St Mary's Church on the 17th inst., Mr John Beck, innkeeper, Rickergate, to Mrs Mary Graham, Etterby Street.[2]

Etterby Street is in Stanwix, a highly respectable area on the north side of the city. Now an attractive suburb, Stanwix was described in a house sale advertisement, carried by the *Carlisle Journal* in February 1841, as the 'pleasant and improving village of Stanwix, near Carlisle.' Though terraced, the houses of Etterby Street have individual style and character. This is not the sort of street built for industrial workers. Number 28 was advertised to be let in April 1842, containing seven good rooms, with a small garden in front and another behind.[3] The previous September number 5 had been for sale and was described as having two sitting rooms, four bedrooms, kitchen, pantries, cellar 'and other conveniences.'[4]

Although Mary's long-term annuity was not substantial she would at the time have been benefitting from other income from the estate. Regardless of whether she owned or rented the property, or even had rooms in part of a house, it seems likely that Mary's legacy was sufficient to provide her with a comfortable home.

It is possible that it may also have set her up in business. The following advertisement appeared in the *Carlisle Journal* of 13th February 1841:

> To be SOLD by PRIVATE CONTRACT a convenient Freehold DWELLING HOUSE, situate No 10 ETTERBY STREET, STANWIX with a convenient HATTERS' WORKSHOP attached, with every convenience for carrying on the business of Hat Manufacture.

As we do not know Mary's address in Etterby Street we have no particular reason to think that she bought this property but it is tempting to speculate that she may have been the purchaser. There must have been a reason why a woman who had spent her entire life in the countryside chose to move so close to the city. From a census return many years later we know that one of Mary's daughters worked in the millinery trade. Might she have learned her craft from her mother? However this speculation may be fanciful, since, as that year's census shows, Mary remained in Grinsdale for at least four months after the date on which this advertisement was placed. And, although she had an income from her late husband's estate, purchasing such a property may have been beyond her means.

When Mary lived there, Etterby Street was only partly developed. A row of seventeen houses had been built by 1837 and others were added in the 1840s. A hawthorn hedge, growing along the southern side, remained in place until that side of the street was developed in the 1890s.[5] Stanwix was still a village and Etterby Street, though close to the city centre, would have had a largely rural aspect. Today much of the land alongside the River Eden is public parkland, still grazed by sheep and cattle, but much also has been built on since Mary's time. In the nineteenth century it was all agricultural land, part of the Duke of Devonshire's estate – an expanse of countryside near the centre of the city.

Whenever she walked into the city from her home in Etterby Street, Mary would have passed – or even crossed – these green fields. She would then have crossed the river over the stone arches of Eden Bridge, a structure that had been erected within her lifetime. Rickergate was only a short walk from her home but very much part of the busy city centre.

We might wonder how she first became acquainted with Mr John Beck, the landlord of a Rickergate tavern. The location of her home suggests that she was receiving sufficient income from her husband's estate to be able to live comfortably without the need for menial employment. She may possibly have set up her own business but it seems unlikely that she had become an employee at the Wheat Sheaf.

If her son was still with her perhaps she and John were walking by the river one day when they met John Beck and his sons doing the same. Or perhaps while visiting the Carlisle shops she met him in the city.

Or it is possible that Mr Beck was acquainted with Mr John Bell, the proprietor of another Rickergate inn, the George and Dragon, who owned property in Etterby Street. It is conceivable that Bell may even have been Mary's landlord. Perhaps John Beck accompanied him when he was visiting his tenants. Or if Mary was in the millinery trade perhaps Mr Beck was in need of a hat!

John Beck must have thought that Mary Graham, an attractive young widow with an income large enough to enable her to live in Etterby Street, was well worth his interest. We must suppose that he realised that some of the benefits Mary received would cease upon her remarriage. She was nonetheless the mother of the boy who would inherit the Knockupworth estate and, since John was still well short of the age of twenty-one, this might, for the next few years at least, be a situation of some benefit. As we shall see, Mr Beck saw at least one opportunity to try to turn it to his advantage.

On the same day that the newspaper reported the wedding there appeared an announcement that Mr Beck was moving from the Wheat Sheaf to the Three Crowns. Whether or not Mary still had her own son with her, she was taking on the upbringing of her husband's three boys. The youngest was about four years old.

Mary who had been born at Bewcastle, a village so remote it makes Grinsdale seem almost urban, was to spend the rest of her life in cities.

And now we will digress from the story of the Grahams of Knockupworth and turn our attention to the trustees of John's will, his friends John Graham of Kirkandrews (confusingly bearing the same name but apparently not a relative) and Thomas Sibson – the men John trusted more than his wife to manage his estate and educate his son. Sibson, may have been the same man who suffered a severe beating by assailants outside Mr Thomlinson's farm in 1827. He would have been in his mid-thirties at the time of John's death.

Victorian village life was far from simple and it seems that the course of the trustees' partnership did not run smoothly. John Graham of Kirkandrews had a sister called Ruth. Ruth had obviously caught the eye of unmarried Thomas Sibson, to whom she was distantly related, but Ruth's passion lay elsewhere. In August 1841 the *Carlisle Journal* reported a case in which Ruth was suing Sibson for slander:

> the plaintiff being of good character was about to be married to Mr William Robinson of Cargo; and the defendant, to injure and defame her, had used certain malicious words which were set forth in the declaration.[6]

The defence lawyer said the words 'had been uttered in a moment of disappointment and mortification.' Sibson had withdrawn the remarks and offered a humble apology. Miss Graham's counsel said that she had received 'the deepest injury to her reputation as a virtuous woman, which is to a lady dearer than life.' Her object was not 'to put money in her purse, or put damages in her hands' but 'to establish her character and vindicate her virtue.' In accepting the apology on her behalf, her counsel said 'he trusted the passing cloud which had darkened the morning of the young lady's life would be dispelled, and her happiness, now that it had passed away, would be brighter.' The plaintiff was awarded forty shillings.

This was not a good start for the stewardship of Knockupworth but the incident was dwarfed by what was to follow.

Notes

1 Family Search
2 *Carlisle Journal,* 22nd November 1845
3 *Carlisle Journal,* 16th April 1842
4 *Carlisle Journal,* 27th September 1841
5 Carlisle Encyclopedia (http://www.carlisleshistory.co.uk/page27.htm)
6 *Carlisle Journal,* 7th August 1841

CHAPTER FOURTEEN

A Dark Tale of Poison

John Graham senior, who witnessed John Graham of Knockupworth's will in 1839, was the father of trustee and executor John Graham of Kirkandrews. Though they were apparently not related to the Knockupworth Grahams, the two families were obviously well acquainted. John Graham senior was a Grinsdale farmer who, after their daughter's marriage, lived alone with his wife, Ruth. He may well have been the 'useful yeoman' with the good reading and singing voice that Walter Fletcher commended in his Diocesan Book in 1818. It was later said of him that he 'was a man well and generally known and universally respected as an intelligent, industrious, thrifty, amiable yeoman.'[1] By the 1840s John's second son, Sibson Graham, had taken over the farm in the village but John, now well into his seventies, still helped out. John Graham junior rented another farm, also owned by his father, at nearby Kirkandrews-on-Eden.

On Tuesday 20th May 1845 John Graham senior died in suspicious circumstances, showing possible symptoms of arsenic poisoning. Two days later an inquest was opened at Mr Graham's house by coroner Mr W. Carrick. One of the inquest jury was David Wright the tenant farmer of Knockupworth. The inquest was attended by several friends and relatives and by the vicars of Grinsdale and Burgh by Sands. Witnesses on the first day of the inquest included the dead man's widow, Ruth, his younger son, Sibson, and a number of servants and neighbours. The day's hearing concluded at six o'clock and was adjourned, to be recommenced at Carlisle on 30th May.

Suspicion fell on some 'yeasted cake' made by Mrs Graham from flour, yeast and salt butter and baked for her in a neighbour's oven. Mr Graham had become ill after eating some of the cake for supper. His wife also suffered sickness to a lesser degree. Though suffering from repeated bouts of sickness, Mr Graham had continued to work on his son's farm over the next few days. Several other people, having heard talk of the cakes being poisoned had, in a rather cavalier manner, tasted them in order to dispel the rumours. Fortunately, despite becoming sick, they all lived to regret it. Mr Graham's condition worsened over the next few days. Dr Anderson who visited him did not at the time suspect poison, believing that he may have been suffering from cholera. The old man died on the following Tuesday.

It was remembered that one day during the previous February Mr Graham, his wife and his elder son, John, had all become violently sick after eating a potato pot for dinner. Dr Anderson had been sent for and had prescribed emetics. The potato pot had been thrown on to the dung heap without being analysed.

The finger of suspicion was already pointing towards Mr Graham's elder son who had visited the house while the cakes were being made. But if John had wanted to kill his father, and (apart from the early acquisition of his supposed inheritance) there seemed little motive for him to do so, surely he could have chosen a more efficient method than one that was likely to wipe out several other people as well? Besides on the occasion of the potato pot poisoning he had himself been the most violently sick of all.

John Graham was questioned. He informed the court that he had sold his stock and given up the farm. He was now lodging in the Kirkandrews farmhouse with Mr John Beswick, who had taken over the tenancy. After visiting his parents on the Thursday he had caught a train to Newcastle where he was intending to meet friends and look for a place to keep cattle. While he was away he was informed that his father was gravely ill and had returned home. The inference drawn from this seems to have been that his journey may have been a means of removing himself from the scene while the cakes were consumed. He had tried and failed to persuade his mother to accompany him on his trip to Newcastle. Was it suspected that this was an attempt to get her out of the way while his father ate the cakes?

Benjamin Mitchell, a farm worker, reported that around last hay time he had found a package in the turnip shed that he suspected contained rat poison. After hearing rumours that old Mr Graham had been poisoned he had checked that the parcel was still there. It was, still unopened. He had taken it indoors where the housekeeper had opened it to reveal a white powder. Mitchell had tasted it before spitting it out and the housekeeper had then burned it all on the fire.

Mitchell told the court that when he heard about this John Graham flew into a rage and said,

'Oh Ben! Oh Ben! What have you done to me?' It seemed that he feared he would be implicated by the discovery of rat poison on his property.

The dead man's daughter, Ruth, who it seems had not married Mr Robinson of Cargo after all, but was now the wife of saddler William Cannell of Carlisle, had visited her parents while they were ill. She said that she believed both her brothers to be on good terms with their father.

The autopsy report of Mr Elliot, surgeon, and Dr James concluded that Mr Graham had died of arsenic poisoning.

At this point the inquest was dramatically adjourned and a new inquest opened into the death of John junior's wife, Margaret, who was generally known as Peggy. After her death the previous November rumours had circulated and it was now realised she had been suffering from very similar symptoms.

Mrs Graham's body was exhumed from Kirkandrews graveyard and was found still to be in very good condition. The presence of arsenic, a substance used in early embalming fluids, would, it was thought, have helped to preserve the body. Her brother, Richard Hind, and a friend, Jane Hetherington, had the grim task of confirming the identity of the corpse. Extensive tests carried out by Mr Elliot, Dr James, Dr Cartmel and Dr Tinniswood – they were praised by the coroner for their thoroughness – found large quantities of arsenic. Following the autopsy John Graham was arrested on suspicion of the murders of his wife and father.

The new inquest continued with the same jury. Much was made of the fact that John Graham had refused to allow anyone but himself attend to his wife while she was sick. Medical opinion seemed to be that the poison had not been administered in a single dose but had been fed to her on separate occasions over a period of days.

There were allegations that Graham had been in a relationship with a servant girl called Margaret Rickerby who had left his employment on the previous Martinmas[2]. There had been occasions when Miss Rickerby had been heard to speak insolently to her mistress and John Graham had not reprimanded her. She denied that she had left at Mrs Graham's insistence.

There were several occasions when the coroner, Mr Carrick, grew impatient with the evasive and inconsistent answers of a number of witnesses, including Margaret Rickerby. There had been meetings between Graham and Rickerby in various public houses. On one occasion they had travelled to Haltwhistle to meet at an inn. On another they had both spent the night at an inn called The Grapes, though the landlady had refused them a double room. Although Graham's bed was said not to have been slept in, Rickerby denied that they had slept together.

Dr Oliver, one of two physicians to have treated Peggy Graham in the days before her death, stated that he had previously treated her between 1st March and 16th April for an ulcerated sore throat, which had been so severe it had attacked the soft part of the palate. Under questioning Dr Oliver reluctantly revealed that he believed that this may have been caused by syphilis but he had 'avoided enquiring into the previous history of the case.' He was, he said 'in a delicate position, and so is every medical man in such a case.'

Several witnesses reported that John Graham had been extremely agitated at the prospect of his wife's body being disinterred. According to Reverend Isaac Dodgson, the curate of Beaumont, he had said that: 'taking up poor Peggy was more than he could bear.' Jane Hetherington reported that he: 'said he would rather be shot than that she should be lifted.' While it might be considered reasonable for any bereaved husband to find the prospect distressing, the inference drawn from Graham's agitation was that he must have had something to hide.

Superintendent of Police, John Sabbage reported that when he was arrested Graham had been anxious to know if officers had been to Newcastle. This led them to carry out investigations in that city where they discovered a druggist who remembered, some months earlier, selling rat poison to a man of Graham's description.

Mr Carrick's summing up left little doubt that he thought John Graham had a case to answer. He again alluded to the uncooperative nature of some of the witnesses. He said:

> 'It is clear and manifest that their oaths have been grossly violated, the truth perverted, and suppressed to an extent seldom witnessed in any Court of Justice. It is painful to witness such scenes of moral depravity, but the more so when the effect is to conceal and hide one of the most horrid crimes under heaven.'

The coroner did not speculate as to the reasons behind the evasiveness and insubordination of these witnesses. If they were trying to protect John Graham this would seem to contradict the evidence of Reverend

Dodgson who said that Graham claimed that 'his friends had all forsaken him.' It may have been their own reputations that they were trying to protect. Or had they been bribed or intimidated? It was perhaps more than likely due to a natural instinct of these rustic people not to cooperate with authority.

The inquest jury concluded that Margaret Graham died from taking arsenic that was deliberately administered by her husband.

The inquest into the father's death was then resumed. This time the coroner urged the jury to be cautious. While it might be reasonable to suppose that if Graham had murdered his wife he was also responsible for the death of his father, the evidence in this case was less conclusive. Anyone who was cleared of a crime because of insufficient evidence could not be retried if new facts came to light. Guided by Mr Carrick's directions, the jury decided that the deceased, John Graham, died from the effect of poison wilfully administered to him but recorded a verdict of wilful murder against some person or persons unknown.

There was then yet another dramatic turn of events. Superintendent Sabbage decided to examine the waistcoat that John Graham had been wearing on the day he had visited his parents' home. The garment, hitherto disregarded, and been left hanging in the accused man's house. Traces of arsenic were found in one of the pockets. It is not difficult to work out – as did the trial judge – that Sabbage himself or someone else with malicious intent could have planted this evidence, but it was sufficient for Graham to be charged with his father's murder.

The case, it was said in the *Carlisle Journal*, 'continues to be the engrossing subject of interest in Carlisle and throughout the county.'

John Graham appeared before the magistrates on Saturday 19th July 1845. Given the opportunity to speak he said nothing except that he was innocent. He was sent for trial at the next assizes.

When the trial was held on Wednesday 6th August the defence lawyer, Mr Wilkins, appealed for the case to be postponed until a later date because the advance publicity might prejudice his client's right to a fair trial. This request was rejected. He was first tried for his wife's murder. During the trial, which was completed in a single day, much of the inquest evidence was repeated.

Mid-nineteenth century justice did not allow defendants the right to speak in their own defence. In this particular trial perhaps this was just as well. John Graham might have been well advised to remain silent, his lawyer fearing that he would incriminate himself.

Mr Wilkins made out a case for his acquittal. John Graham had hitherto always been regarded as being of good character. John had borrowed £200 from his father-in-law, which he was required to pay back if Peggy died childless. As they had no children her death would not be in his interests. Members of Mrs Graham's family, the Hinds, appeared – or so the lawyer claimed – to bear a grudge against their brother-in-law. (Hardly surprising we might think if they believed he had murdered their sister.)

Mr Wilkins continued with his defence. None of the witnesses had been able to positively identify the woman he had been seen meeting as Margaret Rickerby. Neither the Newcastle druggist nor his son could be absolutely certain that the man to whom they had sold rat poison several months earlier was John Graham – though both had red whiskers. Finally, the defence lawyer made much of the fact that John Sewell, a Burgh by Sands doctor who had attended Mrs Graham, had sent the prescription for her medication to a pharmacist in a lower class area of Carlisle. Was it not possible, he suggested, that some arsenic might accidentally have been mixed with the medication? The prosecution lawyer countered this by reminding the judge that the very reason the doctor had sent for the medication was that Peggy was already suffering from severe vomiting. Had Mr Wilkins sown sufficient doubt in the jurors' minds to save John Graham from the gallows?

After deliberating for an hour the jury returned a verdict of not guilty. It was decided to proceed with the trial for the murder of his father on the following day. This time the trial ran into a second day but the jury took only fifteen minutes to acquit him.

After extensively reporting the inquest hearings and trials over a period of four months the *Carlisle Journal*'s concluding report on Saturday 16th August consisted of a single sentence:

> John Graham remained in gaol on Friday night, after his acquittal, and left early the following morning, by mail, for Glasgow.[3]

John Graham senior is buried in Grinsdale churchyard along with his wife, Ruth, and an infant daughter. Ruth lived to be eighty-nine, a considerable age in the mid-nineteenth century. Sibson Graham and his wife lie in a grave nearby.

A belief has grown up among some who have taken an interest in this story that after his departure on the Glasgow mail coach John Graham was never seen or heard of again. This can be dispelled by a visit to the graveyard at Kirkandrews-on-Eden, for John is buried there with his wife. The date of his return is unknown; as is the nature of his reception from the family and friends whom he believed had forsaken him in the days before his arrest. His stay in the village was to be brief. In November 1849, four years after his trial, he died at the age of forty-eight. The cause of death was recorded as an obstruction of the bowels from which he had been suffering for a year. He was described on his death certificate as a yeoman.

His death was witnessed and reported to the registrar by Edward Hetherington whose wife, Jane, had identified Peggy Graham's corpse when it was disinterred and later gave evidence about John's state of mind. Edward Hetherington had been a gunner in the Royal Horse Artillery and was a veteran of the Battle of Waterloo.[4]

Notes

1 *Carlisle Journal,* 14th June 1845
2 Martinmas: 11th November
3 The above account is based on Petra Mitchinson's transcripts of the *Carlisle Journal* newspaper reports of the inquests and trials: [CUMB] Carlisle Journal 1845 – The GRAHAM Poisoning Cases by "Petra Mitchinson."
4 Information about Grinsdale and Kirkandrews-upon-Eden graves courtesy of Bridget Casson.

1. Artist's impression of Knockupworth Hall in the nineteenth century, by James Bainbridge

2. River Eden at Grinsdale

3. Gateway to Grinsdale churchyard

4. St. Kentigern's Church, Grinsdale

5. Knockupworth graves in Grinsdale churchyard; courtesy of Bridget Casson, Feb. 2016

6. First Graham gravestone

7. Second Graham gravestone

8. James Robson of Knockupwards memorial

9. Hannah's sampler; courtesy of Liz Johnson

10. Mary and Jane Sewell

11. Mary Beck (daughter), back row, first on right; courtesy of Liz Johnson

12. Margaret Ann Lancaster, nee Beck; courtesy of Liz Johnson

13. Mary Beck's grave,
Toxteth Park Cemetery

14. Grosvenor College group;
W.S. Graham fourth from left,
front row

15. Rugby team (probably Grosvenor College); W.S. Graham front row, centre

16. Family group outside Knockupworth Hall; left to right, William, Mary Sewell, John, Jane, Robert

17. John Graham
(1864–1948)

18. R.H.
Graham
(1865–1922)

19. Richard Graham
(1867–1935)

20. W.S. Graham
(1870–1920)

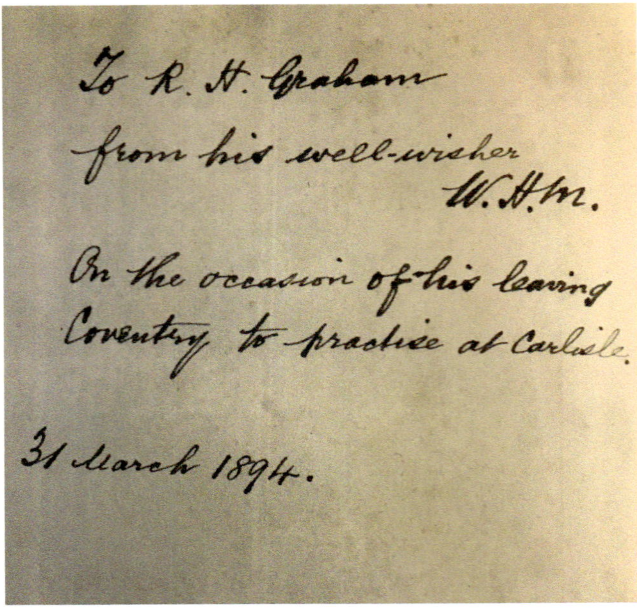

To R. H. Graham
from his well-wisher
W. H. M.

On the occasion of his leaving
Coventry to practise at Carlisle.

31 March 1894.

21. Inscription inside poetry anthology presented to R.H. Graham

22. John Graham (on right) with bank employee outside Aspatria branch

23. Isabella Holmes/Graham

24. Knockupworth Farmhouse; Isabella Holmes and son Edward on right

25. Harvest at Knockupworth; R.H. Graham on far right; Isabella Holmes and son Edward, third from left.

26. Cyril and Jack Graham

27. Cyril Graham

28. Richard and Robert Graham

29. John Graham with shorthorn bull

30. Phyllis and Dick Graham

CHAPTER FIFTEEN

Exhibition, Empire and Exile

On Saturday 24th June 1837 the *Carlisle Journal* gave details of the death, four days earlier, of William IV and of the proclamation of Victoria as the new Queen.

So began what was to be the longest reign in British history until exceeded by her great-great granddaughter Elizabeth II. This period of history has become known as the Victorian Age. However as Trevelyan says, we must not think of these years 'as having a fixed likeness to each other merely because more than sixty of them were presided over by "the Queen".' He goes on to say that the unity of the Victorian era is found in the lack of any great external threat from war or catastrophe and in the prevailing 'seriousness of thought and self-discipline of character.'[1]

Trevelyan defines the Victorian Age as the period between the Great Reform Bill of 1832 – five years before the Queen's accession – and the end of the nineteenth century. In terms of the Graham family history the onset of Victoria's reign roughly coincides with the family vacating Knockupworth Hall in early 1837. When they returned she was about to enter the final decade her life. For the Grahams, the Victorian Age was mainly a time of exile from their ancestral home.

It was a period of great social, political and economic change. Later in the century further Reform Bills would extend the franchise to the majority of the male population but the 1832 Act only resulted in one man in seven being able to vote. The right to vote depended on having a legitimate claim to property. Britain did engage in wars – in Crimea, Afghanistan, Africa and elsewhere – but they were fought in distant lands and hardly needed to concern the farmers of rural Cumberland. The threat of invasion that had been so much part of life during the times of 'Weaver John' and his children had become a distant memory.

Ships that had been designed for military conflict found peaceful service. It was an age of exploration and discovery. A few months before Victoria's accession, HMS Beagle had returned from its five-year voyage, surveying the coast of South America and circumnavigating the world. On board was a young naturalist, Charles Darwin. It would be over two decades before Darwin would publish his treatise, *On the Origin of Species*. His findings on evolution are so embedded in our thinking today that it is difficult to imagine how revolutionary and controversial they were at the time, or how vigorously they were opposed, even by many within the scientific establishment.

A few weeks before the dying John Graham made his will in the Knockupworth farmhouse, the *Carlisle Journal* briefly announced preparations for another momentous voyage of exploration. This was James Clark Ross's expedition to the Antarctic Circle 'for the purpose of making magnetic observations in the southern hemisphere.'[2] The Carlisle press then seems to have ignored Ross's arduous but ultimately successful voyage until the ships returned in 1843. Then the *Carlisle Patriot* reported that:

> The acquisitions to geology, geography, but above all towards the elucidations of the great mystery of terrestrial magnetism, raise this voyage to a pre-eminent rank among the greatest achievements of British courage, intelligence and enterprise.[3]

Less than two years later the same two ships, Erebus and Terror, were being fitted out for an Arctic expedition with the aim of discovering the elusive North West Passage. The *Carlisle Journal* announced this 'New Polar Expedition' in a very brief paragraph in its 'Art and Science' column on 22nd February 1845, and a month later produced a fuller account, which listed the senior crew members of the two ships.[4] The actual departure of Sir John Franklin's ill-fated expedition seems to have escaped the attention of the Carlisle press. Its readership was soon to be gripped by what seemed at the time to be a more sensational story closer to home. On 20th May, the day after the ships set sail, an elderly farmer died in Grinsdale. His death and his son's subsequent trial for murder would make gripping reading for several weeks to come.

However, towards the end of the year, Carlisle's newspapers began publishing occasional reports on the early stages of the expedition's progress. As time went by, references to the news – or rather lack of news – concerning the voyage became more frequent. The reports, at first reassuring, became increasingly pessimistic until, years later, it became clear that all of the men had perished in the ice. This tragedy was a rare blow to the confidence of Victorian Britain.

By 1845, the year of the Grinsdale murder trial and Mary Graham's marriage to John Beck, the Queen had reigned for over seven years. For five of those years she had been married to her German cousin, Prince Albert, and she had given birth to the first four of their children.

The massive industrial expansion that Britain experienced during this period was the result of the exploitation of natural resources such as coal and iron and the development of transport. In the early days of the Industrial Revolution canals had enabled the movement of raw materials and manufactured products. They were soon to be superseded by a faster and more efficient means of transport. The railways had a huge impact on industry, agriculture and social life. Not only could trains carry manufactured goods, but also fresh produce could be rushed from rural producers to city consumers. In most respects this was to the advantage of farmers but later in the century there would be a downside: better transport meant that American grain could be imported more easily; and after the Corn Laws were abolished in 1846, farmers no longer enjoyed the benefits of protectionist policies. One result of the 1832 Reform Act was that the interests of merchants were now represented in Parliament – the dominance of landowners had been broken. There was now an irresistible pressure for free trade. Rural life, seemingly unchanging for generations, could not escape its impact.

The nineteenth century saw a transformation from a countryside that was largely self-sufficient to one that was inextricably linked with towns and cities. Rural people had not only grown their own food they had also made most of their own possessions. Now, with better transport links and an expanding economy, the people of the countryside became both suppliers of food to the urban populations and consumers of their products.[5] Itinerate traders dwindled in number as village shops became commonplace. Goods that had once been the monopoly of rural craftsmen could now be made in factories and, as incomes rose, more people could afford to buy them.

Even today Grinsdale is still a country village. But, being only a few miles from Carlisle, the resilient people of earlier times would have regarded the city as being within easy walking distance. And the occupants of Knockupworth Hall would not have needed to walk. The grounds in front of the house contained a turning circle for a horse and carriage. The marked division between town and countryside may have applied less to Grinsdale than it did to more isolated villages of similar size. But, for country and town alike, life was undoubtedly changing.

By 1851 the population of Carlisle had risen, from fewer than ten thousand at the turn of the century, to over twenty five thousand. It had truly become an industrial city. The cotton mills flourished during the early part of the century but later fell into decline. However, the city had a broad industrial base, which included heavy engineering, biscuit making, printing, brewing and brick making.

As in other cities, industrial progress did not promote the well being of the factory workers who produced the goods. Most received low wages and many lived in poverty and squalor, and like most cities, Carlisle was ill-equipped to cope with its expanding population. Reporting on the insanitary conditions, the *Carlisle Journal* said that Carlisle had once been described in the House of Commons as 'one of the most healthy places in the kingdom.' About half a century ago it had ranked very highly in 'the health and comfort of the community.' It was feared this was no longer the case: 'The population had greatly increased and manufactories had extended; but the means of carrying off offensive matter had not kept pace with the increase of the town.'

The problem, it was claimed, was largely due to part of the city having been built on the ruins of the ancient town. Water from sewers was able to force its way into wells:

> Whenever drains were stopped, or did not act properly, there fevers were almost sure to prevail. This had been the case in Rickergate and George Street, where the inhabitants were frequently annoyed by stagnant water. In the course of the present year there had been upwards of 200 cases of typhus fever in the town and much of this [...] could be ascribed to our want of proper drains.[6]

This indicates that there was still confusion between typhus and typhoid, it being the latter that was caused by contaminated water. And there was by now another devastating disease that shared this source of infection. Although Carlisle was less affected by the sporadic outbreaks of cholera than many other towns, it was not entirely spared. In January 1849 the Carlisle Journal reported:

> One or two persons have died in Carlisle this week of diseases having much the appearance of cholera. They were persons living in crowded rooms, and in the midst of filth and uncleanliness. If they were cases of cholera it is gratifying to add that so far there are no appearances of further progress of the disease.[7]

Even when the disease was not present in the city the threat of an outbreak was a constant fear. The local press kept readers informed of outbreaks in other parts of the country: 'The ravages of the Cholera are again upon the increase – especially in the metropolis.'[8]

Of 2,796 deaths in London during the last week of August of that year 1,663 were from cholera. And the disease was much closer at hand. 'Fearful ravages' were reported in Workington and Maryport but 'In Carlisle we are happy to say there are at present no signs of the disease.' In September 1853 the newspaper reported that extensive precautions were being taken in Carlisle after an outbreak in Newcastle.[9] It is perhaps unsurprising that Dr Anderson, visiting a sick Grinsdale farmer in 1845, should have mistaken the symptoms of his patient's arsenic poisoning for a case of cholera.

At least the Carlisle authorities were aware of the health risks and were taking steps to remedy them, and in particular taking note of Edwin Chadwick's 1842 Parliamentary Report on an inquiry into the Sanitary Conditions of the Labouring Population of Great Britain. In his book *Georgian and Victorian Carlisle* Sidney Towill reports that:

> The first positive step taken in Carlisle to obtain an adequate domestic water supply of unpolluted water, which was also adequate to service a sewerage system of a type proposed by Chadwick, was the formation in 1846 of a joint stock company to supply the city with water from the River Eden at a point adjacent to its junction with the River Petteril.[10]

Towill goes on to say that, 'by 1849 760 private dwellings at £10 and above, and 2619 dwellings at under £10 were connected to the supply.'

By 1852 there were over seven thousand miles of railways in England and Scotland, and Carlisle had, by degrees, become very much part of this network. The Newcastle and Carlisle Railway was completed in 1838 – taking what was for passengers a rather inconvenient route to the south of the city in order to transport coal to the canal basin. In 1843 the Maryport to Carlisle Railway was opened and the Lancaster to Carlisle line completed in 1848. Lines from Scotland were developed between 1847 and 1851. Carlisle Citadel Station, built in 1847, had by 1851 become the city's main railway station.

Although industrial expansion had been the driving force behind the railways they also had a huge impact on social life. Coupled with road improvements they provided new affordable opportunities for ordinary people to travel. And in 1851 London became a major destination for thousands of these new travellers.

Largely the vision of Prince Albert, the Great Exhibition provided Britain with an opportunity to show off its standing as the major industrial and economic power in the world. Held in the great iron and glass structure of the Crystal Palace in Hyde Park, it was the first international exhibition of manufactured goods. A hundred thousand exhibits from over fifteen thousand contributors were displayed along a distance of more than ten miles. Queen Victoria opened the exhibition on 1st May 1851. At first, admission was £3 for gentlemen and £2 for ladies but from 24th May the masses were allowed in for a shilling a head. They came in thousands. Special excursion trains were laid on to the capital. A third class ticket from York cost five shillings. Third class carriages had initially resembled open cattle trucks, but the 1844 Regulation of Railways Act had decreed that third class passengers should be protected from the weather and provided with benches to sit on. By the time it closed on 11th October the exhibition had attracted over six million visitors, making a profit £186,000.

Britain's industrial expansion depended on trade and in the nineteenth century this to a great extent depended on the expansion of its empire. The American colonies had been lost; it was now largely in the east that this expansion lay. Until its collapse the East India Company pursued Britain's commercial interests in India. With its colonial influence in Africa and Australasia and its continued presence in Canada and the Caribbean, Britain had become the world's main imperial power.

While industrialisation led to urban expansion, farming itself was becoming increasingly mechanised. At first this amounted to simple horse-powered machines, such as harrows, iron ploughs and threshing machines; but steam power, the driving force behind the Industrial Revolution, was soon to play an important role in the English fields.

The Great Exhibition had given manufacturers an opportunity to showcase a range of agricultural machinery. Steam traction engines, mechanical reapers and mowing machines were to transform harvesting. In *Victorian Country Life* Janet Sacks states that between 1871 and 1900 the proportion of cereals cut by machine increased from 25% to 80%.[11]

Steam driven threshing machines were expensive and usually hired from contractors. We do not know when they were introduced at Knockupworth but there is photographic evidence of the Grahams using them there in the early years of the twentieth century.

For several decades after 1839 the Grahams did not farm the Knockupworth land themselves but the hall and the farm still provided much of their income. And, with a growing need to feed the urban population, a mixed farm with a dairy herd is likely to have been profitable.

Despite the changes that were taking place across Britain, rural Cumberland retained its own distinct character. Nowhere was this more evident than in the sporting activities that were pursued by its inhabitants. In an online article depicting Victorian culture in Cumberland, Guy Woolnough says:

> Sport is just one area of culture where Cumbria has long differed from the rest of England. Hound trailing, sheep dog trials, fell racing and Cumberland and Westmorland wrestling were all Cumberland inventions which enjoyed growing popularity in the 19th century.[12]

These sports were well supported and highly regarded by the whole community. Pugilism – bare knuckle fighting – was, on the other hand, considered disreputable. Cock fighting became illegal when the Prevention of Cruelty to Animals Act was passed in 1849 but it did not immediately die out. Woolnough says that it had a strong following in Victorian Cumberland and its supporters resented the law and the interference of the police with their sport. Cock fighting had supporters among all classes, illegal fights were attended by gentlemen and some magistrates were sympathetic. Many other Cumbrians condemned the sport as 'depraved and immoral.' Woolnough describes the paradox that: 'Prize fighting was reviled, wrestling was revered and cock fighting divided opinion.'

For many, interest in sport was driven by gambling. Pugilists, wrestlers, runners, dogs and fighting birds could make or lose money for those willing to wager on their success. And the railways provided new opportunities for gambling men; racecourses, such as York and Doncaster were now within reach of Carlisle.

One of the highlights of the 1851 racing calendar was the 'Great Match' or rematch between Voltigeur, the dual Derby and St. Leger winner of 1850, and The Flying Dutchman, who had performed the same feat in the previous year. Voltigeur's St. Leger victory had come as the result of a rerun after dead heating the first race. Over the next two days the colt was entered for two more races at the Doncaster meeting. The first was the Scarborough Handicap, in which he walked over. Then he lined up against The Flying Dutchman in the Doncaster Cup. Although Voltigeur won the race by half a length, his opponent's jockey was said to have ridden a poor race, allegedly after a night of heavy drinking. And so it was arranged that a rematch should be held at York Racecourse in the following spring.

The 'Great Match' was held on 13th May 1851. It drew an estimated 100,000 spectators – the largest crowd seen at the Knavesmire since a public hanging in 1759. The race, over a two-mile course, resulted in revenge for The Flying Dutchman.

Small-scale events could be arranged closer to home, providing gambling opportunities that required little organisation and were subject to little regulation. Cumberland is famous for fell running but even around Grinsdale, which can hardly be described as fell country, impromptu 'foot races' had a following. All that were required were two men prepared to run against each other and groups of followers willing to wager on the result. Some of the participants acquired a degree of local fame.

An article in the *Carlisle Journal* of 14th June 1859 begins in a somewhat nostalgic tone:

> Some four or five years ago, when it was a common thing in Carlisle to witness a foot race, or two or three in a week, great interest was manifested in the sport, and Carlisle was at that time frequently the scene of some of the most noted pedestrians of the day. However, like everything else that is too much wrought upon, and where "too much of a good thing is good for nothing," the interest in the sport naturally flagged, the foot-racing fraternity "finished their course," returned to the less exciting pursuits of private life, and since then a foot race has become a rare occurrence.

The article goes on to report on a recent attempt to revive the sport, when, on the previous Saturday night, it became known that four men were planning to run two foot races at Newby Cross, an event that clearly did not meet with the approval of the law.

When they arrived in cabs along with their backers, 'they were very cordially received by two policemen, who had orders to prevent the "event" taking place.' They decided to go to Knockupworth, which was presumably beyond the range of the local officers, and, arriving there at about six thirty, began to prepare for the races: 'The first was a quarter mile race for £3 a-side between "Gwordie Rigg" and "Bill Sawyers", alias the "Buffer"'.

After the "Buffer" had overtaken his rival and reached the post about twelve yards in front:

> It was generally supposed that Rigg's trainers had been too liberal in their allowance, and that Rigg was too stout for the work. A large amount of money was laid, the "Buffer" being the favourite. It is said that another match is in contemplation between them, the "Buffer" to be handicapped.

Apparently there was much less money invested in the second race between Jim Bulman and a 'knight of the bodkin, named Sewell.' Sewell's occupation in the cotton industry suggests that the runners were industrial workers from the city rather than country folk.

Knockupworth seems to have been a frequent scene for such races. A few months earlier, Rigg – then obviously much fitter – had beaten the favourite, Robert Sanderson, in a one hundred yard race. On this occasion it was Sanderson who 'appeared to be in bad condition.'[13]

Curtailing illicit foot races was one of the lesser problems facing the officers of the law. The byways of Cumberland could be dangerous places. Incidents of violent crime made news that spread beyond the county's borders. On 3rd March 1849, the *Preston Chronicle* reported on 'daring attempts at highway robbery' in the suburbs of Carlisle – a man being stopped 'on the brow betwixt Coal Fell Hill Workhouse and Knockupworth, by a fellow who presented a pistol at him and demanded his money or his life.'

Travellers along this road faced other problems besides the threat of robbery. On 29th March 1850, the *Carlisle Patriot* reported on the poor state of the road between Coal Fell Workhouse and Knockupworth, and also other roads nearby. This apparently was not the responsibility of the authorities. Local surveyor, Mr John Pattinson, said that these were 'allotment roads' and the owners had ignored his frequent requests to repair them. Crime and road surfaces figured highly in the concerns of the Victorians, just as they do today.

The 'self-discipline of character' that Trevelyan attributes to the Victorian era is what modern politicians sometimes describe as 'Victorian Values.' And yet the crime reports in contemporary newspapers paint a picture of life that is neither highly moral nor self-disciplined. The behaviour of Victorian youth could be disturbingly close to problems of modern society. The following example was reported in the *Carlisle Journal* of 1854:

> The swans which grace our river are well cared for in all respects, and we believe everybody above the condition of a ruffian takes a personal interest in their security from molestation; but we are sorry to hear that while some of the flock were feeding near the village of Grinsdale they were pelted with stones by some thoughtless and mischievous boys, and so mercilessly that one of them was killed. A reward of two sovereigns has been offered for the discovery of the offenders.'[14]

All of this took place during the Grahams' long exile from Knockupworth. The Hall had been let to John Wright and his family in early 1837 and though John Graham returned – presumably to the farmhouse – his death in 1839 marks the end of the family's residence on Knockupworth land for nearly fifty years. What became of John's father, Thomas Graham, we do not know. Though I have conjectured about entries in the 1841 census and newspaper announcements about men with the same name, Thomas's actual fate is unknown.

John's infant son's education had been assigned to two trustees, one of whom was John Graham of Kirkandrews, who had been tried for the murders of his wife and his father in 1845. John's widow, Mary, was now remarried to Carlisle publican, John Beck. She continued to benefit from her annuity but her claim to any of the surviving Knockupworth furniture may have ended with her remarriage. However, there was at least one item that she salvaged. Hannah Graham's sampler has been passed on through Mary's second family. The sampler may have been more to Mary than a reminder of her first marriage. If she arrived in Grinsdale as a teenager she would have been acquainted with her future husband's sister. Mary would have been about three years older than Hannah – hardly a great age gap between two teenage girls. Hannah's tapestry may have evoked memories of both a husband and a friend.

And now we again take up Mary's story.

Notes

1 G.M. Trevelyan, *English Social History*, p.509
2 *Carlisle Journal*, 30th March 1839
3 *Carlisle Patriot*, 23rd September 1843
4 *Carlisle Journal*, 22nd March 1845
5 Janet Sacks, *Victorian Country Life*, (2012) p.39
6 *Carlisle Journal*, 28th April 1838
7 *Carlisle Journal*, 5th January 1849

8 *Carlisle Journal,* 7th September 1849
9 *Carlisle Journal,* 16th September 1853
10 Sydney Towill, *Georgian and Victorian Carlisle,* p.90
11 Janet Sacks, p.27
12 Guy Woolnough, Blood Sports in Victorian Cumbria – Journal of Victorian Culture online, (Keele University) 22nd October 2014
13 *Carlisle Journal,* 16th November 1858
14 *Carlisle Journal,* 21st April 1854

CHAPTER SIXTEEN

The Life of Mary Beck

In November 1850, Mary and her new husband moved up in the world, exchanging the Three Crowns for the 'more commodious' Angel Inn and London Tavern in English Street.[1] We do not know if her son, John, was still with her but he was not recorded as being on the premises in the 1851 census. The census records John Beck, aged 41 and described as an innkeeper, his wife Mary (37) and John's three sons – William (16), an engineer, and two schoolboys, Thomas (13) and John (9). Mary had just given birth to the first child of their marriage, a daughter, also called Mary, who on the night of the census was only weeks old. It also lists two female servants living on the premises.

1851 was the year of the Great Exhibition and in December of the previous year a public meeting was held at the Angel Inn at which John Beck was appointed secretary of a subscription club to which members contributed one shilling per week to enable them to travel to see this spectacle.[2] It may be that Mary made this journey to London, travelling in a draughty railway carriage, but it seems more likely that the expedition was an all-male affair.

The Angel Inn and London Tavern may have been a relatively upmarket establishment but running it was not without its troubles. On September 5th 1851 John Beck wrote an indignant open letter to the *Carlisle Journal*, addressed to the magistrates who sat at the town hall for the renewal of licenses. He had been reported for having disorderly company in his bar. A party, who had come into the bar for refreshment, had been attacked by a gang who had rushed in from outside. The landlord protested that he had done everything he could, calling the police and closing the bar, and that he could hardly be held responsible for the behaviour of people who weren't even drinking in his bar.

That Mary had been unable to enjoy the privilege of being mistress of Knockupworth Hall may be an indication that her first husband was experiencing some financial difficulties. However, John Graham's assets were sufficient for him to avoid the bankruptcy that had befallen his father. In her second marriage Mary was not so lucky. On Friday 5th March 1852 the *Carlisle Journal* carried a report of John Beck's arrest for insolvency.

The insolvency hearing at the County Court on 22nd March was reported in detail by the same newspaper on Friday 26th. John Beck stated that he did not know how much he owed when he moved from the Three Crowns to the Angel at Martinmas 1850. It might have been two or three hundred pounds. His circumstances improved because of an increase in business. He had spent £10 on travelling expenses going to see The Great Exhibition and had been to York Races to see the great match between The Flying Dutchman and Voltigeur. He had also been to Doncaster Races and to Carlisle where he had lost money on the Cumberland Plate. He had not considered himself to be insolvent at the time but 'was not, however, very full of money.' He admitted: 'I never looked into my affairs at all.' He had signed a bill for £62 for his brother, an out of work London hairdresser, having, he said, no reason at the time to believe that his circumstances were not good. He admitted that nine or ten years ago he had been lent £40 by the Odd-Fellows.

John Beck said that his customers were principally betting men and he had gone to London at their request. They gave him money to lay out on betting and it was more on their business than his own that he went. The Angel, which was a larger house than the one in Rickergate, had required more furniture and stock and that accounted for the increase in his liabilities. He had the prospect of having a better business and if his creditors had given him time he had no doubt that he would have been able to pay them. He had also borrowed £14 to pay the rent.

It was alleged that £150 was unaccounted for and that some bottles and bundles had been clandestinely removed from the premises. The bundles, it was said, were primarily Mrs Beck's clothes. A bedstead and some carpets had also been removed. The articles had, however, all been returned.

The newspaper reported that 'His Honour strongly remarked on the indefensible conduct of the insolvent, referring to the utter carelessness with which his business had been conducted, and the gambling life which he appeared to lead.' It was believed that 'his wife was not dependant on him for her maintenance. She had an annuity.' Mary still benefited from the legacy of being John Graham's widow.

John Beck was unable to satisfy his creditors' demands for five shillings in the pound or to provide security. Bail was refused and the case was adjourned until the next court day.

On the same day, John Beck wrote a letter from the debtors' prison to the editor of the *Carlisle Journal* protesting that from the newspaper report:

> It will no doubt appear as I possessed two or three hundred pounds of my creditors' money which I have not accounted for in my profit account from July 1851. Now I would most respectfully wish the public to suspend its judgement thereon until the re-hearing of my case when I will be enabled to prove, by accounting for every gallon received on the premises, and the cash I have paid from the above date, that I cannot possess any of their money.[3]

By the end of April, having already suffered over a month's imprisonment, John Beck was still unable to make any proposal to his creditors. Before the case was adjourned for another month he remarked that the accusation brought against him that he was a betting man was a 'fabrication from beginning to end.'[4]

On the 28th May 1852 the *Carlisle Journal* reported on the reopening of the case. Mr Donald on behalf of the insolvent said that despite what had been said Mr Beck was not a habitual betting man. His Honour said that nevertheless it would have been better if he had remained at home and paid some of his creditors instead of attending Doncaster Races. He granted him his release but said that 'notwithstanding what had been said the insolvent had acted very improperly, and if he ever came before him again he would be more severely dealt with.'

And so, John Beck was again a free man, returning to the tenancy of the Angel Inn and London Tavern. Mary must have held the fort during his absence as well as caring for their one-year-old daughter. Beck's experience in the debtors' prison seems to have left him undaunted. Four months later he attempted to take advantage of his wife's situation to secure political gain. His name appeared on a list of men claiming to be entitled to vote, being landowners:

> JOHN BECK registered as owner freehold house and land at Knockupworth. The land belonged to his wife and to her son when he came of age. Objection was taken by Mr Hough that the interest

of Mrs Beck in the land was in the form of an annuity. The objection was sustained.[5]

John Beck does not appear to have learnt his lesson when it came to gambling. On Saturday 28th May 1853 the *Carlisle Patriot* stated that he had been anonymously reported for running an illegal Derby sweep.

The landlord of the Angel Inn seems to have had a habit of being on the wrong side of the law but a few weeks later the Becks themselves became victims of crime:

> ROBBERY: On Monday last some person abstracted £10 10s in gold and 7s in silver from a box in an upper room of the "Angel Inn" the property of Mr Beck the landlord. In the morning Mrs Beck had counted £30 in the box, £24 10s in gold and the rest in silver. At one o'clock the money was safe but soon after five p.m. the first mentioned sum was missing. Information was given to the police and a man was apprehended soon afterwards on suspicion but, on searching his pockets, they were found to contain only 2s 6d and as there was no means of incriminating him he was released.[6]

In view of Mr Beck's previous character we might be inclined to wonder if there was more to this incident than meets the eye and question why the thief did not take all of the money. However, if this was a genuine robbery it was a substantial sum to lose.

John Beck's experience in the debtors' prison does not seem to have caused long term damage to his reputation and, despite his misfortunes, he appears to have retained a position of high standing. In December 1853 his name appeared on a list of subscribers to the Royal Agricultural Society.[7] This might seem an unusual step for a pub landlord. For a man who wished to be regarded as the owner of the Knockupworth farm it made a great deal more sense. In December 1854 and January 1855 meetings of the innkeepers of Carlisle were held with Mr John Beck of the Angel Inn in the chair.[8] By October 1856 he was secretary of the Licensed Victuallers' Association.[9]

The Angel Inn appears to have been thriving, enjoying a good reputation and attracting a high quality clientele. On Friday 3rd October 1856 the *Carlisle Journal* reported that on Tuesday last the Carlisle Union Cricket Club 'sat down to a sumptuous spread, the preparation of which conferred infinite credit on its worthy host.' And on Friday 13th March 1857 the same newspaper reported that the anniversary supper of the Cumberland Lodge of the Odd-Fellows was held at the Angel Inn where the guests 'sat down to an excellent supper provided by the worthy host and hostess.'

John and Mary's lives were flourishing in another sense too. About this time Mary gave birth to their second child, another daughter called Margaret Ann. In the 1861 census she is listed as Mary Ann, which would give her the same first name as her sister – obviously a copying error by the census official.

But this good fortune was not to last. On 10th February 1857 John Beck again found himself before the court. On Friday 13th February the *Carlisle Journal* reported the case of Lennox v John Beck, Angel Inn. Lennox was suing him for repayment of £5. John Beck claimed that it was not a loan but part repayment of £40 betting debts that the plaintiff owed him. On this occasion the case had a positive outcome for the court found in John Beck's favour.

However, the incident shows that Mary's husband was still involved in gambling and financial troubles never seem to have been far from his door. On September 16th 1857 the Angel Inn was advertised to be let from the following Martinmas.[10] This marked the end of John Beck's life in the licensing trade. He became a book canvasser. Years later his daughter, Margaret Ann, on her marriage certificate, described him as a stationer. Today we would probably call him a door-to-door salesman.

On Tuesday 7th February 1860 Mr Robert Peat, junior, of Seaville was crossing the mires between Abbey Holme and Bromfield when he came across a body lying face down in the marsh. The man had apparently fallen whilst walking. Mr Peat hurried on to Bromfield and a horse-drawn cart was taken to the spot. The body, which had been dead for several hours, was taken to the house of Joseph Fiddler where, two days later, an inquest was held. *The Carlisle Journal* of 10th February reported that the man:

> had called on Monday afternoon about 4 o'clock, on Joseph Fiddler, and had enquired of him the way across the meadows to the Abbey station and had not got more than half a mile on his road before he had fallen in a field in the occupation of Mr Baxter. The jury returned a verdict of "Found dead, and died from natural causes."

The man was John Beck. At the age of forty-six Mary was again a widow.

Notes

1 *Carlisle Journal*, 22nd November 1850
2 *Carlisle Journal*, 24th December 1850
3 *Carlisle Journal*, 26th March 1852
4 *Carlisle Journal*, 30th April 1852
5 *Carlisle Journal*, Friday 8th October 1852
6 *Carlisle Patriot*, 16th July 1853
7 *Carlisle Patriot*, 24th December 1853
8 *Carlisle Patriot*, 6th January 1855
9 *Carlisle Journal*, 24th October 1856
10 *Carlisle Journal*, 18th September 1857; *Carlisle Patriot* 19th September 1857

CHAPTER SEVENTEEN

His Advancement in Life

On the night of 30th March 1851 a 55 year-old grocer, Margaret Knox, and her grown-up son and daughter were sharing their home in Back Street, Brampton, Cumberland with a thirteen-year-old lodger called John Graham. This is the only John Graham of the correct age, with a Cumbrian birthplace, neither living with other members of his family, nor in an unlikely occupation, that I have found anywhere in England or Scotland on the night of the census. In other words, he seems the most likely candidate to be the son of the late John Graham and his widow, now Mrs Mary Beck.

The boy is described as a scholar, so if this is Mary's son perhaps there was a school in Brampton where he was, in accordance with his father's wishes, being 'educated in a proper manner suited to his condition in life.' His birthplace is given as Carlisle. On later censuses John accurately gives his birthplace as Thursby. If he had been living in another part of the country 'Carlisle' might be considered accurate enough, but in a town only a few miles away we might have expected the answer to be more specific. Perhaps Mrs Knox did not want to wake her sleeping lodger to ask where exactly he had been born. Or perhaps at this stage of his life John was unsure of his birthplace. He can only have been a small baby when his parents took him to Grinsdale. He may have thought he was born there. He would have known that his ancestral home, Knockupworth, was close to the city. In a case of uncertainty 'Carlisle' would seem a reasonably safe answer. On the other hand this might not be our John Graham at all.

A short distance away at Little Corby, Brampton, a visitor called John Graham was staying with farmer Nichol Wilkinson and his wife Frances. This boy gives his birthplace as Burgh by Sands. Burgh is close to Grinsdale but there is no reason to believe that John would think that he had been born there.

A very attractive possibility is a John Graham listed among the boarders at a school at Green Row, Holm Cultrum, Wigton, under the care of schoolmaster John Saul. This seems just the sort of establishment in which we might imagine John to be receiving his education. This boy was born at Cargo, which is tantalisingly close to Grinsdale, but the River Eden separates the two villages and there is no bridge between them. John might have mistakenly thought he was born at Grinsdale but not in a village on the other side of the river.

Finally, at Catterlen, Penrith, farmer William Head was employing a young farm servant called John Graham. It was quite normal in these times for young working class boys and girls to be in service miles away from their homes and such work might well have been useful experience for a future farmer but it seems unlikely that the heir to Knockupworth would find himself in such a situation. However this boy's birthplace is given as Wigton, which is the nearest town to Thursby.

But none of the latter three John Grahams are quite the right age. All are described as fifteen. John would have been a couple of months short of his fourteenth birthday when the census was held. His age is unlikely to have been recorded as more than fourteen at most.

Even if Mrs Knox's thirteen-year-old lodger is our John Graham it still leaves a frustrating gap in our knowledge of his history. For how long was he in the care of his mother? Did her marriage to John Beck affect their relationship?

My mother believed, correctly as we have learned, that John's mother remarried. She also understood that the boy was brought up by trustees and that he had once lived at Park Farm, which was the Grinsdale home of the Sibson family. She also believed he had spent time away at school. The source of her information was her uncle, who was John's son. We must suppose that his knowledge of his father's upbringing was fairly accurate. I think my mother inferred from his remarks that the boy's mother had abandoned him but it is clear from his father's will that it was the trustees who were given responsibility for rearing him. Mary still lived locally but she may have had very little influence over the decisions that were made regarding her son.

So who did bring him up? One of the trustees survived a murder trial when the boy was about eight years old and died before he had reached his teens. John appears to have had few close relatives on the Graham side. Disregarding his mother's family – and it seems likely that the Littles *were* disregarded – he had no siblings, no living aunts or uncles and no first cousins. We cannot be certain how long his grandfather, Thomas, lived or where he went after the family moved out of Knockupworth. The various relatives his father mentioned in his will may or may not have been close but there is no reason to think they took a particular interest in young John's upbringing.

None of which answers the question of what part Mary played in her son's life. We do not know precisely when she moved to Etterby Street or if her son went with her. He may even have lived with her for a time after she married. On the other hand a trustee may indeed have brought him up. After being spurned by Ruth Graham, Thomas Sibson remained unmarried, but in 1851 he was living with his aged mother and two unmarried sisters. There were women in the house who could have taken care of young John.

The Sibsons were a prosperous and long-established Grinsdale family whose ancestors lay in historic tombs in the churchyard. Park Farm was one of the largest in the neighbourhood. One of Thomas Sibson's brothers, James, was a successful timber merchant. Another brother, George, was the solicitor who had drawn up John Graham's will – the will that had appointed Thomas as one of the trustees of the Knockupworth estate and established his influence over the infant John. If there were objections raised to the boy being brought up in a public house by a gambling innkeeper who would spend time in a debtors' prison Mary may have had little power to withstand them. It may be that John Beck, with three sons of his own for Mary to take care of, would also have seen the advantages of his stepson being raised elsewhere. The family story, that John spent part of his childhood at Park Farm, may well be correct.

When he went to live in the Sibson household is a matter of conjecture. If John lived with his mother until her marriage in 1845 he would have spent his first eight years with her. Thomas Sibson, now effectively the sole trustee and, surrounded by female family members, was in a strong position to provide the boy with a home. That he may have exploited this position for his own financial gain is a story, whether true or not, that remains in the Graham family folklore. If, as seems almost certain, John was receiving an education away from home at the time of the 1851 census Sibson had at least met his obligations in respect of the boy's 'advancement in life.'

And it may have been through his time at Park Farm that John acquired a genuine interest as well as an aptitude for farming that would have been unlikely to develop if he had been brought up in

Carlisle public houses. When he placed his education in the hands of the trustees, his father may not have believed John's future lay in farming, nonetheless Thomas Sibson's actions ensured that it did.

If at the age of thirteen John was living away from home in order to receive his education, the town of Brampton is certainly one possible source of his learning. It is said that between 1829 and 1901 there were at least ten private boarding and day schools in the town, including the 'renowned' Croft House Academy.[1] Established in around 1840 by Joseph Coulthard, the school 'provided a standard of education that attracted not only pupils from the locality, but also from across the county and abroad.'[2] John may indeed have been the scholar lodging with Mrs Knox.

Hopefully Mary and her son at least remained in close contact. The fact that a space was left for her name on the family gravestone surely suggests that they were not totally estranged.

Wherever John was on the night of the 1851 census, his ancestral home and farm were in good hands. John Wright, the tenant of the Hall, drew an income from a farm he owned at Castle Sowerby. He shared the Hall with his wife, Ann, two of his surviving daughters and a son, William, who, like John's grandfather, was a spirit merchant.

The respectability of the Wright family was challenged by what was later claimed to have been an erroneous newspaper report in October 1847. Son William, who would then have been twenty-three, was reported to have been involved in an incident in which he and Thomas Story of Carlisle were each fined twenty shillings and costs for firing a gun on the highway near Kirkandrews-on-Eden thereby causing two horses to bolt and then compounding this by using abusive and threatening language.[3] On October 27th William wrote a letter to the *Carlisle Patriot* in which he insisted that this was 'totally untrue, as I was in no way connected to the case.'

Another son, David, was living in the farmhouse and is described in the census as a farmer of 130 acres. David seems to have been highly respected, serving on the Board of Guardians of the Carlisle Union. He had, of course, been one of the jurors at the inquests into the Grinsdale poisonings in 1845.

Respectable and respected he may have been but David Wright's character was not without blemish. On 24th March 1854 the *Carlisle Journal* reported on a 'Greyhound Case: David Wright v John Murray.' David Wright was in dispute with his friend, John Murray, over the ownership of a greyhound. Mr Wright claimed that his friend had given him a greyhound used in coursing but later claimed it back. Mr Wright was now willing to give up the dog but was claiming 2s 6d a week for its keep. To laughter, the judge commented, 'Why you could keep a child for less than that.' Mr Wright's lawyer replied that, 'A greyhound is more expensive than a child sometimes,' but the judge considered it to be a spiteful action between friends who had fallen out and awarded him nothing.

Farmers were then, as now, at the mercy of the weather. At the beginning of the eighteen-fifties a succession of wet winters caused severe flooding in Grinsdale and the surrounding area. On 6th January 1851 the *Morning Post* under the headline 'Great Floods in the North' reported that about a thousand acres near Carlisle were under water and that the waters of the Eden, Caldew and Petteril had not risen to this height since 1822. Sheep had to be rescued and a mud cottage at Knockupworth was levelled by the storm.

Two winters later came another deluge. The *Carlisle Journal* of Friday 17th December 1852 reported: 'Many fields were under water, and amongst others, one below Grinsdale belonging to Mr Thomas Sibson containing a crop of unpulled turnips.' Again sheep were rescued:

> Men, horses and carts were pressed into service, and the sheep were, after much exertion, swung off, the water being already half way over the cart wheels. What is known as the island at Grinsdale was no island on Sunday last. Not an inch of it was to be seen.

It is impossible to assess how these storms compare with the devastating floods that have befallen Carlisle during the early years of the twenty-first century, when we are told we have had unprecedented rainfall. Certainly the population of the city was smaller then, so fewer people are likely to have been affected. But we know from earlier reports that it was commonplace for floodwater to enter properties especially in the Rickergate area. Cumbrian residents, rural and urban alike, have for generations suffered the consequences of the county's often torrential rainfall and the city has always been at the mercy of the three rivers along whose banks it was built.

The Carlisle Canal was a short-lived success. As a means of transport the new, faster railways were surpassing canals. Railway lines, opened in the 1840s, took freight and passenger traffic away from the canal.

Only thirty years after it opened, the canal closed in August 1853. The water was drained and iron rails were laid on the canal bed. From 22nd July 1854, instead of sedate barges, the residents of Knockupworth could watch the passing steam trains of the Carlisle and Port Carlisle Railway. In contrast with the fanfare that had greeted the opening of the canal, the new railway line seems to have attracted little attention. Railway historian, Stephen White remarks: 'There were no demonstrations, speeches or dinners on this momentous occasion.'[4]

Port Carlisle, which had never lived up to its expectations as an industrial harbour, sank into insignificance and, after an extension was built from Drumburgh to Silloth, the main function of the railway became the transportation of holidaymakers and day-trippers to the seaside.

The Carlisle to Silloth line receives only a cursory mention in George Bradshaw's railway guide of 1861 but Bradshaw is much more expansive about Carlisle itself, which he depicts as a flourishing industrial city. He comments on the considerable quantities of cotton goods produced there and remarks on the height (305 feet) of Dixon's chimney at the Shaddongate mill.

Bradshaw also recommends that tourists to the city pay a visit to Messrs. Carr and Co's biscuit factory where they will be astonished by the manufacturing process.[5]

Carr's biscuit works would continue to flourish but another of the city's above-mentioned industries was about to go into decline. The waters of the Caldew may have been ideal for the manufacture of cotton but, in comparison with the Lancashire mill towns, Carlisle was geographically disadvantaged. With the failure of the canal, the docks at Port Carlisle had come to nothing and a planned expansion of the harbour at Silloth, turning the town into an industrial port, had similarly failed to materialise. The city's outlying location away from major port facilities was compounded by an over reliance on a single product.

It is reported that the ultimate failure of the industry was in large measure due to the abolition of slavery in the United States. It was not, as might be supposed, the result of losing the exploited labour force that harvested the raw material but because a ready market for the manufactured product had been lost. Plantation owners had bought a large quantity of ginghams to clothe their slaves. Whenever other orders were slack, the Carlisle mills had been kept busy supplying this American market. But the liberated slaves wanted to select their own apparel and the manufacturers of Carlisle failed to adapt to this new situation. A historian, writing at the end of the Victorian era when the city's cotton industry was in its final death throes, said, rather poetically, that 'the streets will cease, as in great part they have already done, to re-echo to the clattering clogs of countless millgirls going to and from their work.'[6]

In September 1858 two very similar advertisements appeared in Carlisle newspapers. Both concerned property owned by John Graham, who had recently reached the significant age of twenty-one. He was now living in Grinsdale, quite possibly at the home of Thomas Sibson.

One announcement concerned the Knockupworth estate that had just come into his possession under the terms of the will:

> To be let for a term of years, and entered upon at Candlemas next all that desirable farm situated at Knockupworth, in the Parish of Grinsdale, containing 107 acres or thereabouts, of superior arable and meadow land, with suitable farmhouse and buildings: within one and a half miles of Carlisle, and all lying adjacent to the buildings without any intermixture with other land.
>
> Also to be let, either together or separate from the above, all that genteel dwelling house with garden, stable, coach house etc. suitable for the residence of a respectable family, now in the occupation of John Wright Esq. Particulars may be known by applying at the office of James Sibson, Timber Merchant, George Street, Carlisle or to John Graham of Grinsdale, the owner.[7]

This advertisement raises a number of questions. The first, the reason why David Wright was quitting the farm, is perhaps easily answered. Just before Christmas, the following advertisement appeared: 'To sell by auction, all stock, crop etc. of Mr David Wright who is declining farming.'[8] It may be that David Wright was already in poor health for he died soon afterwards.

It is rather more surprising that the Hall was also being put up to be let because, as things turned out, the Wright family continued to occupy it for many more years. David and John Wright died within a short time of each other but John's widow, Ann, was to remain in the Hall for over two more decades. Whatever had been intended, something – probably her husband's death – caused Mrs Wright to change her plans.

An even more intriguing question is why John had chosen to lease out Knockupworth Farm to new tenants. Within three years he was himself farming but not on his own land. Why did he choose not to return to Knockupworth but instead to rent a farm elsewhere?

My mother believed that John, who was her grandfather, had owned two farms but had been unable to farm either of them because they were let out under long-term leases. He had instead rented a farm at Whitrigg near Bowness on the Solway marshes. But the above advertisement shows that he could have had access to Knockupworth as early as 1858. And what of the second farm? As there was no mention of another farm in his father's will John must have acquired it in his own lifetime. So how had he come by this second farm?

When she was very old, her memory beginning to fail, my mother told me that she thought that this other farm was called the Flatt – or it was at a place called Flatt. In this it seems she was correct, as the second advertisement shows:

> FARM TO BE SOLD OR LET, with possession at Candlemas next, all that desirable Freehold ESTATE and DWELLING HOUSE with suitable farm buildings, containing 60 acres or thereabouts, situate at FLATT in the parish of Kirkbampton now in the occupation of Mr. Thos. Armstrong, who will show the premises. Three acres of the estate is covered with well-grown Scotch Fir Timber, and the remainder is all Arable and Meadow Land in an excellent state of cultivation, and all lying convenient to the Buildings.
>
> Particulars may be known by applying to the Office of JAMES SIBSON, Timber Merchant, George Street, Carlisle or to JOHN GRAHAM of Grinsdale, the owner.[9]

Here is proof that John did own a second farm and, as my mother thought, the farm was at Flatt. Now aged twenty-one and in control of his own affairs he could decide how to exploit his ownership of the two farms to his best advantage. There may be many reasons why he chose to pay rent on a third farm rather than take over one of the ones that he owned. He may have felt that, as a single man, he was not ready to occupy the spacious Hall. There would seem, however, to be no reason why he could not have moved into the Knockupworth farmhouse. He was willing to sell the farm at Flatt but was also happy to let it to tenants if it failed to find a buyer. This arrangement must have suited his long-term plans. Knockupworth Farm had been leased to tenants since his father died nearly twenty years earlier. Both the farm and the Hall might be in need of financial investment. The income he received from the two farms he owned and the profits from the rented farm at Whitrigg would build up his capital, giving him the means to marry and one day to take his bride back to his ancestral home.

This does not explain how the farm at Flatt came into John Graham's possession. However, we know from the Quaker records that in the eighteenth century John's ancestors on his great-grandmother's side lived at Flatt, a small, scattered community near Thurstonfield and Kirkbampton. We do not know for how long they continued to own property there, but it does not seem fanciful to think that John may have acquired this farm, perhaps as a legacy, from a member of the Sharp family. As will become clear, this would also go a long way towards explaining one of the mysteries of the gravestones.

Notes

1 www.cumberlandcountyhistory.org.uk
2 https;historicengland.org.uk/listing/the-list/list-entry/1335530
3 *Carlisle Patriot*, 22nd October 1847
4 Stephen White, *Solway Steam*, 1984
5 *Bradshaw's Descriptive Railway Handbook of Great Britain and Ireland, 1863*; HarperCollins 2014 edition, p.63
6 T. Bulmer & Co., *History, Topography and Directory of Cumberland*, 1901 edition, p.839
7 *Carlisle Journal*, 7th September 1858
8 *Carlisle Journal*, Friday 24th December 1858
9 *Carlisle Patriot*, 4th September 1858

CHAPTER EIGHTEEN

Whitrigg John and the Doctor's Daughter

The 1861 census finds John Graham farming at Whitrigg, a community on the Solway marshes near Bowness. His address is given as Whitrigg, Fingland. John, aged twenty-three is described as an unmarried farmer of 173 acres, employing eight men. Two ploughmen, a female house servant and a dairymaid share the farmhouse with him. The servant is called Elizabeth Little. It is tempting to think that John might be giving employment to one of his mother's relatives, which would suggest that Mary continued to play a significant role in her son's life, but there is no great reason to suppose that the farmer and his servant were related.

The farm at Whitrigg was of a larger acreage than Knockupworth and considerably larger than the one at Flatt. Even allowing for the rent he was paying, the profits from the farm, with its lush Solway grazing land, along with the income he was drawing from the properties he owned, must have put him in a healthy financial position. Even if there is some truth in the anecdotal family stories about him having been cheated by his trustees, he was now free of Thomas Sibson's influence.

Recently widowed Ann Wright continued to live in Knockupworth Hall, while the farm was in the tenancy of Robert Thomlinson. Thomlinson, who in 1861 was living in the farmhouse with his wife and four small sons, may have been related to Thomas Thomlinson whose night soil cart had caused so much offence in the thirties but I have not established a direct connection between the two men.

John may have been an absentee landlord as far as Knockupworth was concerned but he was still taking an interest in the estate. In 1862 he used his position as owner to support the charitable work of the

Carlisle Board of Guardians, which was responsible for the administration of the local workhouse. At a meeting in early October:

> Mr Sibson handed in the surveyor's estimate of some work at Knockupworth Hall, which had been procured for the unemployed. Mr Graham, of Knockupworth Hall, having kindly consented to give £10 towards it, though the result of the work, the levelling of some uneven ground, was a matter of indifference to him beyond its looking better. The cost of the work would be £18. Mr Sibson observed that such work was far more profitable and preferable to stone breaking – the expenditure of the sum proposed was agreed to.[1]

The headline for the article was 'Paupers' Work'. The workmen would have been inmates of the workhouse. Victorian charity was dispensed in return for hard labour. John Graham's motives may indeed have been entirely charitable. As Mr Sibson observed, this was better than breaking stones and John was contributing the lion's share of the cost. However, we may wonder if he was really so indifferent to the work that was being done. He must have been astute enough to realise that he was getting the job done for eight pounds less than the actual cost and, visually at least, the outcome was an improvement to the farm.

He ended up paying rather more than he had initially agreed. In November it was reported to the Board of Guardians: 'that the work at Knockupworth was finished and the Clerk was instructed to send an account to Mr Graham for £12 10s for the work done.'[2]

This may have been a minor improvement but John was surely looking ahead to the time when he would take over his ancestral home – Knockupworth Hall and the farm that had by now been in his family for over a century. Still a single man, he was, for now, content to rent the farm at Whitrigg, while drawing income from the two farms that he owned.

Being some distance from the city, John's farm at Whitrigg was fairly isolated. Knockupworth's location, only a short walking distance from the edge of Carlisle, made it a magnet for crime. The felons among the urban poor had to travel only a short distance to find easy pickings. In July 1862 weaver, John M'Quiggan, was jailed for fourteen days for uprooting and stealing potatoes from Knockupworth land – the property of Mr Thomlinson.[3]

Four years after the potato incident another weaver, John Holliday, was convicted of stealing a duck from Robert Thomlinson, even though its owner was unable to swear that the duck in his possession was the same duck that he had lost.[4]

Crime was rife but punishments were severe. Fourteen days imprisonment for potato theft was relatively lenient. In January 1864 five boys, aged between eleven and fourteen, were convicted of stealing groceries from an itinerant trader's cart at Knockupworth and sentenced to be whipped with a birch rod.[5]

Such punishments may seem excessive but they were not always effective. One of the culprits, a boy named Roscow, was soon in trouble again. Under the headline 'Another Whipping Earned' the *Carlisle Journal* reported:

> John Roscow a lad who was recently flogged for larceny at Knockupworth by order of the county magistrates was today convicted of stealing pears from Mr David Graham's garden at Willow Holme and ordered to receive another castigation.[6]

There were those among Victorian youth who accepted such beatings as part of life.

While John was farming at Whitrigg his mother, Mrs Mary Beck, was living in St Nicholas Street, Botchergate, Carlisle. Recently widowed for the second time, the 1861 census records her living here with her two daughters and two of her stepsons – Thomas, now a twenty-three-year-old cabinet maker, and John, a nineteen-year-old marble mason. She was supplementing her income by taking in two female boarders. We might wonder how often John travelled into Carlisle, a journey from Whitrigg of rather more than twelve miles, and whether he was in the habit of calling on his mother in Botchergate. He must have regularly visited Knockupworth, which was a relatively short distance from Mary's home.

Whatever the troubles of his childhood, John Graham seems to have become a successful farmer, a man with sound financial sense and a good education. And he had sufficient charm and sophistication to attract a doctor's daughter.

Jane was the daughter of John Sewell, the Burgh by Sands doctor who had attended poor Peggy Graham when she was dying from arsenic poisoning and who by his choice of pharmacist had unwittingly contributed to her husband's acquittal. Dr Sewell had married Jane Hodgson who gave birth to four sons before Jane, their elder daughter, was born in 1840. Two years later Jane's sister, Mary, was born.

Dr Sewell had died in 1850 while in his mid-forties. John and Jane were married in April 1863, the event being announced in the *Carlisle Journal*:

> At Burgh-by-Sands on 21st inst. by Rev John Lowry, John Graham of Whitrigg, only son of the late John Graham Esq. of Knockupworth, to Jane, elder daughter of the late Dr Sewell, of the Hill, Burgh-by-Sands.[7]

Over the next seven years the marriage was to produce four sons. The first, born on 1st February 1864, was, like his father, grandfather and great-great grandfather, named John. John was also the name of Jane's late father and of one of her brothers.

A second son was born eighteen months later on 12th August 1865. He was named Robert Hodgson. Since for very nearly a hundred years no male member of the Graham family had been given any name other than Thomas or John, this was a radical break with tradition. The choice of name indicates the influence of the Sewell family. One of Jane's brothers was called Robert, and Hodgson was her mother's maiden name.

John's life as both tenant and landowner seems to have provided an income that gave his family financial security. But troubles were never far from a farmer's door. In January 1866 the area was ravaged by an outbreak of cattle plague, a disease that has now been eradicated but which at the time was regarded as more deadly than foot and mouth disease. The disease, also known as rinderpest, was triggered by a virus related to those that cause measles in humans and distemper in dogs, though at the time there was speculation that it might be linked to smallpox. From newspaper reports it seems that John's herd may have escaped unscathed but several of his neighbours were affected and John was appointed to represent Fingland on the Bowness parish committee to carry out the provisions of the Cattle Diseases Act. In December he was recorded as having donated £3 to the Cattle Plague Compensation Fund.[8]

John and Jane's third son, Richard, was born on 24th June 1867. Again there was no tradition of boys being named Richard within the Graham family but it was the name of another of Jane's brothers. We might sense that the marriage of John and Jane was on a much more equal footing than that of John's parents. Jane was an intelligent literate woman, the daughter of a respected local doctor. Some people may have thought both his father and his grandmother had married beneath them. John and Jane's marriage – like that of his great-grandparents, John and Hannah – was one of solid respectability. And Jane, like Hannah, was a wife who could be entrusted with responsibility. In the event of his death John would have no concerns about his own sons receiving a good education. His wife would make sure of that.

John had another, if somewhat less important, reason to celebrate in 1867. Whatever tribulations the cattle farmers around the Solway may have had in recent months, John Graham experienced some equine success. At the Annual Show of the East Cumberland Agricultural Society, at Selby's Field in Warwick Road, Carlisle, his was one of two entries to be highly commended in the Hackney Prize 'for the best Hackney of any age, height not to exceed 15 hands 1 inch to be brought into the ring mounted.'[9]

Meanwhile, his own farm at Knockupworth was still being managed by Robert Thomlinson. Two colourful incidents from around that time illustrate some features of rural life in what today we have come to regard as the highly moral Victorian Age. In April 1865 the farm had made the news when the headman, Jacob Thomlinson (quite possibly a relative of his employer), appeared before the magistrates accused of assaulting William Inglis, a boy who was a fellow servant. The boy complained that the defendant had thrown him into the pond, threatened to drown him and also kicked him. His complaints were corroborated by a number of witnesses and he was said to be very sore from his bruises. In Jacob Thomlinson's defence it was stated that the boy had rubbed his cap in some manure. The bench considered that too much violence had been used and fined the defendant one shilling plus costs.[10]

In 1867 the following court case was reported in the *Carlisle Journal*:

> SATURDAY, AUG 17 1867
>
> Illegal dismissal – Robert Thomlinson of Knockupworth was charged by Wm Irving with unlawfully dismissing him from his service. The plaintiff was a very "moral man", and asserted that he could not obtain sufficient sleep being a very light sleeper on account of the doings of two other servants, a male and female. Unfortunately for his assertion of morality it transpired that he had been drunk three days in succession, and voluntarily left his employment.

Life at Knockupworth Farm does not seem to have been dull!

When Richard was baptised in 1868, his godparents William and

Sarah Donald, farmers from nearby Longcroft, presented him with a bible and prayer book. Inscribed in each were the words:

'Richard Graham
Whitrigg –
From his Godparents
W & S Donald
Longcroft
1868 –
Proverbs chap 10 ver: 1'

Verse 1 of Proverbs chapter 10 reads: 'A wise son maketh a glad father; but a foolish son is the heaviness of his mother.'

Nineteenth century life could be hazardous, both in towns and in the countryside. This was illustrated by an incident at the end of July 1870, which was picked up by several local newspapers but reported most fully by the *Penrith Observer*.

An elderly greengrocer, named Elizabeth Ramsey, was knocked down and seriously injured by a Volunteer Fire Brigade engine on its way to a fire at Knockupworth. Considering the amount of combustible material kept on farms and the use of naked flames for cooking, heating and lighting, it is unsurprising that there should have been frequent reports of fires. However on this occasion it is only the *Penrith Observer* that gives full details of the actual fire:

> Late on Saturday night, a fire broke out in the stableyard of Mr Thomlinson, Knockupworth farm, near Carlisle. Both the police and the fire brigade engines proceeded to the spot, but on getting there they were no use as no water could be obtained. The fire, however, was confined to the stack in which it originated, which was completely destroyed. It was an old wheat stack worth £40. There was little or no wind astir, hence the other stacks in the yard were easily saved. Hundreds of people assembled at the scene of the accident.[11]

At the time of this dramatic incident John, Jane and their sons were at Whitrigg, well away from any danger. Jane was pregnant with their fourth child. William Sharp was born on 10th November 1870. There seems to be no reason from within the Graham or Sewell families why they named their son William though the name had a long association with the Sharps. And we are now closer to solving the mystery of William's middle name.

John and Jane gave middle names to their second and fourth sons but not to the other two. Robert's second name honours his mother's family, for Hodgson was the name of his maternal grandparents. We now have a partial explanation for William being given the middle name 'Sharp' but it seems unlikely that he would be named after his great-great-grandmother.

John had never known his great-grandmother, Hannah Sharp. However there was one member of the Sharp family of whom he may have had some memory. If Hannah's brother, William, lived with John and his mother at Grinsdale, John would have been nearly four years old when the old man died. Hardly old enough to have developed a deep affection, we may think, or even to have a clear recollection of him thirty years later.

There may however have been a more concrete connection between William Sharp and his sister's great-grandson. This brings us back to the farm that we know John owned at Flatt, near Thurstonfield in Kirkbampton parish. We also know that the Sharp family had once farmed at Flatt; Hannah and her brothers were born there. As the oldest surviving son, William, who was described as a yeoman on his death certificate, would have inherited the farm on their father's death.

Flatt was a tiny community consisting of a few scattered farms. It seems likely that the farm that came into John Graham's possession was the same one that had once belonged to his Sharp ancestors. If both Jonathan and William Sharp died childless – and I have not found a record of either of them having married – then the infant John Graham would not only have been the sole heir to Knockupworth Hall and Farm but heir to the Sharp family property too.

This is speculation, but a desire to recognise this inheritance would surely account for William being given 'Sharp' as a middle name. Indeed, since 'William' was not a name commonly used in either the Graham or Sewell families the full name 'William Sharp' may have been in honour of this benefactor. It is perhaps strange that John waited until the birth of his fourth son to recognise this but it may be around this time that the sale of the farm at Flatt severed his ties with his Sharp ancestors. This may have seemed an appropriate moment to acknowledge the debt he owed to the family.

The 1871 census records John on his farm at Whitrigg, a farmer of 200 acres. He was approaching his thirty-fourth birthday. His wife, Jane, was thirty-one. The oldest of his four sons, John, was seven years old, the youngest, William, just one. Two male agricultural servants and two female domestic servants were sharing the farmhouse with them. My mother believed that John had sold his farm at Flatt and was using the proceeds to refurbish Knockupworth in preparation for a return to his ancestral home. When he had last lived there he had been a baby. He was destined not to return.

John died on 24th July 1872 at the age of thirty-five. His death certificate states that he died from inflammation of the lungs. Of the last four generations of the Knockupworth males who were descended from the millwright Thomas Graham and his first wife not one had lived to be more than forty-five. Two had died in their thirties, one at twenty-three. A doctor had certified John's death, although this was not yet a legal requirement. His recorded cause of death seems very unspecific and could have been brought about by a number of medical conditions. 'Inflammation of the lungs' could have been the result of tuberculosis, the disease that had killed John's father and probably other members of the family. If so, John would have suffered for some time and his health would have been in gradual decline. If, like his father, John's condition was caused by consumption the doctor chose not to record this on his death certificate. There are other conditions resulting in 'inflammation of the lungs' that would have led to a more rapid demise.

Pneumonia and pleurisy – defined as inflammation of the tissue layers lining the lungs and inner chest walls – can result from various lung infections that are treatable today but would be much more likely to be fatal at the time. John, as a working farmer, was frequently exposed to the elements. We might think that July was an unlikely time for him to be subjected to harmful weather but the *Nautical Magazine* for 1872 reports the month to have been wet and sultry with frequent thunderstorms.[12] There is also a condition called Farmers' Lung, which is caused by an allergic reaction to dust and fungal spores in mouldy hay. With frequent exposure this can become a chronic condition.

John's death, when he was planning to move back to Knockupworth, may not have been foreseen. However it is worth noting that, like most of his recent ancestors, he made his will only a few months before he died. This may be coincidental but concerns about his health may have prompted him to make provision for his wife and sons.

John's burial in the family grave is recorded thus in the parish register:

Grinsdale Parish Register: John Graham, Whitrigg, buried July 28th 1872. 35 years.[13]

In his will John, like his father, appointed two friends as trustees but he seemed to be in a much more secure financial position. Whereas his father had been concerned about paying off debts, John gave detailed instructions as to how his money was to be invested. He made provision for his wife and children and any grandchildren who might be born. His mother had been left marginalised by her husband's will. By contrast, Jane was to play the major role in the children's upbringing.

Will of John Graham 1872

John Graham of Whitrigg in the parish of Bowness in the county of Cumberland bequeaths all his real estate to his friends Thomas Irving of Bowness, yeoman, and John Beswick of Raby Cote in the parish of Holme Cultrum, farmer, upon trust.

- They shall from the part of his personal estate consisting of money pay his funeral and testamentary expenses and debts,
- shall invest the residue in the name or names of his said trustees in any of the public stocks or funds or government securities of the UK or any stocks or securities of the Government of India or in any stock of the Bank of England commonly called Bank Stock or upon real or household securities in England or Wales; such securities being held on a term whereof sixty years at least shall be unexpired at the time of such investment [...] or by preference or guaranteed shares or securities of any railway or other company in Great Britain or India incorporated by Act of Parliament or Royal Charter and paying or purporting to pay a dividend on its ordinary stock in shares,
- with power for the said trustees from time to time to vary the said investments into or for others of the same or a like nature and shall stand possessed of the residuary trust monies [...]
- to pay income to his dear wife, Jane Graham, during her life and from and after her decease in trust for all his children living at his decease or born in due time afterwards,
- being a son or sons shall then have attained the age of twenty-one years or being a daughter or daughters have attained the age of twenty-one years or have married, in equal shares.

- If there be only one such child, the whole to be left in trust for that one child provided that if any child should die in his lifetime leaving a child or children who survive him and attain the age of twenty-one they shall take and share equally between them the share which their parent would have taken.
- He empowers the said trustees, with the consent in writing of his wife and after her decease at their discretion to raise any part or parts not exceeding together one moiety of the expectant share of any child or grandchild and apply the same to his or her advancement, preferment or benefit at such discretion as they see fit.
- That the trustees may postpone the sale and conversion of his real and personal estate or any part thereof for so long as they see fit ...
- He bequeaths all estates vested in him as a trustee or mortgagee unto Thomas Irving and John Beswick.
- He appoints Thomas Irving and John Beswick, their heirs executors and administrators subject to the trusts and equities affecting the same.
- He appoints his wife, Jane, during her life and, after her death, the said Thomas Irving and John Beswick the guardian and guardians of his infant children.

Will signed 2nd April 1872. Witnesses: E. Hough, solicitor, Carlisle; I. Sherwood, his clerk.

Proved at Carlisle 30th November 1872 by the oaths of Thomas Irving and John Beswick.

Died on 24th July 1872 at Whitrigg. Under £3,000.[14]

After John's death Jane and her sons moved out of the farm and lived in a cottage at Bowness-on-Solway. From here they would be able to see, and quite possibly use, an architectural feature that had only recently appeared on the landscape and of which today little remains. As part of the Solway Junction Railway, a viaduct had been built across the estuary, linking Bowness with the Scottish shore. The first freight train crossed the bridge in September 1869; the first passenger service began a year later.

Jane seems to have been a very capable woman but she was not a farmer. Knockupworth remained in the care of tenants.

Notes

1 *Carlisle Patriot,* 4th October 1862
2 *Carlisle Journal,* 28th November 1862
3 *Carlisle Journal,* 15th July 1862
4 *Carlisle Journal,* 6th July 1866
5 *Carlisle Journal,* 26th January 1864
6 *Carlisle Journal,* 29th July 1864
7 *Carlisle Journal,* 24th April 1863
8 *Carlisle Journal,* 14th December 1866
9 *Carlisle Journal,* 20th September 1867
10 *Carlisle Journal,* 25th April 1865
11 *Penrith Observer,* 2nd August 1870
12 *The Nautical Magazine for 1872*, Cambridge University Press
13 Cumbria Archive Service
14 Cumbria Archive Service

CHAPTER NINETEEN

Where She Lies

To complete Mary's story and solve the final mystery of the gravestones we must apply a little imagination to the known facts.

On 28th July 1872 John Graham makes a journey that has been made by three generations of his ancestors and will, in their time, be made by several of his descendants.

This time it is a rather longer journey for it begins at Whitrigg near the Solway shore. At last, the horse-drawn hearse makes its way across the fields by the edge of the River Eden and stops outside the wall of Grinsdale churchyard under the spread of the copper beech that may have been growing there since before the Grahams ever came to Knockupworth.

The mourners follow the coffin into the churchyard where John's body is laid to rest.

Almost certainly absent from the proceedings are the two most important women in John Graham's life – his widow, Jane, and his mother, now Mrs Mary Beck. It would have been unusual for respectable Anglican women to attend a funeral in nineteenth century England. They would have other important roles, among them maintaining a vigil with the corpse through the night, and afterwards they would respect a lengthy period of mourning. Funerals were not considered appropriate occasions for women. For one thing, they might display too much unseemly emotion.

But we may imagine that later Jane and Mary walk into the churchyard and stand together by the freshly filled grave. The tall headstone is just over three decades old, still relatively new and un-weathered. And it bears only these words:

'In Memory of John Graham of Knockupworth who died

Novr 23rd 1839 aged 23 years.

> The days of my youth hast thou shortened, among thine elect may I be numbered, Oh Lord.'

Mary stands where she must have stood thirty-three years earlier after her young husband's coffin had been lowered into the ground.

And perhaps it is now that she expresses a wish that she too may be buried here along with her son and her first husband. Perhaps she remembers those few happy years of her youth that were cruelly snatched away. And, in deference to her wishes, Jane instructs the stonemason to leave a space on the gravestone before inscribing the words: 'Also of John their son who died at Whitrigg July 24th 1872 aged 35 years.'

We have no record of the relationship between Mary and her son after 1841, nor of whether she remained on good terms with the Graham family after her marriage to John Beck. But perhaps that space left for her name on the family headstone tells us all we need to know.

And so it would have happened had not Mary's life taken yet another unexpected turn. The 1871 census had found Mary still living in Botchergate but now in Princess Street, with her two daughters and still taking in boarders.

By 1881, now aged sixty-seven and still describing herself as an annuitant, she had moved to Lord Street. Her daughters were still unmarried; Mary, now thirty-one was a dress and mantle maker. Margaret Ann was a felt hat trimmer. She was aged twenty-five. They had a single lodger, a twenty-four-year-old railway clerk. It was over twenty years since Mary had been widowed for the second time.

But then on 20th March 1882 Mary's younger daughter, Margaret Ann, married a Lancashire-born railway guard called Christopher Lancaster and moved with him to Liverpool.[1] Her mother and unmarried sister joined her there, and it was in Liverpool that Mary died in April 1886.

> At 90 Uxbridge Street, Liverpool, on the 11th inst, Mary, widow of the late John Beck, of Carlisle, aged 73 years.[2]

And so Mary does not lie in the seclusion of Grinsdale churchyard but among the ranks of smoke-blackened Victorian gravestones in Toxteth Park Cemetery. This vast necropolis could not be more different from her intended resting place.

Mary's name is inscribed at the top of the gravestone, as is her husband's on that other monument in the little churchyard above the River Eden, the two graves being separated by a distance of a hundred and forty miles. The inscription begins 'In loving memory of Mary BECK, late of Carlisle, died 11th April 1886, aged 72 years.' Unlike the wordy reflection on John's shortened days of youth, Mary's epitaph is only four words long: 'Her end was peace.' It would be reassuring to believe that this implied a peaceful death but it could be given a different interpretation: that her end brought peace after a troubled life. This would not seem an unfitting testimonial.

Other members of Mary's second family are buried with her. The first, an infant grandson, died seven years after her. Her elder daughter, unmarried Mary, was buried here in August 1916, her second daughter, Margaret Ann Lancaster, in January 1921. Finally, Mary's son-in-law, Christopher Lancaster was interred in December 1927. As with most of the surrounding graves, each member of the family has his or her own individual epitaph. That of her grandson bears the words 'He shall gather the lambs with His arm and carry them in His bosom.' The boy died in May 1893. He was three years and seven months old. His name was Alan Graham Lancaster.

Mary never knew this grandson, yet his middle name is unlikely to be coincidental. It suggests that Mary Beck's connection with the family of her first marriage was not forgotten even after her death. Though she had not been called Graham for over forty years the naming of her grandson may have been a tribute to her memory.

Mary's life began in a remote border village. It ended in one of the major cities of Victorian England. She had briefly been the wife of the owner of Knockupworth Hall. Their marriage had lasted for only a little over a thousand days before John Graham had succumbed to his lingering illness. If he had lived, her life would surely have been very different, but there is no saying that it would have been less troubled. John had directed his failing energy not to managing a successful business but to staving off debt. He may have proved no more reliable than Mary's second husband, the wayward publican, John Beck. Widowed twice by her mid-forties, she had also suffered the loss of her only son when he was still a young man.

Mary had outlived her son but she was survived by four grandsons from her first marriage and, by the time of her death, had at least one granddaughter from her second.

Mary Little, the illiterate girl from Bewcastle, is buried far from the Grahams but she had been instrumental in the continuation of the family line.

On a grey November afternoon, nearly one hundred and thirty years after Mary's death, the rain sweeps across the Liverpool skyline. The rows of memorials range from simple gravestones to ornate tombs. The industrial grime has been cleaned from the city's landmark buildings but it remains on the monuments to those who lived and died in the Victorian age. The Beck/Lancaster memorial is of blackened sandstone with a round top and curved shoulders. There is a crack in the stone through which the rainwater is seeping but the lettering is clear and easily readable.

And it is here, among the graves of Toxteth Park Cemetery, that we find the reason why the wife of one John Graham and mother of another does not lie with her first husband and her only son in the soil of Grinsdale churchyard. It is here that we end our search for the missing lady.

Notes

1 Information courtesy of Liz Johnson
2 *Carlisle Patriot*, 16th April 1886

CHAPTER TWENTY

The Four Brothers

The winter of 1880–1881 was exceptionally cold. In January the waters of the Solway estuary froze at the edges and ice built up in the Eden and the Esk. When the thaw came, the melting snow from the fells caused the rivers to surge down towards the sea carrying blocks of ice that were said to be between six and ten feet thick. Some of these smashed into the pillars of the Solway viaduct causing extensive structural damage that took three years to repair.

It was during this harsh winter that Jane Graham and her four sons left Bowness-on-Solway and went to live in Carlisle. Why did Jane choose this particular year to move with her family into the city? Her motive may have been concerned with her sons' schooling. Unlike his own father, John did not specifically refer to his children's education in his will but he must have known that this was something that could safely be entrusted to his wife. The eldest son, John, attended an ancient boarding school at St Bees, on the Cumbrian coast. But now John was seventeen, had left school, and was employed as a clerk at the Cumberland Union Bank in Carlisle, the first step on what was to be a successful banking career. Living in the city would be more convenient for John but I doubt if this would have been an important consideration. If, as commonly happened, working class children of the time could leave home at fourteen there was no reason why a seventeen-year-old boarding school boy could not have found suitable lodgings. He was, after all, used to living away from home.

The move is more likely to have been determined by the educational needs of John's brothers. Jane's finances had not run to sending her other three sons to an expensive boarding school. They were to complete their schooling at Grosvenor College, a respected private school in Carlisle, run by Mr R.J. Baillie and this may be the reason Jane felt it necessary to move into the city.

However, the timing of the move is puzzling. By that winter Robert would have been fifteen and approaching the end of his schooling. Richard was thirteen. It must by now have been apparent that, while all of Jane's sons were intelligent, it was William who was the brightest. It may be that it was her determination to give her youngest son the best possible education that inspired her decision to send them all to Grosvenor College.

There is, I believe, a more satisfactory explanation, although I have no concrete evidence to support it. We must consider where the three younger boys began their schooling. While John was benefitting from a private education at St Bees, would Jane have been content to leave her other sons in the hands of Bowness Village School?

There is anecdotal evidence that some children from the next generation of Grahams attended Annan Academy, a highly respected school over the Scottish Border. This was made possible by the railway viaduct over the Solway, an option that ceased when the bridge finally closed in the 1920s. Did Robert, Richard and possibly William also make this daily journey to attend school in Annan? If they did, then the extensive damage that the viaduct suffered during the winter of 1880–81 would have disrupted their education. Finding a different school would have been a matter of urgency. Grosvenor College would have been an obvious choice and a home in the city would then be much more convenient.

My mother recalled her Uncle John telling her that the family moved from Bowness to Carlisle during the very bad winter when the River Eden froze. He did not, as far as I know, say anything about his brothers' early schooling but there must have been a reason why it stuck in his mind that this was the year that they moved. If the effects of the bad winter were the cause of their move to Carlisle this would explain why he remembered it so clearly. But without evidence this remains speculation.

The census of 1881 records the family living at 16, Myddleton Street, Rickergate. With them is Jane's unmarried sister, Mary Sewell. Both are described as living on 'income from property'. In Jane's case this would largely refer to the Knockupworth estate. Mary must have inherited hers from the Sewell family. Jane was now forty-one. Mary was actually only two years younger but in the census she gives her age as thirty. As the householder, Jane must surely have gone along with this subterfuge. They repeated the deception in the census of 1891. It may be that Mary had moved in with her sister when they were living at Bowness after John's death. Her help would have been invaluable in bringing up the four boys.

At Knockupworth, the farm was in the hands of John Martindale. On the night of the 1881 census the farmhouse must have been bursting at the seams. As well as the farmer and his wife, there were seven sons and daughters, aged between twelve and twenty-six, a three-year-old granddaughter, a female visitor and two farm servants. Meanwhile next door, only Ann Wright, her twenty-six-year-old granddaughter and two domestic servants, occupied the spacious Hall. Mrs Wright was now ninety-three and had outlived most of her children.

Ann Wright died in the following year. This might have been an opportunity for Jane to reclaim possession of her husband's ancestral home but she did not do so. The family remained in Myddleton Street until at least 1887, for in March of that year Jane's youngest son, William Sharp Graham, of that address, was reported as having satisfied the Cambridge University board of examiners and to have received a distinction in drawing at Grosvenor College.[1] While she had a son still attending school in the city it may have been more convenient for Jane to postpone the family's return to Knockupworth.

During the years between Ann Wright's death and the time that the Grahams resumed their occupancy, the Hall must have been let to other tenants on a short-term lease. It seems unlikely that it was left standing empty for long. It was too valuable an asset not to be used as a source of income.

At the Border Union Agricultural Society Bull Show and Sale, held at Kelso in early April 1885, Alexander G. Nicholl of Knockupworth Hall is listed as having entered both non-pedigree bulls and shorthorn pedigree bulls.[2] Since his address is specifically given as 'Knockupworth Hall', Mr Nicholl would seem to have been its tenant at that time.

During that same year the farm, though not the Hall, was again advertised to be let. It was at the time being farmed by a Mr Greenup:

> KNOCKUPWORTH NEAR CARLISLE
>
> To be LET, with entry at Candlemas next, a most desirable FARM, situate at KNOCKUPWORTH, in the parishes of Grinsdale and St Mary's about one mile from Carlisle, consisting of Dwelling House, Outbuildings, and 120 Acres or thereabouts of Arable, Meadow, and Pasture Land, mostly lying in a ring Fence.
>
> The present tenant, Mr Greenup, will show the Farm, and written

> proposals will be received from Mr THOMAS IRVING, Bowness-on-Solway, or Mrs GRAHAM, 16 Myddleton Street, Carlisle and the tenant declared as soon as an adequate offer is made.[3]

Even if John had left them comfortably off, the rent from the Hall and the farm must have been vital to pay for the boys' education. My mother believed that, to help fund their schooling, Jane also took out a mortgage on the property. Her decision to move to a terraced house in the city could well have been motivated by economics as well as by location. Her children's private schooling had put a strain on the family's finances and she was eager for her youngest son to follow an academic career.

Grosvenor College provided Robert and Richard with an education that would enable them to emulate their older brother by taking up respectable professional careers but it was William who really excelled at the school. In 1887 the *Carlisle Patriot* reported on the Grosvenor College presentation, held at the County Hall, at which the school orchestra played and the choir sang:

> The prizes were distributed by the Principal, Mr R.J. Baillie, and as the boys came up to the platform, one by one, they were greeted with rounds of applause; this was especially the case on Graham, the school captain, coming up to receive the gold medal.[4]

William, a successful and popular figure, had already qualified to go to Cambridge, though it was a few years before he began his university career.

Unlike their father, who had perhaps been more truly a farmer than any of his ancestors, the four brothers had received an upbringing that had given them little experience of farm life. At the time this hardly seemed to matter. The brothers would follow different paths, forging careers that would make them financially independent. Knockupworth Farm was in the hands of experienced tenant farmers. The rent from the farm provided an income and, once Jane had provided for her sons' education and they were earning their own livings, would again leave the family in a healthy financial position. The prospect of them moving into Knockupworth Hall must have been discussed and looked forward to, especially in the late 1880s when the promised move drew closer to reality.

The River Eden was one of the great assets of the Knockupworth land. A half-mile stretch of river provided a rich harvest of salmon, river trout and young sea trout, known locally as herling. These attracted the attention of many besides the legitimate landowners and there were frequent press reports of poaching. It seems that there were times when a blind eye was turned to those who fished illegally but in 1886 a noteworthy case was brought before the Carlisle magistrates. This raised a number of issues regarding fishing rights, one of which concerned the question of whether the river was tidal at this point.

Thomas Irving, the Bowness farmer who had been appointed as one of the trustees of John Graham's will, had let the fishing rights of the Knockupworth stretch of the river to the Cumbrian Angling Association. On 14th August a Carlisle French polisher, named Alexander Beattie, was caught fishing there. But Mr Beattie was not a common poacher willing to accept his punishment and go quietly. Mr Beattie hired a lawyer to defend him.

When the case came before the magistrates the defence lawyer, Mr Ryley, said that several witnesses 'would tell the bench that they had fished in this particular part of the river for years without being molested.'[5]

One such witness was 76-year old Jacob Ryecroft of Queen Street, Caldewgate:

> He had fished in the portion of the river where the defendant was caught ever since he was seven years old. The river at the place was tidal, the tide coming as high as the railway sheds.

The prosecuting lawyer, Mr Errington, said that if Mr Ryley wished to claim a right of fishery he must prove that it was within the ebb and flow of the highest tide, that the river was navigable, and also that the soil was vested in the crown. Angling rights were obviously a complicated matter. After discussion, the magistrates adjourned the case for a week to allow Mr Irving to be present to prove his title to the land.

When the case resumed, Thomas Irving stated that he was the trustee of the Knockupworth Hall estate and, as such, let the fishing in the River Eden to the Cumbrian Angling Association:

- Mr Ryley said Mr Irving had not proved his right to the fishery.
- The Chairman: he has sworn an oath that he is the owner.
- Mr Ryley: he may tell you that on oath, but he may be mistaken. He should have produced the deeds.

- Chairman: We are satisfied with what he has sworn.
- Mr Ryley said even if Mr Irving owned the banks of the river he might not be the owner of the land under the stream.
- Mr Errington: Who is then?
- Mr Ryley: My client is prepared to swear that Lord Lonsdale has the right of fishery there.'[6]

The magistrates were unimpressed by Mr Ryley's argument and decided that Mr Irving was the owner of the land. The lawyer responded that there was no use arguing the matter further but drew their attention to the fact that his client had 'sinned in ignorance.'

Mr Errington said the sole desire of the angling association was to protect its rights and that they would be satisfied with a nominal penalty. Thereupon the bench imposed a fine of one shilling plus costs.

Perhaps the most interesting feature of this case is not the complicated matter of the fishing rights but the fact that, fourteen years after John Graham's death, Thomas Irving was still acting as trustee. John's two oldest sons had by this time reached the age of twenty-one but had not assumed responsibility for the estate. Presumably this situation would continue until 1891 when all four brothers would have attained the age of majority. This was very different from 1776 when, under the rules of primogeniture, 'Weaver' John had, as the eldest son, inherited the whole of the Knockupworth estate from his father.

This court case about fishing rights pales into insignificance compared to the tragedy that occurred on the river less than a month later. On the last Monday of September over twenty soldiers of the Border Regiment, garrisoned at Carlisle Castle, were taking part in a 'hares and hounds' paper chase when they attempted to swim across the swollen River Eden towards Grinsdale. Several of the men got into difficulties and three were drowned. The *Carlisle Patriot*'s report included graphic accounts of the incident by a number of survivors and went on to say:

> The men forming the hounds remained searching for their lost comrades, until other help arrived, and then they were kindly treated at adjoining farm houses, being supplied with fresh clothing and being made comfortable in other ways. The search continued till dark, but without success. The river at that part is full of whirlpools, and flows, especially at flood time at a rapid rate.[7]

The newspaper reported that on Wednesday one man had been found in a pool opposite the church but the other two bodies had not been recovered. They were eventually found over six miles downstream at Drumburgh and Port Carlisle.[8]

The spectre of this tragedy lingered in the village well after the lifetimes of those who witnessed it and it would be spoken of for many years to come.

Notes

1 *Carlisle Patriot,* 11th March, 1887
2 *The Scotsman,* 4th April 1885
3 *Carlisle Patriot,* 13th October 1885
4 *Carlisle Patriot,* 23rd December 1887
5 *Carlisle Patriot,* 27th August 1886
6 *Carlisle Patriot,* 3rd September 1886
7 *Carlisle Patriot,* 1st October 1886
8 *Carlisle Patriot,* 8th and 15th October 1886

CHAPTER TWENTY-ONE

Returning Home

Some time before 1891 Jane did move to Knockupworth, for in the census of that year she is recorded as being the householder of the Hall. This was a return for the Graham family but not for Jane herself for she had never previously lived there. Even her late husband had only spent a short time there as very small child, and then in the farmhouse rather than the Hall itself. The move she and John had planned to make together had been delayed for almost two decades and now Jane was making it alone. Did she reflect on the irony that her late husband, whose business acumen and agricultural skill had restored the family's fortunes, had never enjoyed the privilege of living in Knockupworth Hall?

John Livick, his wife, a niece and two servants, now occupied Knockupworth Farm. The farmhouse was much less crowded than it had been in the Martindales' time.

There was plenty of room too in the Hall. Only eldest son, John, was living there with his mother and aunt, along with a seventeen-year-old domestic servant. John's younger brothers had also completed their schooling and embarked on professional careers, which, in their cases had taken them far from home.

After serving his articles at the office of Messrs E. and K.J. Hough in Carlisle, Robert's law career had taken him to the Midlands. In the 1891 census Robert H Graham, solicitor, aged 25, born at Bowness-on-Solway, Cumberland, was lodging at Croft Villas in St Michael with St John Parish, Coventry.

Richard had served articles for three years with G.H. Dixon, a Carlisle land agent and had become under-steward for Albert Brassey, M.P. at Heythrop Park Estate, near Chipping Norton in Oxfordshire. In 1891 he was in lodgings at Broadstone Hill, Enstone, which is next to Heythrop Park. He is listed as Richard Graham, lodger, aged 24, land agent and surveyor, born in Cumberland.

Jane Graham had done well in securing good educations for her sons and, while none of them followed her own father into a medical career, she saw them all set up in professional lives. Predictably her youngest son, William, was to be the most successful. Before embarking on university life he spent a short time teaching in private schools. In the 1891 census he is described as a boarder, living with schoolmaster John Irwin, his wife and Irwin's two sisters-in-law in Dover Road, Ecclesall Bierlow, Sheffield. As no school is named and no pupils are listed it seems that he may have been lodging at the schoolmaster's house rather than living-in at a boarding school.

Later that year William joined Clare College, one of the oldest Cambridge colleges. The short time he had spent teaching would have provided him with some income but a university education involved considerable expense and William needed help from his family in order to support himself. We know that Robert and Richard advanced him money towards his college expenses. It seems certain that John and their mother would also have made contributions. William graduated in 1894 with a second class BA in mathematics.[1] Under Cambridge University's idiosyncratic degree system this entitled him to become an MA in 1902.

Robert and William both returned to Cumberland in 1894, Robert as a solicitor in Carlisle, and William to teach at Carlisle Grammar School. Among the possessions Robert took home with him were some framed photographs of Coventry and an anthology of poetry by the Irish poet, Thomas Moore. Inside the book is a handwritten inscription: 'To R.H. Graham from his well-wisher W.H.M. On the occasion of his leaving Coventry to practise at Carlisle. 31 March 1894.'[2] Although Moore may be regarded as one of the lighter nineteenth century poets, it is perhaps an insight into the tastes of this rugby playing solicitor that his friend thought it an appropriate leaving gift.

It is likely that three brothers lived together at Knockupworth Hall for a short time in the mid-nineties. There is a photograph of John, Robert and William standing in front of the Hall, along with their mother and aunt.

Richard had also returned to Cumberland, not to Carlisle but as resident land agent or steward at Sir Henry Vane's estate at Hutton-in-the-Forest near Penrith. Richard was to spend six years in this position but we know little of his time there, excepting one tragic incident reported in the *Penrith Observer* in October 1893.

Two masons were repairing the roof of Richard's house on the estate when the ladder on which both were standing suddenly broke. The foreman mason, John Smithson, fell to the ground, sustaining head injuries from which he died on the following day. The ladder appears to have been in a poor state of repair. One step was missing near the top and three others from lower down. His fellow mason, who was himself fortunate to escape without injury, told the inquest that, in his opinion, by stepping over a missing rung Smithson had put extra pressure on the ladder. In his evidence Richard Graham said that he believed the ladder to have been too short for the task. No one had ever complained about the ladder or drawn his attention to its condition. The jury returned a verdict of accidental death and requested that the ladder never be used again. Mr Graham readily agreed.

The dead man was forty-two. He was from the nearby village of Ireby and had worked on the Hutton estate for about six months. According to the newspaper report he was married with one child.[3] Census information reveals that Ireby was home to a whole clan of Smithsons involved in various aspects of stone working. The man I have identified in the 1891 census as the likely victim of this tragedy had two daughters. One may have died soon after the census or the newspaper report may have been incorrect in stating that he had only one child. The man's identity may not seem particularly important to the history of the Grahams but, several years later, the name John Smithson was to resurface in Richard Graham's life.

Jane's eldest son, John, who had remained with her while his brothers lived miles away, was now about to move, though only a short distance into West Cumberland. His reasons for leaving home were both professional and personal.

The 1891 census records that a thirty-three year old solicitor and bank agent, called Thomas Rigg, was living in the High Street, Wigton cum Woodside, with his wife, Mary Jane, and their five children. With them, in what must surely have been a large house, were his mother-in-law, sixty-year old Mary Isabella Barnes, and two of his wife's sisters, along with three domestic servants. Mrs Barnes had been a farmer's wife and had a large family but she had been widowed for many years.

It may be that John Graham and Thomas Rigg were associates in the banking world and that that is how John became acquainted with Thomas's twenty-four year old sister-in-law, Sarah Ann Barnes. John and Miss Barnes were married in Wigton in 1894. In July of 1895 John gained promotion, becoming manager of the Aspatria branch of the Cumberland Union Bank.

Robert and William continued to live with their mother and aunt at Knockupworth Hall. On 2nd December 1896 the *York Herald* reported that R.H. and W.S. Graham won second prize in the Old English Game Cock category at the York Christmas Fat Stock Show. Gamecocks were by now show animals rather than fighting birds and the brothers' involvement with quality poultry suggests that, while they may not have been farmers, they were taking an interest in respectable country pursuits. Robert was to become well known as a breeder of Old English Game poultry.

Towards the end of the century Richard again moved south, becoming resident agent for the trustees of the Earl of Strafford at Wrotham Park on the border of Hertfordshire and Middlesex. His appointment was announced in the *Penrith Observer* on 11th April 1899.

Richard was at Wrotham Park at an eventful time. He went there just over a year after the Third Earl died. The Earl's brother succeeded him but, a month after Richard's arrival, the Fourth Earl was killed by a train at Potter's Bar. Various newspapers reported on the inquest, which recorded a verdict of accidental death, the Earl having been subject to epileptic fits. The third brother, Francis Edmund Cecil Byng became the Fifth Earl. An ordained priest, he had been Queen Victoria's chaplain and from 1874–89 was Chaplain to the Speaker of the House of Commons. Now one of the largest houses inside the M25 motorway, Wrotham Park is today sandwiched between Barnet and Potter's Bar. It would then have had been in more rural surroundings. The 1901 census finds Richard lodging at nearby Hadley Highstones, Monken Hadley, with a widow whose three sons are all employed in dairy work.

A short time before Richard began his spell at Wrotham Park his aunt, Mary Sewell, died. Jane's younger sister had lived with them at least since they had moved to Carlisle at the beginning of 1881 and possibly before that too, when they were living at Bowness-on-Solway. Their aunt must have played a big part in the brothers' lives. She died in November 1898, aged fifty-six, and was buried in the Sewell family grave in Burgh by Sands churchyard.

Jane may have lost her sister but by the early years of the twentieth century she again had all her sons near her. John was only about twenty miles away. In 1901 he was living in the Bank House, Midtown,

Aspatria with his wife, Sarah, and their two sons, five-year-old Cyril and two-year-old John Hubert.

Robert and William were with their mother at Knockupworth Hall. After a spell teaching at Carlisle Grammar School, William had, in 1898, at the age of twenty-seven, become principal of Albert House School. The inscription on his gravestone records that he became principal of Grosvenor College in 1895 but this is clearly incorrect. R.J. Baillie remained at the college until 1897 and the 1901 edition of *Bulmer's History and Directory of Cumberland* lists William S. Graham as principal of Albert House School. It would appear from that year's census that he continued to live at Knockupworth Hall.

Richard was also about to return. He left Wrotham Park in 1902 with the following testimonial, written by the Earl of Strafford's son, Viscount Enfield:

> 5, St. James's Square.
> S.W.
> 22nd February 1902
>
> Mr R. Graham has acted as Agent for the Wrotham Park Estates for more than two years and a half & in that capacity has collected Rents, paid work people, kept the Estate accounts, prepared plans and generally performed his duties with care and ability. Mr Graham is an accurate book-keeper & a good draughtsman and I should be glad to hear that he has obtained a suitable appointment.
>
> Enfield.[4]

Richard did not obtain such an appointment, deciding instead that his future lay in running his own business. In July of that year he issued a letter to potential clients from an office at 31, Bank Street. He begins by saying: 'SIR, I beg to intimate that I have commenced business as an ESTATE AGENT, SURVEYOR, &c., at the above address.' He goes on to outline his experience on the estates in Oxfordshire, Cumberland and Middlesex, summarising his capability by saying: 'I have had 17 years experience in all branches of Estate Management.' However personal merit was clearly not enough. Good family connections were also important. Richard concludes his letter by saying:

> As regards stability, my eldest brother is a Bank Manager in Aspatria; my second, a Solicitor in Carlisle; and my other brother Principal of Albert House School, Carlisle.

> I can furnish good references and also produce testimonials from my former employers.
>
> In conclusion I need not say that any work entrusted to me will receive my most careful attention, and I shall endeavour to give every satisfaction.[5]

Richard was later to become a partner in William Wood's land agents business in Lowther Street, Carlisle. Mr Wood died soon after Richard joined the firm but the business retained the name of Wood and Graham. After he returned to Carlisle, Richard lived at the Hall along with his mother and two of his brothers, Robert and William.

William was the second of the brothers to marry. He had been engaged to a young woman from Burgh by Sands, called Minnie Borthwick, but, during a spell in hospital with a minor condition, he fell in love with an Irish nurse, Clara Alma Laing (also known as Clare.) William broke off his engagement to Miss Borthwick. He and Clara were married in Dublin in 1902. It would seem that William and his bride must have lived together at the Hall for a while because the 1904 edition of the *Oxford and Cambridge Yearbook* gives William's address as Knockupworth Hall but they would not remain there for much longer. Their marriage may have been the incentive for him taking the next decisive step in his career.

Grosvenor College had closed after R.J. Baillie moved to Glasgow in 1897. William reopened it in 1905 by transferring the Albert House staff and pupils to new premises and adopting the name of his old school. Grosvenor College had enjoyed high prestige in its former incarnation and had only been closed for a few years. If William could take advantage of its reputation it would enhance the status of his own establishment.

William may have capitalised on the school's existing reputation but his own character and professional skill were undoubtedly pivotal to its success. It was stated in his obituary that: 'He had personal qualities which made a strong appeal to boys, and easily won their confidence and respect. He had a kindly nature and a pleasant address which gained him many friends.'[6] In his professional life William retained the popularity and charisma that had once elevated him to the position of school captain.

It is noticeable that William's name is sometimes written as William Sharpe Graham. The addition of a letter 'e' to the family name of Sharp only appears on occasions when William would have written it himself, such as on census returns, on the marriage register or in literature connected with his university place or his role as school principal. I can only think that he believed that the name looked more distinguished with the final 'e'.

Robert, in addition to his legal practice, was taking an interest in local government and was a member of the Carlisle Rural District Council and chairman of the Belle Vue Parish Council. In this role 'he took an active part in opposition to the extension of the City boundaries.'[7] He was also clerk to Longtown Rural District Council. Robert followed his father's example in supporting the poor and was elected as Belle Vue's representative on the Board of Guardians, which was responsible for overseeing the administration of the Poor Law. He also became clerk to that body.

The early years of the twentieth century found the brothers well established in their professional careers. They had become successful in very different spheres. Not one of them had become a farmer– and, in time, this would have implications for the future of Knockupworth.

Notes

1 *Cambridge Independent Press,* 8th June 1894
2 Library of James Bainbridge
3 *Penrith Observer,* 10th October 1893
4 Family papers
5 Family papers
6 *Carlisle Journal,* November 2nd 1920
7 *Carlisle Journal,* March 14th 1922

CHAPTER TWENTY-TWO

The Sporting Grahams

If Jane had hoped that some of her sons might have followed their maternal grandfather into the medical profession, she, nevertheless, can hardly have been disappointed in them. She may well have made sacrifices to ensure that they received a good education. The terraced house they lived in Myddleton Street was hardly grand. Their private schooling also undoubtedly played an important part in the development of their sporting prowess. As fit young men living at that time, in that part of the country, an interest in Cumberland and Westmorland style wrestling would have been almost obligatory, and the Graham brothers would certainly have participated in this sport. However, it is in the areas of athletics and team games that we have records of their achievements. And for the three younger brothers their sporting talent was nurtured on the playing fields of Grosvenor College.

For William, growing up as the youngest of the four, his three fit older brothers must have been important role models and sibling rivalry may have honed his competitive spirit. Robert, over five years his senior and a stalwart of the rugby field, must have been a particularly iconic figure but in sport, as well as academically, William was to outshine his brothers.

Our first record is of fifteen year-old William (W.S. Graham) scoring a try for the victorious Grosvenor College rugby team against Croft House Academy in March 1886.[1] In October of that year William played in a Combined Schools team (Grosvenor College and Carlisle Grammar School) against Eden Wanderers.[2] It was the practice for former pupils to return to Grosvenor College to take part in sporting fixtures against the current school team. That summer Robert and William had played against each other in a cricket match. In October, twenty-one year-old Robert turned out for a team of former pupils against the school rugby team. The *Carlisle Patriot* reported the match thus:

> The annual match between the past and present pupils of Grosvenor College was played on the College Ground in Waterworks Lane, on Friday afternoon. The present boys played a good game throughout, but proved no match for their opponents, who won by two goals to a goal. The tries for the old boys were gained by Strong, Jackson, Burgess and RH Graham while W Graham ran in for the school.[3]

At the time of the match William was a few weeks away from his sixteenth birthday.

The following February, William captained the Grosvenor College team to victory over the Grammar School, scoring two of the tries:

> from near the half-way Graham dashed through the forwards, and handing off the backs in beautiful style, gained a try between the posts.

And in the second half:

> Jackson [...] passed to Graham, and the Grosvenor captain ran round the opposing backs and planted the ball between the posts.[4]

Mr R.J. Baillie, the principal of Grosvenor College, took a keen interest in rugby and was president of the Eden Wanderers club. Small wonder then that his current and former pupils should be encouraged to join their headmaster's team. The *Carlisle Patriot* reported, in March 1887, on a match in which both R.H. and W.S. Graham played in a winning Eden Wanderers team against Penrith.[5]

A fellow member of the Eden Wanderers team was James R. Philips, a Cambridge graduate and son of Archdeacon Philips. Ten years later Philips was to be one of 'nine British citizens, most of them distinguished servants of the Queen' massacred on the River Niger while on 'a peaceful mission' from the Benin coast.[6]

William Sharp Graham's sporting exploits were by no means confined to the rugby field. On 8th April 1887, the *Patriot* reported on the Grosvenor College sports. W. Graham won the high jump with a jump of four feet eleven and a half inches. He also won the 100 yards and the 220 yards. The latter was a handicap race, William giving a fifteen-yard start to the second placed runner and a twenty-yard start to the boy who came third. The *Patriot* described: 'A capital race. Johnson led until about thirty yards from the post, when he was passed by Graham by about five yards. Time 25.2 seconds.'

He also won the broad jump (which we now call the long jump) with a leap of seventeen feet six inches, and came second in the throwing the cricket ball event. Some events that now seem more appropriate for primary school sports days were then taken seriously by sixteen year-olds. Along with his partner, F.W. Johnson, William won the wheelbarrow race and came third in the Siamese (three-legged) race.[7]

The principal Mr R.J. Baillie presented the trophies:

> The silver cup, which was this year given to the best athlete, was won easily by the captain of the school, W.S. Graham who, on receiving it, was loudly cheered.[8]

By June, William had turned his attention to cricket. During the previous summer he had opened the batting for the college eleven. Now, having dropped to number five, he scored nine runs in Grosvenor College's exciting four run defeat by the Grammar School.[9] It is a measure of young William's sporting prowess and the esteem in which he was held that he was captain of the school's cricket and rugby teams for four successive years.[10]

The story of the Graham brothers' sporting achievements focuses mainly on Robert and William. This is partly because they may have been the most successful, but also because their double initials make them easily identifiable in newspaper reports. Where the name J. Graham or R. Graham appears this may be John or Richard but it is difficult to be certain. John, of course, developed his academic and athletic skills, not at Grosvenor College, but at St. Bees School on the west coast. However he may still have joined Mr Baillie's team and could have been the J. Graham who played at half back for Eden Wanderers against North Berwick in January 1886. John was certainly an ardent sportsman. He was, according to tributes paid to him on his retirement, distinguished in rugby and cricket as well as being a keen tennis player. Where the name R. Graham appears on a team-sheet this presents the same problem: this may or may not be our Richard Graham. However we know for certain that he played rugby with his younger brother. There is a team photograph in which both Richard and William appear. In the match against Penrith, reported by the *Patriot* on 9th December 1887, the Eden Wanderers' team-sheet included W.S. Graham at three-quarter back, R. Graham at half back, and R.H. Graham as a forward. It is likely that this was an example of the three former Grosvenor College Graham brothers playing together in the same team. William, though still only seventeen, was already captaining the Eden Wanderers team.

We are now so aware of rugby as a traditional sport that we perhaps need to remind ourselves that at the time that the brothers were playing it was relatively new. It had evolved from games of football played at various public schools but it had only recently been organised into a sport played across the country and its rules were still evolving. When the Graham brothers turned out for Eden Wanderers the Rugby Football Union had been in existence for less than twenty years.

The late 1880s saw a period of great change for the Graham family. It was at about this time that they moved back to Knockupworth Hall – probably coinciding with William completing his schooling at Grosvenor College. But Jane was to lose the company of three of her sons. At the time of the 1891 census only John was living with her at the Hall. His brothers had all moved away. And they were not only a loss to Jane but also to Eden Wanderers and the Carlisle rugby scene.

After moving to the Midlands Robert Hodgson Graham wasted no time in joining Coventry Rugby Club and made an immediate impression with the rugby reporter of the *Coventry Times*:

> Graham who hails from the Lake District is a distinct acquisition. He works well and dribbles cleverly and as he wears red stockings and is easily distinguished he generally gets all the credit for all he does.[11]

The highlight of Robert Graham's rugby career so far was surely Coventry's victory over Leicester in the final of the Midland Counties Cup played at Rugby in April 1891. The *Coventry Herald* reported that the match was played before eight thousand spectators and this was the first encounter of the season between the two sides. Despite neither team having had a very good record that season the game seems to have exceeded expectations, both in the quality of the play and the sportsmanship of the players. The *Herald* reporter declared that 'the game was played with a gentleness and a generosity unfortunately not often seen.'

He went on: 'From the beginning the players adopted loose and passing tactics, as opposed to the tight scrimmaging and mauling of earlier years.'

The half backs, of which R.H. Graham was one, were singled out for special praise: 'The skill of the Coventry half backs went a long way towards obtaining the victory.'[12]

It seems that the result was rarely in doubt, with Coventry dominating the closing stages and Robert Graham getting on the score sheet.

That year William joined Clare College Cambridge. Unsurprisingly he became involved in the university's strong sporting traditions though he may have been up against stiffer competition than he had experienced in his home county. In the Clare College sports of March 1892 he came second in the long jump with a best jump of eighteen feet and half an inch. In the three hundred yards freshers' race he finished alone in a time of thirty-seven seconds.[13]

The following year, in the university handicaps, W.S. Graham won heat two of the 200 yards and, with a fifteen-yard start, also won heat two of the quarter mile handicap. However, on the following day, he could only finish second in the finals of both races.[14]

On 10th March of that year the newspaper reported that at the Cambridge University Athletics meeting W.S. Graham had, on the previous Saturday, won the second heat of the quarter mile but could only finish third in the final on the following Monday.

Our best source of information regarding William's sporting achievements while at university is a 'Portrait Sketch' of him published in the *Lancashire Evening Post* in 1901. This portrait comments that while at Clare College 'he kept up his athletic acquirements with even greater success' and held the position of President of Sports. It goes on to say that 'though he took part while at Cambridge in so many branches of sport, his best love was the Rugby game.'[15]

In October of 1893 he is recorded as having scored a try for the stripes in a trial match against the whites. He then played at half back in Cambridge's first match of the season, a 30 – 0 win over Guy's Hospital,[16] and he was also selected to play against Old Leysians, St Thomas's Hospital and Middlesex Wanderers.[17] In Cumberland, William normally played as a three-quarter back, where his pace would have been a distinct advantage. At the university his position was half back.

During his years at university and Robert's spell in the Midlands, Cambridge played an annual match against Coventry Rugby Club. In 1893 Robert played in the match at Coventry but William was not included in the University team.[18] Nor did he play in that month's match against Oxford University. His absence from these games was down to very unfortunate circumstances.

The 'portrait' of W.S. Graham in the *Lancashire Evening Post* says that he played several matches for the university but:

> just prior to the event which would have secured him his "blue"[19] – the inter-Varsity match – he had the misfortune to sustain an accident to his collar-bone, which kept him out of the field for a while.[20]

It seems that William's rugby career at university was curtailed by injury and he never did achieve his Cambridge Blue.[21]

For these few years it seems that Robert's rugby career may have been even more distinguished than that of his younger brother.

Having won the Midland Counties Cup in 1891 Coventry retained it for the next two seasons. In the final of 1892, played at Leicester, they inflicted a heavy defeat on Mosely. After scoring a try in the semi-final Robert was listed in the team for the final.[22] Reporting on the final, the *Coventry Herald* printed this quote from *The Daily Post*:

> It was indeed, a finely-won match, and excellent as many of the displays of the cupholders have been in the course of their long career, it is doubtful if they have ever given a finer all-round exhibition of the game than at Leicester on Saturday.[23]

In March 1893 Robert played as a forward in the semi-final of that year's cup, in which Coventry beat Old Edwardians by one goal and one try to nil in front of three thousand spectators at Birmingham County Ground.[24] In his third cup final appearance Coventry beat Burton by one goal and three tries to nil. It was, according to most accounts, a disappointing game. In an article reprinted in the *Coventry Herald*, "Great Scott" from *Athletic News* was particularly venomous:

> Coventry can thank Tuke and Slater for the cup, but they didn't deserve to win the trophy on the form shown. It was altogether too bad to be true. And the same remark holds good for Burton. It is absurd to believe that neither team can rise above the mediocre show they gave here. That's the opinion of yours truly, and those who don't like it can do the other thing.[25]

The match was held at Leicester's Welford Road ground and watched by a crowd estimated to be between eight and ten thousand, many of whom had arrived on special trains. Railways were by now an integral part of the country's social life.

The final may have been disappointing in terms of entertainment but it seems to have been just reward for the team's performances over the season. The same edition of the *Coventry Herald* congratulated the team in the following way:

> For the third successive season the Coventry Football Club has won

the Midlands Counties Cup. The achievement is a fitting conclusion to a record of victories upon which the team may be congratulated.

And a week later it quoted from an article published in the *Birmingham Mail*:

In the Midland District Coventry have managed to keep to the front with the best team that has been seen in the district for many years, though at the beginning of the season dissention in the ranks threatened to break it up.[26]

The report does not give any indication of what form this dissention had taken and whether it was on or off the pitch. There was no hint of dissent when the annual dinner of Coventry Rugby Club was held at the Queen's Hotel on 4th May 1893. There was every reason for good humour, the team having lost only six of the thirty matches it had played that season.

The players who had played in any of the three cup finals were each presented with a gold medal; among them was R.H. Graham.

The speeches that were made at the dinner reflected a country that was confident about itself; a confidence based on its imperialism. Victorian Britain saw a close correlation between military success and sporting achievement. Proposing a toast to the success of the club, the chairman, Alderman Hill, declared that:

England's greatness was to be attributed in great measure to the game of football, and other popular pastimes in which the soldiers and sailors and others whose duty it was to fight for the liberties of the country engaged in while young. If they were to judge from the conversation that they heard not only in the streets, but on all occasions, even when coming out of places of worship they would find that it was nearly always about football.[27]

The Coventry M.P., William Ballantyne said:

There was no doubt, as the chairman had said, that it was owing to athletics that they had made the Empire so powerful. It was an old saying, very often repeated, of the Duke of Wellington, that "the Battle of Waterloo was won on the playing fields of Eton." He was glad to say that such playing fields had considerably extended since 1815.

It was a time of success but also a time of change for Coventry Rugby Club. The club captain was retiring, one of the officials was standing down; and, as he sat listening to the speeches, Robert

Graham must have known that his time in the Midlands was drawing to a close.

Robert's contribution to the successful Coventry team was not forgotten. On 25th August 1894 the *Nuneaton Advertiser* reported that 'Mr R. Graham who played with the Coventry Football Club for several seasons has been elected captain of the Carlisle Football Club.'

Having graduated from Cambridge, William Sharp Graham also returned to Cumberland in 1894 and resumed his participation in local rugby. Eden Wanderers had by now amalgamated with its bitter rival, Carlisle Football Club, and it was for Carlisle that the brothers played the rest of their club rugby.

William's return heralded an even more successful period in his playing career. In February 1895 he was selected as a three-quarter back in the Cumberland team to play against Devonshire.[28] The following month he played in another county game against Midland Counties at Workington. Very much in the thick of the action, it seems to have been a somewhat frustrating match for William in a personal sense, though Cumberland ran out winners by fourteen points to nil. A pass 'was cleverly taken by Graham who made a fine dash across the centre line but was bowled over by Butlin. Graham immediately afterwards made another good run.'

And later: 'Graham obtaining the ball from Fletcher just failed to force his way over the line.'[29]

William was again selected to play for Cumberland against Durham at Gateshead on Saturday 26th October.[30] It may have been in recognition of his county status that he was promoted to the captaincy of the Carlisle team. When the brothers played together in the team that defeated Jed Forest in November it was William, not Robert, who was the captain.[31]

William was undoubtedly a star of his club side and distinguished himself when representing his county. He was later described as possessing 'a sturdy physique, and was a very strong and fast runner, and a clever dodger. He was one of the best half backs in the North of England and did invaluable work for Cumberland when it was challenging the supremacy of Yorkshire in the county championship competition.'[32] However a star player does not always make the best captain. That William took over the captaincy of the Carlisle club may also tell us something about the characters of the two brothers. William may have been the more outgoing; he did, after all, have the leadership qualities to be the proprietor and headmaster of a school at the age of twenty-seven. His obituary said this of W.S. Graham's sporting character:

> No player of his generation was more generally liked and more highly esteemed as a good sportsman, who played the game in the true spirit, and whose personal modesty won almost as much admiration as his skill.[33]

1897 was an eventful year for William at both club and county level. As the 96–97 season drew to a close he drew a rave review from the reporter despite Carlisle's defeat in strong wind and 'drenching rain' at Aspatria.[34]

Now, in his mid-twenties, he may have lost some of the pace needed for a three-quarter back but he had gained the experience and footballing intelligence to operate in the playmaking role of a half back.

When the club's records were published at the end of that season it was revealed that W.S. Graham was the leading try scorer with ten tries – more than double the total of any other player. R. Graham had scored one try.[35] The omission of the second initial suggests that this may have been Richard rather than Robert but, as the third brother is little mentioned in reports, this is by no means certain.

The Annual General Meeting of the Carlisle Football Club was held in August at the Great Central Hotel. R.H. Graham, as secretary, read the report to an audience of about seventy members. He reported that the club's financial position was good, the team's performances on the pitch less so, having won only eight out of twenty five matches. However, four of the team: T.D. Bell, D. Elliot, A. Smith and W.S. Graham had represented the county, the first three regularly. W.S. Graham was again elected club captain.[36]

And he was again selected to play for his county in their next game against Lancashire.[37]

The high point of William's playing career came the following month when he was selected to play in an international trial match for the North against the South. Announcing his selection, the *Patriot* declared:

> The honour of a North cap has, through a variety of circumstances, been rather slow in coming Graham's way but it is none the less well-deserved, and the Carlisle captain's many friends hope to see him do himself justice.[38]

Sadly, the North lost the match, a result that may have dashed William's hopes of a full international cap.

William's career in county rugby football and his hopes of international glory were soon to be brought to an end, not by injury or loss of form, but by a bitter dispute between his club and the Cumberland Union. And the Graham brothers, Robert and William, would be at the very heart of this conflict.

Notes

1 *Carlisle Patriot*, 26th March 1886
2 *Carlisle Patriot*, 22nd October 1886
3 *Carlisle Patriot*, 29th October 1886
4 *Carlisle Patriot*, 25th February 1887
5 *Carlisle Patriot*, 4th March 1887
6 *Carlisle Patriot*, 15th January 1897
7 Siamese Race: I assume this refers to the three-legged race. Today, the term would be considered inappropriate.
8 *Carlisle Patriot*, 8th April 1887
9 *Carlisle Patriot*, 3rd June 1887
10 *Lancashire Evening Post*, 12th October 1901
11 *Coventry Times*, 13th November 1889
12 *Coventry Herald*, 10th April 1891
13 *Cambridge Independent Press*, 4th March 1892
14 *Cambridge Independent Press*, 24th February 1893
15 *Lancashire Evening Post*, 12th October 1901
16 *Cambridge Independent Press*, 20th October 1893
17 *Sporting Life*, 21st, 25th, 28th October 1893
18 *Sporting Life*, 15th December 1893
19 Cambridge 'Blue': awarded to students who have competed against Oxford in a major university sport. Among the privileges is the right to wear a 'Cambridge Blue' scarf.
20 *Lancashire Evening Post*, 12th October 1901
21 *Carlisle Journal*, November 2nd 1920
22 *Nuneaton Advertiser*, 9th April 1892
23 *Coventry Herald*, 8th April 1892
24 *Coventry Herald*, 31st March 1893
25 *Coventry Herald*, 8th April 1892
26 *Coventry Herald*, 14th April 1893
27 *Coventry Herald*, 5th May 1893
28 *Carlisle Patriot*, 15th February 1895
29 *Carlisle Patriot*, 15th March 1895
30 *Carlisle Patriot*, 25th October 1895
31 *Carlisle Patriot*, 8th November, 1895

32 *Carlisle Journal,* 2nd November 1920
33 *Carlisle Journal,* 2nd November 1920
34 *Carlisle Patriot,* 2nd April 1897
35 *Carlisle Patriot,* 30th April 1897
36 *Carlisle Patriot,* 27th August 1897
37 *Carlisle Patriot,* 26th November 1897
38 *Carlisle Patriot,* 17th December 1897

CHAPTER TWENTY-THREE

The Cumberland Difficulty

Shortly before William Graham played in the North v South international trial, the Cumberland Union had themselves arranged a trial match for selection to the county team. This would deprive Carlisle of several players for their club game on the same day. William made his position clear:

> The Carlisle captain, W.S. Graham is also among those chosen for the trial match, but he declares his intention of playing for his club on Saturday, no matter what the consequences may be. He held himself aloof from county football last season after playing against Durham; but he has agreed to turn in again this season if selected which there is not the slightest doubt he will be.[1]

As the above extract suggests, William was already being selective about his appearances in the county team. This may have been for genuine professional reasons; he was teaching at Carlisle Grammar School and may have already been in the process of setting up Albert House School. His career would necessarily take precedence over his participation in amateur sport. He was now ready to play for the county again but not on any terms. He may well have thought he had done enough to justify his selection without having to take part in this county trial game. The reporter clearly thought that W.S. Graham was a sufficiently valued member of the team for the County Executive to overlook this snub and William himself must have shared this view. It seems they were right. In the following month he scored a try in Cumberland's narrow victory over Cheshire. But, in a dispute that the press would come to refer to as 'The Cumberland Difficulty'[2], the rumblings of discontent were already stirring. And when the conflict erupted William Graham would nail his colours firmly to the mast of his club.

Rugby Union in Cumberland was already under threat from the

emergence of the Northern Union – the forerunner of what is now known as Rugby League. This gave men the opportunity to play professionally and its popularity grew in Yorkshire and the North West. As membership of the Cumberland Union became depleted by defections to the Northern Union, Carlisle became the major – and eventually the only – club left playing rugby union in the county. Its officials and players began to believe that its dominance should be reflected both in the committee room and on the playing field.

In January 1899, W.S. Graham wrote to the county executive recommending that several of his teammates should be included in the Cumberland team. Among them was his half back partner Jack Fleming who had hitherto been overlooked.[3] This might have been well-received but it seems that the Carlisle captain may have gone a little too far by implying that unless his fellow club players were included he would not be playing either.

The executive ignored W.S.'s advice and his implied threat, called his bluff and selected him for the Yorkshire match without his Carlisle teammates.[4] However, in the following match against Northumberland, Fleming played alongside him in the team.[5]

The end of the playing season in 1899 did not bring to an end the growing hostility between the officials of the club and those of the county. At the annual meeting of the Cumberland Rugby Union the Carlisle members tried unsuccessfully to have the elections of the officers postponed.[6] This was followed by a proposal at Carlisle's annual general meeting for the club to sever its links with the Cumberland Union. The motion was heavily defeated but it would not be the last time the matter was raised.[7]

Carlisle began the following season badly. 'Oh what a difference from last year,' said a report in the *Lancashire Evening Post*. The forwards had not 'got into their methods' and of the backs '"Billy" Graham was about the only one that did play.'[8] But, despite his club's poor form, despite his confrontational letter about the non-selection of his team mates, and despite the ill feeling between his club and the officials of the Cumberland Union, "Billy" Graham's place in the county team did not seem to be in jeopardy: 'The half-back position may cause some difficulty. Graham is a certainty of course; but who will partner him?'

Then, a few days after this was written, the simmering hostility boiled over. Mr Westray, the Cumberland Union President, triggered the crisis by requesting that each club should submit the names of players it considered worthy of selection for the county team and mark them in order of merit. Carlisle's response was that it was unreasonable that they should be expected to mark their players in order of merit. Mr Westray saw this as a 'palpable lack of moral courage on the part of the Carlisle committee.' According to the press reports 'the discussion got more and more fire in it as it proceeded.'[9] Strong language had been used. Rumbling discontent had turned into positive ill feeling.

Mr Westray was a formidable man. In the words of *Lancashire Evening Post* correspondent, Carel Cross: 'The Cumberland President has made himself famous as a strict disciplinarian, and he is one of those men who will boldly assert what he believes to be right and will courageously follow it whatever the consequences.'[10] There were men of equal obstinacy on the Carlisle side, among them its secretary, R.H. Graham.

W.S. Graham and Jack Fleming had been selected for the forthcoming county match against Durham. Neither of them played. Though it is impossible to think that this was unconnected to the heated meeting of a few days earlier, they did not directly refuse to play. Each of them cited work commitments as the reason for their absence. The situation was compounded by the fact that, having declared themselves unavailable for the county match, they requested permission to play in Carlisle's game against Jed Forest on the same day.[11] This was not as unreasonable as it sounds, since the club match was at home, while the county game involved a long journey to Spennymoor. However, when the Cumberland Union objected, the Carlisle Club decided to challenge the County Executive's authority and wrote a letter to the Rugby Union.[12]

The County Executive was in no mood to be charitable. When the team was selected for the next match against Cheshire, Graham and Fleming were omitted from the team sheet.[13]

William may have offended the Cumberland officials but their wrath was directed more towards his brother who had been responsible for the letter. Under the threat of suspension, Robert and the club chairman E.A. Strickland were called upon to withdraw the accusations and apologise. Neither was in any mood to do so. In appealing against their suspensions Robert further inflamed the situation by raising the objection 'that the County Executive was an "invalid and illegal committee" and consequently not competent to adjudicate on the matter in question.'[14]

The ruling of the Rugby Union Emergency Committee came down

mainly on the side of the county though it annulled the suspensions of the two Carlisle officials.

In September 1900 the members of the Carlisle club again voted (by 30 votes to 11) to continue membership of the County Union, much to the displeasure of the secretary, R.H. Graham, who said 'this decision would only mean more trouble.' He went on to say that the annual report of the County Union 'was a direct insult to the Carlisle Club.' He contended that 'owing to the position of the Carlisle Club in the county' – they were virtually the only team left playing – they ought to have another representative on the County Committee.[15]

Cumberland continued to select players from Carlisle but there was no place in the side for W.S. Graham. The Carlisle captain's continued omission may have been largely due to the animosity between his brother, the club secretary, and Mr Westray.

The antagonism between the Cumberland Union and the Carlisle club continued, with disputes over fixture clashes adding to the general ill feeling. But in January 1901 there appears to have been a change of heart regarding W.S. Graham because the Carlisle captain was selected to play alongside his club teammate Jack Fleming for the county match against Yorkshire.[16] This was claimed by the County Executive to be a move towards reconciliation, though it might also be seen as an attempt to test the resolve of both the club and the player.

We will never know for certain if W.S. Graham might have played against Yorkshire. The match did not take place. On 22nd January 1901 Queen Victoria died and that Saturday's sporting programme was cancelled.

It seems that the moment had passed. William Graham's next move was to burn his boats in the most dramatic fashion:

> When the team against Northumberland came to be chosen on Thursday night it was reported that W.S. Graham, the Carlisle captain and old North half, whose recent selection for the subsequently postponed match with Yorkshire was welcomed on all hands, had written to say that he had "no intentions of playing," and that the County Union "had no authority" to select him. The President (Mr Westray) remarked that the selection was made with a view to reviving, as far as possible, harmonious relations, but when a player, after receiving an intimation from the secretary as to his selection, replied in this manner he did not see what more they could do.[17]

Mr Westray then made a comment that conflicts with everything we have hitherto heard said about one of the county's most respected sportsmen: 'We think a player who would send such a reply is guilty of gross impertinence and unworthy to be classed among good sportsmen.'

Of all those who were suffering as a result of the dispute perhaps no one was affected more than William Graham. His wound might have been largely self-inflicted but it was felt that his action was denying him deserved rewards. It was thought that if he had been playing for his county, an international cap might well have come his way. 'But the present attitude of "W.S.G." renders his selection impossible.'[18]

Despite the above comment about William Graham's 'present attitude', and Mr Westray's earlier claim that he was unworthy to be classed among good sportsmen, it was only a few months later that the *Lancashire Evening Post* published its 'Portrait Sketch', which was full of praise for the Carlisle captain's reputation. It made little reference to his part in the dispute, merely stating that: 'the unfortunate "difference" between some of the officials of the Carlisle club and the County Executive has caused him to decline to play for two or three seasons in higher circles than club football.'[19]

That summer brought a change of attitude among the members of the Carlisle club. Another vote, held at that year's general meeting, resulted in a huge majority of 48 votes to 4 deciding to sever the club's connection with the Cumberland County Union. A major factor behind this decision was its perceived under-representation on the committee.[20]

The Cumberland Union requested that the English Rugby Union hold an inquiry into the allegations the club had made in its resolution. When the two sides failed to reach agreement the Rugby Union Committee suggested a compromise. It proposed that a new committee be constituted, 'consisting of seven members three of which will be representatives of the Carlisle Club.'[21]

This seems to have been a major concession in Carlisle's favour but things had gone too far for there to be any reconciliation. Personalities were now involved. The club was not prepared to cooperate with the County Union so long as Mr Westray remained its president.[22]

Carlisle's withdrawal from the County Union had a devastating effect on the fortunes of Cumberland rugby. A severely weakened county team suffered a series of embarrassing defeats. And this was not the only consequence. Cumberland had played most of its home matches on the Carlisle ground. The club would no longer allow it to use its Warwick Road pitch. It started to arrange matches at Keswick but other counties complained that the town was inaccessible.[23] The expulsion of Cumberland from the County Championship became a real possiblilty.

By December the Rugby Union had considered its sub-committee's report into the crisis but it seemed unable to do anything to resolve the situation:

> The inquiry appears to have been abortive, for while the Carlisle Club have established their claim to increased representation on the Cumberland Union, the crux of the whole trouble, the election of the president, remains, apparently, unsettled.[24]

Early in 1902 a letter appeared in *Lancashire Evening Post*, dated January 23rd, and signed 'Spectator'. The letter was a vitriolic attack on the Cumberland Union and its president, and also on the Rugby Union authorities for their handling of the crisis.

'Spectator' pointed out what, from a Carlisle perspective, was the absurdity of having the County run by representatives of clubs that no longer had teams, when they themselves were the only side still competing under Union rules:

> The Rugby Union then decide that Aspatria is a club, entitled to representation, the reason being that it has a banking account. They admit that it could not place a team in the field, yet, because it has a banking account, they allow it to be represented, and in this case practically to control it [...] The Rugby Union decision means that a club may have no players, no matches, ground &c, but, so long as it has a banking account it is the equal, in the matter of representation, of the strongest club that ever lived.

He stated that the antipathy towards the President dated back fifteen or sixteen years and that there was good reason for it. Finally, he pointed out that of the twenty or thirty clubs that had once formed the County Union, all except Carlisle had joined the Northern Union and 'the Rugby Union seem as if they wished by their short-sighted policy, to drive it over also.'[25]

The letter may have been written under the pseudonym 'Spectator' but it does not feel like the work of an onlooker; rather it has the tone of someone on the inside of the Carlisle Club, someone capable of analytically studying the Rugby Union rules and of presenting a rational and well-argued case, someone with the mind of a solicitor, perhaps – someone like the Carlisle secretary, R.H. Graham.

Opinion was now turning against the Carlisle club. Its officials may have had some valid points but by ignoring overtures towards reconciliation they were losing the sympathy of the newspaper correspondents of the day.

The dispute continued for another two years – two years in which Carlisle players continued to boycott the county team. But by the beginning of 1904 support for the club's stance was crumbling from within. New young, talented players were arriving on the scene and, like their more senior teammates, they were being denied the opportunity of achieving deserved county honours. By now William Graham was playing fewer club games and had relinquished the captaincy. As well as his increasing professional commitments he had a wife and a young son.

In February 1904 the club's united front finally cracked. Ironically one of the first players to break ranks was Jack Fleming, the half back and now club captain, who had been the subject of W.S. Graham's indignant letter of support and who had been so deeply involved in the early stages of the controversy.

> That the Carlisle players are anxious to play for Cumberland cannot be denied; and today's team against Northumberland promised to yield some interesting results as regards its construction, both Fleming and Jennings, two of the three or four lights of the Carlisle team, having signified their willingness to play for their county, and were joyously accepted.[26]

This was the turning point – the beginning of the end for the club's stubborn resistance to the County's authority and its boycott of the Cumberland team – and for the rest of the county it heralded a new mood of optimism.

In the boardroom of Carlisle Football Club, the mood was blacker. The club's rebellion against the authority of the Cumberland Union was now being subjected to a counter-rebellion by some of its players against its own authority. There was now disunity amongst the membership. Those who wanted the offending players 'chucked out' of the club were out-voted by those who favoured a more tolerant attitude. There is no doubt which side of the fence the Graham brothers were on.

In October the club chairman Mr T.H. Hodgkinson resigned.[27] Then under the headline: 'CARLISLE CLUB RUPTURE' the

Yorkshire Post reported on the refusal of the committee to keep the offending players out of the Carlisle Club team and that the chairman's resignation 'has this week been followed by that of Mr R.H. Graham, the late secretary.'[28]

Two weeks later it was reported that 'Rugby Union football in Carlisle and the broader Cumberland may well be said to be progressing towards recovery,' and that Cumberland's recent victory over Durham 'did the Border County a good deal of good.'[29]

William Sharp Graham was a man of strong principles, determination and stubborn loyalty. It is doubtful if he ever played for Carlisle again. But he was not finished with rugby football. When he was over forty he was still turning out for the Grosvenor College team and he was to have a long influence over the sport in the city and the county. As principal of Albert House School and later of Grosvenor College, he encouraged boys to take part and nurtured their talent. In January of 1904 the *Lancashire Evening Post* had published an article about a promising Carlisle player called H. Bewsher. He was now recognised as one of the club's best forwards. But:

> His energies were for a long time latent; but when W.S. Graham, the captain of the Carlisle club, started up Albert House School, Bewsher went there to finish his education. "W.S.'s" football enthusiasm quickly spread to his pupils, and they have all along been eager players.

The article goes on to say that Bewsher:

> was amongst Mr Graham's scholars whose ambitions went towards football as well as to the serious part of school life; and their master always believed in educating them in the game he so well liked, and in which he himself was so proficient.[30]

When Robert Hodgson Graham resigned as club secretary in 1904 he may have turned his back on rugby football forever.

He was about to turn his attention to agriculture.

Notes

1 *Shields Daily Gazette*, 8th October 1897
2 *Sporting Life*, 27th December 1899
3 *Lancashire Evening Post*, 21st January 1899
4 *Manchester Times*, 27th January 1899
5 *York Herald*, 6th February 1899
6 *Lancashire Evening Post*, 4th August 1899
7 *Leeds Mercury*, 1st September 1899
8 *Lancashire Evening Post*, 7th October 1899
9 *Lancashire Evening Post*, 14th October 1899
10 *Lancashire Evening Post*, 14th October 1899
11 *Lancashire Evening Post*, 21st October 1899
12 *Athletic News*, 20th November 1899
13 *Athletic News*, 6th November 1899
14 *Bradford Daily Telegraph*, 2nd December 1899
15 *Yorkshire Post and Leeds Intelligencer*, 3rd September 1900
16 *Lancashire Evening Post*, 18th January 1901
17 *Athletic News*, 4th February 1901
18 *Lancashire Evening Post*, 23rd February 1901
19 *Lancashire Evening Post*, 12th October 1901
20 *Athletic News*, 2nd September 1901
21 *Lancashire Evening Post*, 19th October 1901
22 *Lancashire Evening Post*, 26th October 1901
23 *Athletic News*, 23rd December 1901
24 *Yorkshire Post and Leeds Intelligencer*, 16th December 1901
25 *Lancashire Evening Post*, 24th January 1902
26 *Lancashire Evening Post*, 6th February 1904
27 *Lancashire Evening Post*, 20th October 1904
28 *Yorkshire Post and Leeds Intelligencer*, 27th October 1904
29 *Lancashire Evening Post*, 12th November 1904
30 *Lancashire Evening Post*, 9th January 1904

CHAPTER TWENTY-FOUR

Lengthening Shadows

The members of the Graham family who had been alive at the beginning of the nineteenth century had known only one king; those who saw the end of it had spent their entire lives during the reign of one queen. Queen Victoria's sixty-three year reign ended on January 22nd 1901. The new century brought a new king. As Prince of Wales, Edward VII's reputation had been almost as bad as that of his great uncle, George IV, but as king he embarked on a course of diplomacy designed to hold together the fragile peace of Europe.

The new century had, like the previous one, begun with the country at war. The Second Boer War had broken out in October 1899 and was to last until May 1902. Many young men had been eager to enlist, including several of William's teammates at Carlisle Rugby Club. But this war was fought far away in South Africa, did not involve conscription and did not lead to the carnage of the conflict that was soon to follow.

The Grahams had been restored to Knockupworth for over a decade; Jane and three of her sons were in residence at the Hall. William may have continued to live there with his wife, Clara, for a short time after their marriage but in the next census he gives their first son's birthplace as Carlisle. Born in November 1903, the boy was rather grandly named John St Clare William Laing Graham but was subsequently known as Bill. Laing was his mother's maiden name. Once William had taken over Grosvenor College, which was a boarding school, the family went to live at the school. Their daughter, Alma Mary, born in 1906, was the first girl to be born into the family since Hannah, ninety years earlier.

Jane lived to see four of her grandchildren – John's sons and William's two oldest children. She died on 10th February 1908, at the age of sixty-eight, and was buried in the grave where her husband had been laid thirty-six years earlier, and her husband's father thirty-three years before that.

The last tenant farmer, Philip Tweddle, left Knockupworth sometime after the 1901 census. Robert and Richard had decided to end the succession of tenants and take over the farm themselves. It is not known precisely when they undertook this venture but it may have been as early as 1904, while their mother was still alive. Stocking the farm required a substantial financial investment and this may have been the occasion when a further mortgage was taken out on the property.

For a time the brothers employed a farm bailiff. This might have seemed like a sensible compromise, bringing someone with agricultural experience to work alongside them in managing the farm, but it turned out to be a less than satisfactory arrangement. In October 1909, at Wigton Petty Sessions, a bastardy order was imposed on John Smithson, the farm bailiff at Knockupworth Hall.[1] The plaintiff was Miss Sarah Robinson of Bank House, Aspatria. This was the address of Robert and Richard's older brother, John. If I have identified her correctly in census records, she was a farmer's daughter from Workington and part of a very large family.

The defendant was not present at the hearing but the magistrates were satisfied that Sarah's claim was corroborated by other evidence and awarded her 3s 6d per week until the child reached the age of sixteen, and also £1 9s 6d to cover her costs in obtaining the order.

The details of the relationship between Miss Robinson and the Grahams' farm bailiff are not clear and the reason why she should be living at the home of their bank manager brother is open to speculation. Perhaps the most likely sequence of events is that Sarah had been an employee at Knockupworth and had become pregnant while she was working there. John Graham may have taken her in after she left; perhaps he felt that the family bore some responsibility for her predicament. He and his wife normally had a domestic servant living with them at Bank House and they may have provided Sarah with temporary employment, though by the time of the 1911 census she was back with her family on the farm at Workington. It is likely that John was instrumental in guiding her in making the application for the bastardy order.

Was it coincidence that Knockupworth's disgraced farm bailiff had the same name as the workman who had tragically fallen from the roof of Richard Graham's house sixteen years earlier? If the stonemason had had a son, we might think that Richard, feeling responsible for the man's death, had taken this son under his wing and given him employment. But census information suggests that Smithson only had daughters. He appears to have had a nephew called John and it is possible that it was he who became the Grahams' farm bailiff, though it is unlikely that Richard would have felt the same degree of responsibility for a nephew that he might have done for a son.

Following their experience with John Smithson, Robert and Richard decided to dispense with the services of a bailiff. They would run the farm themselves while at the same time maintaining their professional roles in the city. John is believed to have counselled against the decision. Later opinion within the family was that they would have been better heeding his advice. Farming may have been in their blood but it was not in their upbringing. If their father had lived and they had been brought up as a farmer's sons their lives might have been very different.

That is not to say that they did not take farming seriously. Richard had in his possession a copy of *Stephens' Book of the Farm (Division II)*, a standard agricultural textbook of the time. Henry Stephens F.R.S.E. gave detailed and often very scientific advice on a range of important farming matters, among them feeding animals in winter, building chicken coops, applying liquid manure to the soil and the workings of what must then have been innovative farm machinery.[2] They were, nonetheless, part-time farmers whose upbringing had hardly equipped them for the role.

William and Clara's second son, Percy Reginald, was born in 1909. The 1911 census, held around six years after the re-opening of Grosvenor College, recorded that William and Clara were both aged forty-one and had been married for eight years. Clara's seventy-six year old mother, Margaret Laing, was staying with them at the school. She was, like her daughter, born in County Mayo. Their eldest son was seven, their daughter four, and Percy Reginald just two years old.

Three schoolmasters, all in their early twenties and one of them Australian, were also in residence. There was one female servant living in at the school. Grosvenor College catered for boarders but it seems that it mainly served local families, for only three resident boys are listed in the census. The youngest was twelve-year-old Humphrey Arthur Targheggan from London. The oldest, sixteen-year-old John

Robinson, was much closer to his home in Aspatria. Fifteen-year-old Francis John Bell was from Tottenham – and he has an interesting and tragic story; Grosvenor College was to be touched by the major national disaster of 1912.

Francis John Bell was the son of Joseph Bell, the chief engineer on the Titanic. After leaving school Frank was himself apprenticed in marine engineering at Harland and Wolfe and he accompanied his father on the ship's voyage from Belfast to Southampton. Frank disembarked at Southampton but his father was one of the hundreds who perished when the ship struck an iceberg in mid-Atlantic.[3]

In 1911 John Graham and his wife, Sarah Ann, were still living in the Bank House at 30, King Street, Aspatria. They had been married for sixteen years. Sarah Ann was, I believe, known – at least by John – as 'Ally'. I assume that this came from Sally – a derivative of Sarah, which had then been personalised by dropping the initial letter.

John had not sent his two sons to his brother's college in Carlisle but to his own former school at St Bees. This school, founded in 1583, was a much larger establishment, having, at the time of the census, forty boarders – most of them coming from outside the county. The headmaster, William Alderson, was a single man, running the school with his elder sister. There were five servants living in: a cook, a kitchen maid and three housemaids. John's two sons are listed among the boarders, Cyril being fifteen, his brother two years younger.

As a bank manager, John was very much a pillar of the community. In 1909 the Cumberland Union Bank became part of the London Joint Stock Bank, which would in 1918 amalgamate with the Midland Bank. At the turn of the century John had been in his mid-thirties and, while he may still have been an active sportsman, he was by now turning his attention to other pursuits.

I speculated earlier about whether male members of the family might have been involved in the militia during the Napoleonic War, but I have found no evidence of the Grahams having had any military tradition. However, John was to have a long association with the Volunteer Forces. He had entered the ranks as a private at Carlisle and, in 1900, was responsible for the formation of the 'H' Company of the Border Regiment at Aspatria. He became a lieutenant and later succeeded to the captaincy on the retirement of Lord Gilford. According to tributes paid to him later: 'he paid exceptionally close attention to duty and never missed a training, while he also attained a very good position as a marksman.'[4]

John's military involvement may have begun as nothing more than a useful hobby but it was to take on a grave implication. King Edward's diplomacy had helped to stave off war for a time but a tangled web of alliances and treaties would soon ensnare the continent in its most deadly conflict. Dark shadows were lengthening across Europe.

In 1911 the two unmarried brothers – Robert Hodgson, aged forty-five, describing himself as a solicitor and farmer, and forty-three-year-old Richard, an estate agent and farmer – were living in Knockupworth Hall with a fifty-two-year-old widowed housekeeper called Jane Slavert.

The farmhouse was now used to house farmworkers. On the census night of 1911 a ploughman, Thomas Oliphant, and farm headman John Herbert were living there. Looking after them was Isabella Holmes. On the census return she declares her occupation as 'housekeeper at farm', clearly differentiating herself from the other housekeeper at the Hall.

Unmarried Isabella was thirty-one and had a six-year-old son, Edward. Isabella had been brought up in the city. She was a daughter of railway carpenter Edward Holmes. Her grandfather had been a skinner at an abattoir. Though they may have been city girls Isabella and her three sisters all ended up spending their adult lives in the countryside. And, despite her urban upbringing, Bella became a proficient farmworker, an asset to Knockupworth in the farmyard and the fields as well as in the kitchen. An acquaintance once told my mother that Bella was the best shepherd in the neighbourhood. Bella's son became close to the brothers, especially to Robert. Young Ted would often accompany him when he was checking the cattle.

I have referred to the brothers Robert, Richard and William by their full names but they were known within the family as Bob, Dick and Will or Bill. Though she never actually met them, my mother knew of her uncles as Uncle Bob and Uncle Bill. Her knowledge of the family came mainly through her Uncle John with whom she lived for many years. And it was from John that she learnt the next part of the story.

One day in 1913 John, on a visit to the farm, observed to Bob that Bella was pregnant. Bob, a bachelor and no doubt less enlightened about such matters than his married elder brother, refused to believe him. If the suggestion of Bella's pregnancy shocked Robert he was to be even more stunned by the events that later unfolded.

On 2nd December 1913, forty-six year-old Richard Graham and thirty-four-year-old Isabella Holmes were married. The wedding was conducted in secret at Carlisle Register Office. It was some days before Richard's brothers learned of the marriage. John passed down the story to my mother and she retold it with slight variations. In one version solicitor Robert discovered the secret wedding when he spotted the couple's names on the marriage list outside the court building. In another account it was only after he had learnt of their marriage that he realised he must have walked past the list several times without noticing.

It is difficult to establish if it were only the marriage that was kept secret or if the brothers were in ignorance of the entire relationship between Richard and Isabella. I suspect the latter. In those days, if it were known that a woman was pregnant to a known father, marriage would be expected. The wedding, secret or otherwise, would hardly have come as a surprise.

On New Year's Eve, Bella gave birth to a son and this led to a strange turn of events, the mystery of which we are unlikely to fully unravel. Bella left Knockupworth, taking with her their baby son, whom they had named Richard Sewell, and nine-year-old Ted. They moved several miles to a cottage at a place called the Ling, in Hesket parish, in the countryside south of Carlisle. Bella took on cleaning jobs to help make ends meet. It seems likely that she also received financial assistance from her husband, for although they were not living together they were not estranged. They continued to meet and during this period of separation Bella, gave birth to their second child.

My mother attributed this strange situation to her belief that the rest of the family must have frowned on Richard marrying a working class woman who was one of their own employees. Bella would not have wanted to stay where she felt unwelcome, but she was a strong woman, more than capable of standing up for herself, and surely Richard would not have allowed his wife to be driven away by snobbery. Besides, my mother always described her Uncle John as a man who was at ease with all social classes and certainly not a snob.

That Isabella already had a son born out of wedlock must, at that time, have raised moral as well as social concerns, but the Graham brothers seem to have shown compassion to Sarah Robinson when she gave birth to an illegitimate child. It would be wrong to assume that everyone brought up in the Victorian era was judgemental.

It is also possible that Isabella's elevation from employee to mistress of the Hall may have caused difficulties with her fellow workers but, while this might have explained a temporary absence, it would not account for the lengthy period of separation that ensued. Disaffected labourers could surely have been replaced.

My own theory requires more imagination and certainly has no evidence to prove it. I have wondered if the two brothers, both bachelors, were rivals for Isabella's affections. If Robert was hurt by the discovery of her secret marriage to Richard she may have felt it impossible to go on living there. This is speculation, but Bella's exile from Knockupworth was to last for over eight years and she would not return until after Robert's death.

During his time as captain of the Border Regiment Volunteers, John secured for the company 'a commodious drill hall' in Aspatria. But in May 1914 he resigned his command. He was then aged about fifty and may have thought it was time to hand over the reigns to a younger man. It may be that his work at the bank was taking up too much of his time. There may also have been a more personal reason for his decision.

One day, while accompanying a friend on a bicycle ride through the hilly Cumbrian countryside, John's wife, Sarah, became unwell. She was diagnosed as having a weak heart. At the time, the treatment for such a condition was long-term rest. For the remainder of her life Sarah would be regarded as 'an invalid'.

Within two months of his resignation, war had been declared and wishing to serve his country, John reversed his decision and asked to be reinstated. But younger men, stirred up by a spirit of patriotism, were offering their services, and it was not until October that he was accepted. He was invited to become Adjutant to the 5th Reserve Battalion of the Border Regiment but, on applying to his employers for permission to take up the post, discovered that he had been selected as manager of the larger Whitehaven branch of the bank. This promotion meant a change of location but it did not mark the end of John's military involvement.

1915 was to be a difficult year for the Grahams. Richard was living apart from his wife and baby son. Robert too may, for different reasons, have been mourning Bella's departure. But for the other two brothers the year was marked by tragedy.

William and Clara's family had increased to five with the births of George Desmond in 1913 and Lionel a year later. But in the spring of 1915 their second son, six-year-old Percy Reginald, developed an infection of the middle ear. This in itself must have been very painful, and distressing both for the small boy and for his parents. But the bacterium that can cause such a condition can also lead to more serious complications and on 10th April Percy Reginald died of meningitis. He was interred in a new grave on the other side of the footpath, a few yards from where his ancestors were buried in Grinsdale churchyard. The gravestone, which was erected several years later, incorrectly gives the year of his death as 1913.

Richard believed that his schoolmaster brother, eager to promote his children's education, had contributed to the boy's death by subjecting him to too much pressure. Though we know now that such an idea was illogical, it was perhaps understandable at the time to suppose that the stress of intensive learning might cause a disease of the brain. Richard's attitude to his own children's education was to be considerably more relaxed.

Initially there had been no shortage of enthusiastic young men eager to enlist for military service but by spring of 1915 recruitments were drying up. On 15th July the government passed the National Registration Act. All men who were not already in military service were obliged to register and give their employment details. Men between the ages of eighteen and forty-five were given the choice of enlisting voluntarily or 'attesting' and being available to be called up later if needed. Those who were not in protected high or scarce skill jobs were likely to be called up. This was not yet full conscription but it was a big step in that direction. The Director-General of Recruitment, Edward Stanley, 17th Lord Derby launched the scheme, and, though it was officially called the Group Scheme, it became known as the Derby Scheme.

After his transfer to Whitehaven John Graham:

> put to good use his military experience and rendered much valuable service in connection with what was known as the Voluntary Training Corps. First acting as an instructor, he trained hundreds of men under the Derby Scheme, many of whom on going forward were, thanks to his thorough and successful handling, almost immediately made non-commissioned officers.[5]

Eventually John took over command of the training corps. Though he was undoubtedly greatly respected, his involvement in military training caused resentment among some local people. Years later my mother reported back to him some comments she had heard about him being a 'war-monger'. His reply was that, since the men were going to be sent into battle, their chances of survival would be much greater if they were properly trained. By the time of John's involvement with the Derby Scheme his military participation had taken on a more personal tone.

The 5th Border Regiment was based at Workington and mobilised there on 4th August 1914. Among the officers present was Second Lieutenant C. Graham. It is hardly surprising that John's elder son, Cyril, should have enlisted only days after the outbreak of war. While it would be unnatural for any parent not to feel some trepidation about a son going into battle, John doubtlessly felt proud to see Cyril as a young officer about to fight for his country. In those early days it was not known how brutal the conflict was to become.

On 25th August the regiment travelled by train to Southampton and embarked for France on SS Manchester. The soldiers' lives were not just about fighting in the trenches. Much time was spent on other duties away from the lines of battle. For the first few months the men of the 5th Border Regiment were scattered at places such as Rouen, Boulogne, Abbeville and Dieppe, performing prisoner of war escort duties. Some two thousand German prisoners were processed and shipped to England under their guard.

But in early April the regiment was moved to Arques to undergo a month's training for trench warfare. They left Arques on 5th May and moved to Droglandt from where they were taken by bus to Brandhoek. Letters from home took only days to reach the troops and Cyril may have learned of his young cousin's death.

On 10th May the regiment came under fire for the first time but survived without casualties. Three days later the soldiers were moved to huts west of Ypres and companies were split up to serve alongside other regiments, occupying nearby trenches.

On 24th May 1915 their trenches were attacked under the cover of poison gas. The attack was repelled but at a heavy cost. One officer and eighteen other ranks were killed. Three officers and 113 men were wounded. One man was posted as missing and ninety suffered gas poisoning. The dead officer was nineteen-year-old Lieutenant Cyril Graham.[6]

The telegram was sent to John and Sarah's old address and John received news of their son's death in a telephone call from the Aspatria branch of the bank. Sarah was confined to bed with her heart condition. When John went in to break the news she is reported to have said, 'It's all right, John. I know you have come to tell me about Cyril. I saw him die. He was shot here.' She made a gesture indicating her head.

On 26th June the *Newcastle Journal* reported on the placing of the colours of the 5th Border Regiment in Carlisle Cathedral and on the regretted deaths of 'a gallant young subaltern, Lieutenant Cyril Graham, and of Major Broadley Smith.'

Like many of his fallen comrades Cyril was at first buried in a grave that bore no identification. After the war John travelled to Belgium and was able to locate his son's grave. The body was exhumed and identified, largely as a result of a childhood injury – a broken arm.

Lieutenant Cyril Graham is buried among the Commonwealth War Graves in Potijze Chateau Grounds Cemetery, near Ypres.

My mother believed that she was conceived in her father's office. Richard and Isabella's second child, Phyllis Anna, was born on 19th July 1916. Her birthplace is recorded as Ling Foot, Hesket. This was during the time that her parents were living apart and, whether or not Wood and Graham's estate agents' office was the place of her conception, it was certainly the scene of her earliest memories of her father. She recalled visiting him in Carlisle with her mother and remembered telling her teacher that she had seen her father and 'he had a bald head.'

Whatever the cause of Isabella's exile from the farm it must surely have been a troubling situation for Richard and may well have put a strain on his relationship with Robert. For the two farming Graham brothers the war may not have had the tragic consequences that it had for John but they were certainly not untouched by it. Farmers were at the centre of food production. In its effort to feed the nation the government demanded greater productivity and drew up legislation to force farmers to plough up more land. In January 1917 the Board of Agriculture was empowered to take over land it considered was being inadequately farmed. Some farmers resisted what they saw as unreasonable instructions to plough good pastureland. In 1918 the Grahams fell foul of this legislation:

> Mr R.H. Graham, solicitor, and his brother Mr Richard Graham, land agent, Knockupworth Hall Farm, near Carlisle, were summoned

> at Carlisle on Saturday for failing to plough a field as required by the County Agricultural Committee. The case was adjourned.[7]

It would appear that this was not an act of defiance on the part of the Graham brothers but rather an indication that they were struggling to manage the farm. When the case was resumed the magistrates accepted their explanation and their reputations were not besmirched:

> At Carlisle on Saturday the resumed hearing took place of the case in which Mr R.H. Graham, solicitor, Carlisle, clerk to the Longtown Rural District Council and Board of Guardians, was summoned along with his brother, Mr Richard Graham, for alleged failure to comply with the requirements of the Cumberland War Agricultural Executive Committee in reference to ploughing a 12½ acre field called Bessie's Croft, on the farm of Knockupworth Hall, near Carlisle, owned and occupied by them. The prosecution alleged that through Messrs. Grahams' failure to plough the field a motor tractor had to be sent by the committee to do the work, but evidence given by the defence showed that the defendants were short of horses and labour, that they made reasonable endeavours to cope with the work, and that in the end they let the field to a tenant who undertook to do the ploughing. The Bench unanimously dismissed the summons, the Chairman (Dr Barnes) observing that there was not sufficient evidence to warrant a conviction.[8]

On 11th November 1918 the armistice was signed and the Great War came to an end. Two of the Graham brothers had lost sons during the years of conflict; John's had perished in battle, William's had died of illness at a young age. For John there was soon to be further grief.

John's wife, Sarah Ann, died in January 1919. John remarried in March 1920. His new wife was Isabella Ward, widow of naval officer Captain Desborough Ward and daughter of wealthy coal and iron master and cattle breeder William Burnyeat of Moresby near Whitehaven. As a bank manager John moved freely among wealthy people and it is not surprising that he should get to know Mrs Ward. It may be that the family's cattle enterprise was instrumental in bringing the couple together, for John was still a farmer's son. Their marriage, little over a year after Sarah's death, might have brought both of them deserved happiness. Instead it seems to have been a case of marrying in haste and repenting at leisure.

Notes

1 Cumbria Archive Service
2 Library of James Bainbridge
3 josephbellengineer.wordpress.com
4 Quotations regarding John Graham's military involvement are taken from tributes paid to him on the occasion of his retirement from bank service in 1927.
5 See footnote 4.
6 www.freewebs.com/7borderandyeo/5thterrier1.htm
7 *Lancashire Evening Post,* 22nd April 1918
8 *Yorkshire Post and Leeds Intelligencer,* 13th May 1918

CHAPTER TWENTY-FIVE

The Final Years

Of the four brothers, John must have had the clearest memories of life on the farm at Whitrigg. He had been eight years old when his father died – old enough to have helped a little around the farm. As a youth he had expressed an interest in following in his father's footsteps. Jane had had other ideas. With her other children to educate, she could not afford to set up her eldest son in farming.

John had a successful career in banking but he retained his interest in agriculture and this may have been what brought him close to the Burnyeat family, who were renowned breeders of shorthorn cattle, and especially to their widowed daughter who became his second wife.

While farming continued to have a personal attraction for John, his financial wisdom told him that the practical running of Knockupworth by an estate agent and a solicitor was not the most sensible business proposition. Besides, it was now over thirty years since their father had refurbished the farm with the intention of farming it himself. The property may have been in need of further investment. And, while the land and buildings belonged to the brothers, re-stocking the farm had required capital outlay. William bought into his brothers' venture. Between 1904 and 1912 he made annual and sometimes twice-yearly mortgage repayments and then in 1918 contributed a lump sum of one thousand pounds. William may not have been personally involved in the running of Knockupworth but the brothers reciprocated his financial commitment by supplying him and the school with produce from the farm. Robert also gave him free legal advice, while Richard applied his bookkeeping skills to the school accounts. It was an informal and seemingly mutually beneficial arrangement. The brothers did not anticipate the problems it would later cause. John, judging that the enterprise was unlikely to be a commercial success, remained on the outside.

By 1920 William had been principal of Grosvenor College for fifteen years. Having lost one son he was the father of four living children, the youngest being about five years old. But now William was gravely ill.

The youngest of the brothers had, only a few years earlier, been playing for the college cricket and rugby teams. Towards the end of 1919 he became unwell and, after medical investigation, the seriousness of his condition became clear: William was suffering from cancer of both the stomach and the liver.

He appears to have received the best treatment that was available at the time and was taken to Edinburgh for a major operation. It is said that some of the doctors were former pupils of his and that, while there, he met King George V who was visiting the hospital with Queen Mary.

William survived the operation and made a partial recovery but 'his health and strength were no longer equal to the performance of his professional work, and he retired to Bowness.'[1]

The relationship between William and Clara was to end as it had begun, with Clara nursing her sick husband. After a year of illness, William Sharp Graham died on 28th October 1920, just under a month short of his fiftieth birthday, at The Pottery in Bowness-on-Solway. He had chosen to live his last days in the village where he had spent most of his early childhood. In death he made a very similar journey to the one his father had made nearly half a century earlier – a journey from the Solway shore to Grinsdale churchyard. Here he was interred with the remains his young son, Percy Reginald. The *Carlisle Journal* gave the following account of the occasion:

> The funeral took place at Grinsdale yesterday afternoon, when the remains were interred in the churchyard in the presence of a large gathering of relatives and friends. The service was conducted by the Rev J A Kitchen, Vicar of Grinsdale, and the Rev L D Mitton, Rector of Bowness on Solway. The chief mourners were Miss Mary Graham (daughter), Mr and Mrs John Graham, Whitehaven (brother and sister in law), Mr R H Graham and Mr Richard Graham (brothers) and Miss Laing (sister in law).[2]

Absent from the list of mourners is William's widow, Clara Alma, but her sister, who had come over from Ireland, attended the funeral. Clara may have stayed at home, not only with her two youngest sons but also with her aged and infirm mother who still lived with them.

Margaret Laing died just two weeks after her son-in-law. She was laid to rest in Bowness churchyard.

William and Clara's eldest son was also unable to attend his father's funeral. At the age of fifteen the boy had, according to family lore, 'run away to sea.' John St. Clare William Laing Graham had joined the Merchant Navy in 1918 and was away from home during his father's fatal illness.

Clara remained at Bowness with her other children. There is anecdotal evidence that some of the children may have attended school in Annan for a while, though the viaduct across the Solway closed to traffic during the following year. Then Clara took her family to Liverpool where she and her sister had trained as nurses. Thus she became the second Graham widow to live in that city. She outlived William by over three decades, dying in Cornwall in 1951, and was brought back to Grinsdale to be buried with her husband and young son.

William's death had implications for Knockupworth. The youngest brother may not have been involved in the practical running of the farm but he had a financial stake in the enterprise. Settling debts owed to William's family would place further strain on a business that was already struggling.

The brothers' efforts to run the farm alongside their professional careers were to be even more severely tested. By the end of 1921 Robert was seriously ill, suffering from nephritis – chronic inflammation of the kidneys. At a low point in his illness he is reported to have said that if Bella were here she would have looked after him. It was perhaps only one of many reasons why his sister-in-law's absence from the farm was a matter for regret.

Then, early in the New Year, came one of cattle farmers' worst nightmares – an outbreak of foot and mouth disease. The story my mother told was that Robert, insisting that his cattle did not have the disease and fearing that the inspectors would carry the infection on to his farm, got out of bed to deny them access to his land. While his neighbours' animals were slaughtered the Knockupworth cattle survived and remained free of the disease. If this account is true, and the Grahams' cattle did indeed survive, it seems that they were extremely fortunate for the newspaper reports paint a different picture. It seems that Knockupworth was at the very epicentre of the Cumbrian outbreak.

> The disease has broken out in a herd of 17 Irish cattle which for the past few days have been in the fields of Knockupworth Farm, about two miles from Carlisle. This farm is owned and occupied by Messrs. Graham and the cattle belong to Mr McCassarty, an Irish cattle dealer residing in Carlisle. The usual steps have been taken, under the direction of the Ministry of Agriculture to deal with the outbreak. Yesterday the inspector of the Ministry was present at the farm and superintended the slaughter of the animals. What the effect of the restrictions will be remains to be seen, as Knockupworth is close to the city, where there are two auction marts. Mr McCassarty's cattle came direct from Dublin.[3]

Two days later, on 1st February, the *Western Daily Press*, under the headlines 'Foot and Mouth Disease', 'Infection Spreads to Scotland' and 'Extremely Severe Outbreak' reported that the infection had been confirmed on over a hundred premises and there were over a hundred unconfirmed reports. The outbreak, it said, was not to be confused with cattle plague, which was a more terrible disease. There had been no outbreaks of cattle plague in this country since 1877. It went on:

> The outbreak at Knockupworth near Carlisle has spread to a herd of 59 Irish cattle grazing in a field adjoining that in which 17 animals, cremated on Monday, were located. Nine of the second herd have been certified and destroyed. All the cattle drank from the same trough. The Irish cattle reached Carlisle from Dublin, via Greenock.

Meanwhile on 2nd February the *Yorkshire Post and Leeds Intelligencer* reported that, at a meeting of Cumberland County Council, Mr Robinson Mitchell declared that the only way to stamp out the disease was to ban the import of Irish cattle for twelve months. The chief constable said that they proposed to issue licenses for fat cattle to be moved for immediate slaughter outside a five-mile radius of Knockupworth, the farm where the outbreaks near Carlisle had occurred.

In March, news reached Bella, at the Ling, that Robert Graham had died. She set off with Dick and Phyllis to make the journey back to Knockupworth. They caught a train to Carlisle and then a tram to Newtown. Walking along the road they were overtaken by a Kirkandrews farmer, named Bill Robson, and his wife, with a horse and cart. Five-year-old Phyllis rode on the cart while her mother and Dick walked alongside. When they reached Knockupworth Hall,

Phyllis fell asleep in a chair. When she awoke her father was in the room. The family was together for the first time.

When, over eighty years later, Phyllis recalled the few months that she lived in Knockupworth Hall her memory was understandably hazy. Nevertheless this is the only first hand description we have of the Graham family home.

There was a big kitchen, which was also used as a living room and had a big fire, a roasting fire and a range. It sounds like a traditional farmhouse kitchen, serving many purposes. From here, she said, you could go into a second kitchen, which also had an oven. This, I imagine, was what is often referred to as a scullery. From there steps led down into a cellar. My mother referred to some back stairs, which seem to have led off the kitchen. There was a small sitting room and a dining room. Both of these rooms had fireplaces. There was a hall and staircase and a long landing. She said that when you went upstairs you turned a corner and came to a room that was still referred to as Uncle Bob's bedroom. This she identified as the room immediately above the hall. When she spoke of the room shared by her parents she referred to it as 'father's bedroom', adding 'and mother's' almost as an afterthought. It had presumably been Richard's room ever since the family moved back into the Hall and would have retained that name even though he now shared it with his wife. She said it was at the end of the house. She did not say in which rooms Phyllis herself or her brother, Dick, slept but she remembered there being bedrooms that were not used. There was no bathroom. They used tin baths. There was an outside toilet and a pump in the yard.

She talked of a part of the house that had been 'built on'. This must refer to the extension on the left hand side of the front elevation. The roof is lower and of a less steep gradient than that of the main part of the house. Although the windows are similar in style the panes are larger and do not match those of the rest of the house. I do not know the date of this extension but one might imagine that it may have been added to accommodate the large Wright family when the Hall was let in the 1830s. Though sympathetic to the rest of the house and certainly not unsightly, this addition destroys the symmetry of the original Georgian design.

There was an oval lawn in the drive at the front of the house. This could be used to turn round a horse and trap. It was planted with spring bulbs. The drive then went down the side of the house on the opposite side from the farm. The farm buildings included byres, pig halls and a place for calves. Phyllis remembered cows being milked. Behind the farmhouse was a cobbled farmyard and a large dairy where she remembered butter being made. Stables divided the big house from the farm. There was another stable in the yard and a place for putting the carriage, which she called a 'digby'. There was no garden behind the Hall, only a farmyard.

We can gain a more detailed impression of the interior of the Hall from the 'Valuation of Household Furniture and effects' produced by the firm of Thomas P. Reed of Croft House, Etterby on 27th July 1922.[4] This confirms that there was a dining room, a 'front sitting room' and a kitchen. There is no mention of a second kitchen or scullery. My mother may have been mistaken about this but it is likely that the house would have had a scullery or 'back kitchen'.

The valuation makes no specific mention of a cellar but there was a washhouse. This contained a mangle, an oil tank, a dolly tub and, surprisingly, a washing machine. The washing machine would have been primitive, probably hand-powered and would certainly not have been electric. It was valued at five shillings – half the price of the mangle.

Five bedrooms are listed. Judging by the amount of furniture they contained, three of them must have been generously sized. The main bedroom contained a mahogany chest of drawers, dressing table, wash stand, night commode and four chairs. Two other bedrooms were also extensively furnished while the others contained little more than a bed and a chest of drawers. Only five bedrooms are listed but it is likely there were more. From the valuation sheet it would appear that the house contained around eight furnished rooms but this may be misleading. When Robert Graham filled in the census return in 1911 he stated that it had twelve rooms. As Reeds' valuation was only concerned with moveable, saleable furniture, it is likely that, at the time of the sale, there were other rooms that were unfurnished.

Standing on a landing on the u-shaped staircase were a grandfather clock and a mahogany bureau. My mother described the sitting room as small but it may have only seemed small because of the amount of furniture it contained. Among other items, it held a couch, five chairs, two tables and a piano and stool.

Much of the furniture may have been as old as the house, though that is not to say that it necessarily belonged to the first Grahams who lived at Knockupworth Hall. During the nineteenth century the family had been absent from the Hall for about fifty years. It is doubtful that the Grahams' furniture remained there during the Wright family's occupancy. Jane may have refurnished the house when she moved there. Much of what her sons regarded as 'the family furniture' may have owed more to the Sewell family than to the Grahams. However it is possible that some of the remaining items had indeed belonged to earlier generations of Grahams. We may wonder about its history, especially about the piano and stool. Could these have survived from the time that the Grahams first occupied Knockupworth Hall? Did young Hannah have musical skill as well as her talent for embroidery? Did Margaret, like her fictional contemporaries in Jane Austen's novels, play the piano to entertain her family and friends?

My mother never alluded to any of the later Grahams having had any interest in music. However I have discovered an entry in the *Carlisle Journal* of 18th December 1891, which reports on a weekly meeting of Holy Trinity Men's Mutual Improvement Society held at the Temperance Hall in Caldewgate. It says: 'Mr Graham of Knockupworth Hall provided a high-class concert, the performers being Miss James, Miss Latimer, Miss J. Latimer, and Mrs Nixon, and Messrs Anthony James and Graham.' The Mr Graham referred to would almost certainly be John, who was the only one of the brothers living at the Hall at that time. This concert and the poetry book presented to Robert on his departure from Coventry are the only evidence I have found of the brothers' interest in the arts. The school distinction that William received for 'drawing' may refer to technical drawing rather than art. However, if he was artistic, it was a talent he passed on to his children, especially to his daughter, Mary, who was an accomplished painter. Musical accomplishment and an interest in the arts in general may have been expected of educated young men at that time but, in the case of the Grahams, it is an aspect of their lives that seems to have been little recorded.

From their new home Dick and Phyllis walked over a mile and a half each day to the village school in Kirkandrews.

But the days of the Graham family's ownership of Knockupworth were numbered. Richard was now the only brother running the farm while at the same time walking into the city each day to conduct his business. And the farm was not thriving. Debts were mounting.

When the sale of the farm became inevitable John made a last-ditch attempt to keep his ancestral home within the family. He, and his new wife, would provide the financial backing to enable John's son,

Jack, to buy Knockupworth. John must have believed that his son had an aptitude for farming that his brothers had lacked. But, to John's disappointment, and perhaps anger, Jack pulled out of the bidding before his price limit had been reached.

It may be that Jack had his own reasons for failing to fulfil his father's wishes. It seems that another property may have been more to his liking. Two weeks later an estate known as 'The Gale' near Abbey Town was sold by auction at Wigton.[5] Surviving correspondence suggests that on this occasion Jack may have been the successful bidder.

The sale of Knockupworth took place in October 1922 and was reported thus:

> The Knockupworth Hall estate was sold by auction on Saturday, at Carlisle, by Mr Fred Telford. The estate comprises a residence, farmhouse etc. and half a mile of salmon, herling and trout fishing in the River Eden which skirts the north side of the property.
> After keen competition, the property was sold in one lot to Mr J.S. Jackson, solicitor, Carlisle, on behalf of a client for £6,800. Mr T. Norman Robinson, Cathedral Chambers, Castle Street, was the solicitor for the vendors.[6]

In 1836 the farm was described as having '100 acres of arable and meadow land of superior quality' and had been 'advantageously occupied as a dairy farm'. Now it seems its most distinctive asset was the river flowing past its land.

And so, after one hundred and seventy years, Knockupworth ceased to belong to the Graham family.

Notes

1 *Carlisle Journal,* November 2nd 1920
2 *Carlisle Journal,* November 2nd 1920
3 *Yorkshire Post & Leeds Intelligencer,* 30th January 1922
4 Family papers
5 Sale brochure, Messrs William Hope and Sons, reproduced by Mick Jane www.cumbrianhistory.co.uk
6 *Yorkshire Post & Leeds Intelligencer,* 31st October 1922

CHAPTER TWENTY-SIX

Reeds' Valuation

After the sale, John sent his brother a typed 'statement of monies paid on completion'. On the back he had copied by hand, in pencil, a letter from the solicitor T. Norman Robinson. It read:

> This sale was completed this morning & I enclose a statement showing how the money has been dealt with. The matter did not altogether go off without a hitch. Before Mr Jackson would complete he insisted upon my giving an undertaking to get rid of the present occupiers of the farm house in addition to the farm man. I also had to give an undertaking to pay the current rates and arrears but as Dick has promised to pay these I presume it will be alright. On hearing from you I will send the receipted bills.
>
> Yours truly,
>
> T. Norman Robinson[1]

John's purpose in reproducing the solicitor's letter may have been as a gentle reminder that his brother had 'promised to pay the current rates and arrears' without having to confront him directly. He must have known that Richard was feeling beleaguered. And turning over the letter to read the statement can hardly have lifted Richard's spirits. The sale total of £6,860 was reduced by the sum owing on the mortgage, interest, property tax, tithes, solicitors' costs and auctioneers' charges to £1,704 4s 7d.

Now that the Hall and farm had been sold, the remaining livestock needed to be disposed of. This was done with varying degrees of success but probably did not add greatly to the proceeds. The *Hartlepool Northern Daily Mail* reported that: 'At a farm sale at Knockupworth, near Carlisle, three horses sold at 10s each but bidding for one goose reached £3.'[2] Meanwhile, the editor of *Dundee Evening Telegraph*'s 'Day by Day', a column that tried to extract wit from the week's news, noticed the poor prices for the horses and the unusual name of the farm. He remarked: 'The three farm horses which were sold for 10s each at Knockupworth did not live up to the place name.'[3]

Having struggled and failed to make the farm viable, Richard might have hoped that the sale would bring an end to his troubles. But, with little of the capital from the sale unaccounted for, the following months were to be a time of financial anxiety, legal dispute and bitter family conflict.

The informal arrangement by which William had received produce and services from his brothers in return for financial investment may have seemed simple during his lifetime but it would prove complex and acrimonious after his death.

Nearly five months before his death in October 1920 William had made a will. The will itself is unremarkable, making fairly standard provision for his wife and children. What is perhaps surprising is that he appointed his sister-in-law, Henrietta Laing, as sole executrix and trustee.[4] William had a brother who was a solicitor and another a bank manager – both experienced in dealing with such matters. Instead he chose his wife's sister, who lived in Ireland where she held a responsible position in the nursing profession. Miss Laing would certainly ensure that her sister's interests would be well represented and Clara Alma may have influenced her husband's choice. But does it also suggest that the relationships between the brothers were already becoming strained?

William had left four children. Henrietta was understandably anxious to see that her sister's family was well provided for. Having failed to find a buyer, Grosvenor College had closed after William's death. Financial security meant establishing what the Knockupworth estate owed his family. And this was a matter of legal complexity, the origins of which dated back half a century.

When the brothers' father died in 1872 his will stipulated that each of his sons should have an equal share of his estate. But these were shares in a property that, once again, was now heavily mortgaged. And the situation was further complicated by the financial contributions William had made towards the running of the farm.

When the process of legal disentanglement began, Robert and Richard were still running the farm together; by the time of Robert's death and the subsequent sale of Knockupworth, the situation was still unresolved. John was largely unaffected. He still owned the share of the estate that he had inherited from their father but, as he had not bought into his brothers' venture, he was not involved in the various arrangements that had been made between the schoolmaster and the farm. Besides John was comfortably off in his own right, had his own home and had a wealthy wife. Richard had his own children to consider and, as the surviving occupant of the Hall, he and his family were in danger of being homeless.

The claim submitted by W.S. Graham's estate was against the sale monies of Knockupworth; against the estate of R.H. Graham who had died earlier that year; against that of their father, John Graham, who had died in 1872; and against Richard Graham.

The £1,000 that William had advanced towards the repayment of the mortgage in October 1918, plus the payments he had made between 1904 and 1912, amounted to £2,037. This formed the major part of his widow's claim, which totalled over three thousand pounds.[5]

Richard replied with a counter claim. You can sense his anger as he compiled his list of the benefits that he considered his late brother had received:

> Potatoes Carrots & Turnips, say 400 stone a year for 22 years, 8800 stone @ -/6d per st: £220.
>
> Mutton supplied at various times, say £20.
> Poultry 20 per year @ 2/6 for 20 years: £50.
> Eggs 30 per week for 8 months a year for 18 years: £72.[5]

And so it went on, with claims for butter, fruit and jam. The produce William had received from the farm over the years as part of a friendly fraternal arrangement was now to be accounted for and set against his widow's claim against the estate. But there had been other assistances too that Richard and Robert had provided for their schoolmaster brother. These may at the time have been performed as personal favours but now Richard saw them as professional services that should be charged at professional rates:

> R. Graham making out school a/c's three times a year & entering up account books: £460.
>
> R.H. Graham legal charges: £50.

In addition Richard had supplied his younger brother with furniture, bedding and books, which he now considered were worth £100. And then there was the money they had advanced him towards his college expenses: £600 from Robert and £220 from Richard. Finally there was a sum of £160 that had been lent to William in 1914. If these had at the time been regarded as gifts they were now to be treated as unpaid loans that needed to be balanced against his widow's claim.

The solicitor, Mr Lightfoot, returned 'R.H. & R. Graham's account against W.S. Graham' on a typed sheet with some of the claims substantially reduced. However the various loans were not disputed. Mr Lightfoot had accepted that the counter claim amounted to around two thousand pounds. We can imagine Richard angrily perusing this sheet and then, suddenly remembering that his brother had owned some animals that had been kept at the farm, picking up a pencil and adding: 'keep of cob, ditto sheep, ditto ewes and lambs, ditto goats.' However he did not go so far as costing the grazing of this livestock.

It seems that, at the end of some complicated calculations, Richard's personal liability towards his younger brother's estate was reckoned to be £174.

The matter was resolved, satisfactorily or otherwise, and by March of the following year John was able to report that 'Will's share has been settled.' But another, even darker conflict was brewing, this time between the two surviving brothers.

As the eldest son, John had become trustee for their father's estate. He was also administrator for the estates of their mother and their brother, Robert, both of whom had died intestate – somewhat carelessly, we might think, in the case of solicitor Robert! It was a responsibility that should not have proved too onerous for this experienced bank manager, but his role was complicated by his personal involvement. The Hall and farm had been sold but not yet the furniture. This was proving to be an obstacle.

John recognised that some of the furniture needed to be sold to pay off debts. He also wanted some of it for himself and had promised some to his son, Jack, for his new home, The Gale. Richard was also entitled to a share. Whatever each of the brothers retained would be properly accounted for and set against the cash each received from the sale of the estate. To bank manager John the matter was clear. His brother saw it differently.

It is difficult to imagine that Richard really thought he was entitled to keep all of the furniture himself. He may have been merely dragging his feet; perhaps resentful at the way his brother was handling matters, perhaps fearful of his own financial insecurity. Perhaps he was finding it difficult to accept the reality of what was happening. But John was finding him decidedly uncooperative and this must have been intensely frustrating for him, both on a professional and personal level.

It appears that by the following March, five months after the sale, Richard was still at the Hall, the furniture still in place. John called to see him in the hope that the matter might be settled but found his brother unwilling to negotiate. John left disappointed. He waited another week but there was no still no sign of his brother relenting. Then, on the 21st March, he wrote a letter on both sides of a sheet of notepaper headed: 'London Joint City & Midland Bank Limited, Joint Stock Bank Branch, Whitehaven.' It read:

Dear Dick,

I came along to see you last Wednesday with a view to settling with you re the furniture, but you would not discuss the matter & in consequence I am very disappointed. I now wish you to clearly understand that a settlement must be arrived at and as you evidently wish to shelve the matter and won't say what you wish to keep I am enclosing a list of what I can do with. You appear to forget that the Gale has to be furnished for Jack, & I fail to see why you should retain the whole of the family furniture. I want my share and I also claim Bob's share but will pay the value into his Estate to meet his creditors. If you want to retain any of it you can do so by paying for it according to Reeds' valuation. If you refuse to accept this valuation then a total sale will be held, but as sole Trustee to Father's Will and administrator to Mother's and Bob's Estates I think you have little say in the matter if I should so decide. If you stupidly cause trouble & delay you will force me to act on my own which I do not want to do if you will be reasonable. I am open to have your views, and to hear what furniture you wish to keep. Failing your complying before Monday, I propose having a lorrie [sic] at Knockupworth on Easter Monday to remove what we settle out you can do without.

Now that Will's share has been settled I am pushing on Bob's affairs & I must have this furniture question settled. I want some here and Jack wants at the Gale. I therefore think that I have reason on my side. I am only asking & wanting what should have been done 15 years ago.

Yours John[7]

The tone of John's letter is of frustration and sadness with a degree of controlled anger. He does not want to fall out with his younger brother but he feels that he has right on his side and is determined to have his way. The event to which he refers in the final sentence is the death of their mother. When Jane died fifteen years earlier the property should theoretically have been shared among her sons. As administrator of her estate it had been John's responsibility to oversee this. But at the time it had been Robert and Richard's home and John had allowed them to retain possession of the Hall and of the family furniture. Once again a friendly family arrangement had led to later complications.

John's enclosed list of 'what I can do with' was roughly written in pencil. Underneath he wrote 'I have kept off everything that might be useful to you' and added that, in claiming his own and Robert's shares he was entitled to £120 worth of furniture. The total of what he was asking for amounted to just under a hundred pounds. He wanted his brother to understand how reasonable he was being.

Somehow agreement was reached. Lists of the division of the furniture were typed out. Richard's share amounted to £60 7s 6d – seven shillings and sixpence over his one-third entitlement. However John claimed the two most expensive items in the Hall, a mahogany bureau and the grandfather clock – each valued at £15. Lorries arrived to take the furniture to its various destinations.

The Grahams left Knockupworth for the last time.

There is a final mystery to add to the story. In the Cumbria Archives there is a record of probate being granted on Mary Sewell's estate in 1925. Mary died in 1898. Had her will lain hidden somewhere in the Hall and remained undiscovered until the house was emptied for sale a quarter of a century later? It seems that Knockupworth may have held one last secret.

Notes

1 Family papers
2 *Hartlepool Northern Daily Mail,* 3rd February 1923
3 *Dundee Evening Telegraph,* 6th February 1923
4 Cumbria Archive Service
5 Family papers
6 Family papers
7 Family papers

CHAPTER TWENTY-SEVEN

North View and Norda Brows

The sale of the Knockupworth estate might be an appropriate place to end this narrative. But two of the brothers were still alive and it seems fitting to bring their stories to conclusions.

Richard bought a plot of land along the road towards Burgh by Sands, a short distance outside Grinsdale village and close to Grinsdale Bridge. He bought two army officers' huts, surplus from the First World War, and had them re-erected to form a wooden bungalow. It had a view over the green vale of the Eden towards the dark outline of the Scottish hills. He called it 'North View'.

While their parents worked on the construction of their bungalow, Dick and Phyllis returned to the Hesket area to stay with Bella's sister, Jane, and her large family, avoiding school until the attendance officer caught up with them. Richard and Bella, together at last after their years of separation, slept in a converted hen house until the bungalow became habitable. Then the children returned to their new home where the house was barely finished, with some of the floorboards still not laid. Phyllis remembered having to walk along the joists.

North View was remote, in the sense that it stood on its own and was some distance from Grinsdale village, but as it was on the road to Burgh by Sands it did at least have traffic going past. Richard added various wooden outhouses around the yard behind the house; in the furthest corner was an outside toilet.

Behind the house, Richard planted an orchard and there was a sizeable garden, much of which was devoted to growing fruit and vegetables. The Carlisle to Silloth railway line, the course of which had once been the canal, ran directly behind the orchard and the smoke from the passing trains drifted among the fruit trees. Although it was no great distance from the city, the house did not have mains electricity until the nineteen-sixties and until then was lit by oil lamps.

Now that they were back in Grinsdale, Dick and Phyllis resumed their education at Kirkandrews Village School. It was now a shorter distance for them to walk. For their father the walk to his business in Carlisle was much longer.

My mother described Richard, her father, as a man who ate very slowly, partly because he had a deformed left hand that had been caused by an infected thistle wound. On the small acreage of land attached to the bungalow he retained an interest in farming, keeping poultry and pigs. He also bred canaries. The 'Canary House', which was a reclaimed gatehouse from Carr's Biscuit Factory, retained its title long after the last bird had sung there. As a young man Richard's work had taken him to Oxfordshire and near to London but after returning to Cumberland he showed no further wish to travel. Apart from going to work he rarely left his home.

John Graham retired from his position as manager of the Whitehaven branch of Midland Bank in 1927. As well as the glowing tributes that were paid to him regarding his career and his sporting and military achievements there were expressions of goodwill towards his future retirement:

> Having always been interested in agricultural pursuits, Mr Graham intends on his retirement to take up as a hobby the breeding of pedigree shorthorn cattle as well as pedigree sheep and that he may long be spared in health and vigour to enjoy that hobby will be the sincerest wish of his many friends in West Cumberland.[1]

John was indeed spared in health and vigour but his retirement was not to be an altogether happy one. His second wife, Isabella, drank heavily. Their deteriorating relationship came to a head one morning when he found her drunk in the bathroom. According to his account she became aggressive and he tried to restrain her. He decided he must leave. John did not drive so he hired a taxi to take him to his son, Jack. His wife, presumably by now sober enough to drive, had got there first and told her side of the story – that John had assaulted her.

When his father arrived, Jack refused to take him in, saying that he would have nothing to do with a man who had struck a woman. My mother believed that Jack had borrowed money from his stepmother and felt obliged to take her side. Perhaps it was she who had funded the purchase of The Gale. Of course my mother only heard her uncle's side of the story. When she talked of him she described him as someone who insisted on punctuality and expected his meals to be ready on time but he was also very kind to her. She lived with him as his housekeeper for fifteen years, greatly respected him and did not believe him capable of ill-treating a woman.

Spurned by his son, John made his way to his brother's office in Carlisle. Any lingering malice from their dispute over the furniture must by now have evaporated, for Richard insisted that John must stay at North View. When John suggested that he should ask Bella first, Richard assured him that she would not mind. If, after their marriage, Richard's wife really had been driven away from Knockupworth by the hostility of her brothers-in-law she must have had a very forgiving nature, for she readily accepted John's presence in their home.

During his stay John paid for a number of improvements to North View, including the installation of a bathroom. Richard drew the line at allowing his brother to have an inside toilet installed, believing such an innovation to be unhygienic.

Meanwhile John was having his own house built at Burgh by Sands, a house that he named Norda Brows[2]. When he moved there in 1933 he took his seventeen-year-old niece, Phyllis, to be his housekeeper. John's hopes of keeping pedigree cattle and sheep may have been curtailed but, after he was found to have developed an allergy to cows' milk, goats were kept at Norda Brows. For the rest of his life his relationship with his son remained strained.

As usual, on Saturday 15th June 1935 Richard walked back to Grinsdale from his office in Carlisle. As he entered the gate he hesitated for a moment. Bella noticed that he appeared unwell and went out to meet him but when he saw his wife he put his hands behind his back and strode purposefully up the drive. Phyllis, who had been visiting, went home and told her uncle of her concern. Next day she and her uncle went together to call on her father.

Richard had been unwell all night but he was never a man to seek medical assistance. He and John talked for some time and then Richard crossed the yard to the outside toilet. If he had accepted his brother's offer of an indoor convenience the story would have been rather different for, while out there, Richard collapsed, falling against the door and trapping himself inside. In order to free him Phyllis had to climb in through the small open window. She then ran into the road, flagged down a passing car and asked the driver to stop at the post office and call for a doctor. But by the time the doctor arrived her father was dead.

Richard was sixty-seven years old. He was buried in a new grave under the canopy of the copper beech and near the grave of his younger brother, William.

John, the eldest of the brothers, lived through the Second World War and died at his home, Norda Brows, in Burgh by Sands on 28th June 1948, at the age of eighty-four. Like Robert he was buried in the family grave but, the headstone being full, his inscription was added to the reverse of the stone.

It was almost two hundred years since the millwright, Thomas Graham, and his first wife, had moved to Knockupworth. Of the descendants of this marriage, John was the first who could be said to have lived to a great age.

Notes

1 Taken from tributes paid to John Graham on the occasion of his retirement from bank service in 1927

2 Norda Brows: north of the brows (hill crests)

CHAPTER TWENTY-EIGHT

Trait and Trace

In his poem 'Heredity', Thomas Hardy reflects on how shared facial features project a family line through generations. We have no surviving portraits to show us what the early occupants of Knockupworth Hall looked like, but there are photographs of the later ones, some dating back well over a hundred years. The four brothers – John, Robert, Richard and William – are represented at various stages of their lives. There is also a portrait of their mother who brought characteristics of the Sewells into the Graham family line. It is likely that somewhere among a vast number of photographs in family albums there is one of Jane's husband John, the Whitrigg farmer, but sadly these photographs are all unnamed and unidentifiable. The Beck family seem to have been more astute when it came to labelling and there are surviving images of John's half sisters, Mary and Margaret Ann. We may hope to see in their faces something of their mother, who began her life as Mary Little, in Bewcastle, while Britain was still at war with France.

Photographs give us an idea of what Hardy calls the 'curve' of their facial features but they are monochrome prints, giving little indication of colouration. There are colour images of later members of the family and we have memories of those we have known in our lifetimes. Then, of course, there are descendants of the family who are still alive today.

From these we may speculate about the appearances of our ancestors. We can be sure that some of their characteristics have been passed down from the Grahams, the Sharps, the Littles and the Sewells, as well as from Thomas Graham, the Carlisle spirit merchant, through whom the family name was preserved.

It seems likely that they mostly had blue eyes, since this is the colour that predominates in later generations. Their hair may often have been fair with a slight tendency towards ginger. The trustee John Graham of Kirkandrews, who faced a double murder charge in 1845, was a friend, not a relative, but we know from evidence given at his trial that he had red whiskers. It is not unlikely that some of the menfolk of Knockupworth around that time may also have had reddish beards. It is possible that, even if they were not closely related, there may have been a distant biological connection between the two families.

We may have some idea of their physical characteristics but what do we know of their characters? We have no surviving diaries or journals to give us insights into their minds – nor, before the twentieth century, any letters. The letter we do have, regarding the dispute between John and Richard over the family furniture, reveals an inflexibility that could arouse friction between family members. In Richard's reaction to the financial claim of his late brother's widow we may also detect a hint of a fiery temperament. William and Robert, in their involvement in the Cumberland rugby crisis, showed similar traits and took actions that may have been highly principled but were hardly wise. William was willing to sacrifice his glittering rugby career rather than bend to the authority of the administrators of the game. And yet, as a schoolmaster, he must have valued discipline and authority. He is also described as being modest and having a kindly temperament, ideally suited to his professional role. There were many facets to the characters of the Graham brothers.

The long exile of Richard's wife, Bella, from the farm suggests another conflict between the brothers, though in this case the cause of the discord is harder to define. But the rifts within the family were usually healed. Richard and Robert managed to run the farm together; John and Richard were reconciled after the furniture dispute.

Where did these characteristics come from? How far back in the family line do they go? We may only wonder what conflicts beset earlier generations of the family and how they were resolved.

The opinions held by members of the family were shaped, not only by inherited characteristics and by their upbringing, but also by the social values of the day. We might detect that the values held by the Grahams in the early nineteenth century were both liberal and philanthropic – Thomas's donation to the Bible Society, his nephew's support for the Reform Society. Such inclinations may have been influenced by the values of the Quaker Sharp family. In later years both 'Whitrigg John' and his son Robert became involved with the Board of Guardians. Victorian benevolence was not always sincere but we must hope that the Graham family's charitable work was inspired by the best of motives.

A biological family line pays no heed to names. If people are biologically related they will have shared characteristics regardless of their surnames. But, since this is a history of a family, the family name is important to us. If Margaret Graham had, in 1814, chosen a different suitor instead of one with the same surname then the story would have been very different.

Researching family history is rewarding but it also has its frustrations. Answers can sometimes lead to new questions that lie beyond the reach of practical research. Is it likely that Margaret Graham was already related to the man she married in 1814? Their shared surname proves nothing but we might wonder how a young woman from Knockupworth Hall with a Quaker background became acquainted with a city spirit merchant. And was their son, John, already related to his bride, Mary Little? We know from his will that John had cousins called Little – probably on his father's side. Did the former spirit merchant, now installed as yeoman at Knockupworth, offer employment to the daughter of one of his relatives? And did that offer result in a teenage girl making the journey from Bewcastle to bring her weaving skills to the farm? We have insufficient information about this Thomas Graham to be able to trace his family. And with names as common in the area as Graham and Little it would be wrong to assume any such connections.

We think of the Victorians as having large families. The Grahams were not typical. The eighteenth century Thomas Graham fathered at least seven children by two different wives but after him offspring were sparse. This was sometimes because one or other partner had a very short life, but 'Weaver' John and Hannah Sharp were married for over twenty years, yet had only two children – at least there were only two who lived to be baptised. And for two generations the family line became a very fragile thread. If Margaret's consumptive son had not lived just long enough to father a son of his own, or if that son had succumbed to one of the many childhood illnesses that were prevalent at the time, the thread would have been broken, the line would have ended and the story would not have been told.

Jane Sewell, herself one of a large family, produced four healthy sons and would very likely have had more if her husband had not died in his mid-thirties. In the end it was not mortality but economic reality that brought an end to the story of Knockupworth.

The Graham name lived on, though less assuredly than might be supposed from the progeny of four brothers who all lived to adulthood.

Robert was unmarried. Richard had a son and a daughter; his son, Dick, had two daughters but no sons, so through Richard's line the name of Graham has also died out. John's surviving son, Jack, had children: a boy with the forenames John Ramsey and a daughter named Agnes Ann Isabel, but known as Inez. In his will John gives his son's address as Montrose, Angus, but I have no further knowledge of what has become of this branch of the family. Despite his early death, William had more children than any of his brothers but only two of them had offspring of their own. His youngest son, Lionel had several children but most were girls. So while there are descendants of the Knockupworth family who still bear the name of Graham they are perhaps not so very numerous.

In 2010 my daughter, Katherine, and a friend were walking along the Hadrian's Wall Footpath, which passes through Grinsdale. The owners at that time had, for a number of years, run Knockupworth Hall as a guesthouse, offering bed and breakfast to weary travellers. Katherine decided that she would like to spend one night in her 'ancestral home'.

While there she told the owners of her connection with the house. They recalled that another member of the Graham family had been there in the past and had left a telephone number. It was a London number. When Katherine returned to her home in London she rang the number.

Michael Graham is a grandson of William Sharp Graham. He is the son of William's third son, George Desmond. His father used to talk of childhood visits to his uncles' farm at Knockupworth and once, while staying in the Lake District, Michael and his wife, Philippa, had looked out the house, talked to the owners and left their number in case anyone else should make enquiries.

About twelve years had passed. Fortunately the same owners were still at the Hall; they had kept the number and remembered that earlier visit. I have now met Michael a number of times. He is a professor in the Faculty of Engineering at Imperial College. Like his grandfather, he studied mathematics at Clare College, Cambridge. His father studied medicine at the same college.

By a remarkable coincidence, while on holiday in Cornwall many years ago, Michael and his family had met and become friendly with a former teacher of mine and had visited him on a number of occasions at his home in Ponteland, the Northumberland village where I grew up. My mother was still living there. They must have been within about a mile or two of each other but they never met.

In the early eighteen-twenties a canal was dug from east to west across Knockupworth land. A few years later it was drained and a railway line was laid along its route. Only traces remain of these once innovative transport links. Grinsdale Bridge, with its sharp turns and blind corners is now a totally unnecessary motoring hazard. But in the twenty-first century a new transport link has appeared. An extension of the A689 takes traffic from the south-west to the north of Carlisle, avoiding the need to drive through the city. A roundabout has been built only yards from the Knockupworth farmhouse. This new road has transformed the landscape. It has divided most of the farmland from the buildings that were once the home of the Grahams. A new farmhouse has been built on the 'cnoc' – the hill from which Knockupworth gets its name.

The changes at Grinsdale Church are, as yet, more subtle and, even when the building is converted, will not be observed by many. When the gravestones are moved to their new positions along the churchyard's eastern wall, the few casual visitors may be unaware that they no longer mark the resting places of the people they commemorate – though the more knowledgeable may wonder why the oldest memorials are not in their traditional location on the southern side of the church.

The closure of St. Kentigern's can be attributed to various causes: dwindling congregations, the building's inconvenient location and the Church of England's need to manage its finances.

The sale of Knockupworth Hall, together with the farmhouse and its land, was also the result of several factors. The early death in 1872 of the last real farmer among the Grahams was undoubtedly a pivotal moment in the family's history. His sons were unable to provide either the necessary expertise or the significant financial investment to make the farm a success. Robert's death was the final straw.

But the two events, almost eighty years apart, had one common feature. The ending of worship at St. Kentigern's and the Grahams' loss of tenure of the land they had owned for one hundred and seventy years were both portended by an outbreak of the disastrous cattle condition known as foot and mouth disease.

My research into the Graham family was largely inspired by four questions. All have been answered, at least in part. The last question

– the reason for William Sharp Graham's middle name – takes us right back into the eighteenth century and the marriage of John Graham, a farmer involved in the production of linen, and a young Quaker woman from Thurstonfield. It seems unlikely that William would be named after his great-great-grandmother but at least we have established the connection between the Graham and Sharp families and we have speculated on a more specific reason for his name.

We have discovered that Hannah, who died at sixteen, and John, who died six years later at the age of twenty-three, were siblings. They were not, as we had first supposed, the children of the Thomas Graham whose name is inscribed on the first Grinsdale headstone but of Thomas's sister, Margaret. Their father was indeed called Thomas Graham but he came from a different Graham family.

And we have not only identified the elusive widow of twenty-three year old John, we have also traced her life story and found her final resting place.

This has been the story of a family. Several of its members suffered early deaths; few had an opportunity to know many of their ancestors or descendants. But as part of a family line they shared common characteristics. They have in them what Hardy calls:

> 'The eternal thing in man,
> That heeds no call to die.'

No matter if they are buried beneath the soil of Grinsdale churchyard, in a Liverpool cemetery, among Commonwealth War Graves, or if they lie elsewhere, they share with those who are still living that common identity that defines their history.

Postscript

I had almost finished writing this history when work began to convert Grinsdale Church into a dwelling. Seven headstones have been relocated. Five of them have been removed to create a parking space in the oldest part of the graveyard. These include the two Graham memorials and the one dedicated to James Robson and his family. As well as the five Georgian and early Victorian memorials, two twentieth century headstones have also been moved to make way for a new gate into the area of land that is still to be used as a burial ground.

The gravestones have all been positioned along the east wall of the churchyard, each one at right angles to the wall and with a spacing of 1.25 metres between them. This arrangement, rather than placing them with their backs to the wall, means that the inscription to the last John Graham, which is on the reverse of the stone, can still be read. The spacing is intended to enable the stones to be viewed without giving a false impression that they mark actual graves.

These changes mean that the description I included in Chapter 1 is now out of date. However, I have decided not to rewrite it. Instead I have left it as a record of how Grinsdale churchyard remained for over two hundred years and as a reminder of what has been lost.

Bibliography

Armstrong A.M., Mawer A., Stenton F.M. and Dickens B., *The Place Names of Cumberland, Part 1. Eskdale, Cumberland and Leath Wards* (1943)

Bradshaw, George, *Bradshaw's Descriptive Railway Handbook of Great Britain and Ireland, 1861* (1901 edition)

Brown, Richard, *Church and State in Modern Britain 1700–1850* (1991)

Bulmer, T & Co, *History, Topography and Directory of Cumberland* (1901 Edition)

Byrne, Paula, *Perdita, The Life of Mary Robinson* (2004)

Dobson, Revd. G.N., *Grinsdale Parish Church, the history of one of Cumbria's smallest parishes* (1981)

Downs, Jonathan, *The Industrial Revolution, Britain 1770–1810* (2010)

Knight, Roger, *Britain Against Napoleon: the organisation of victory 1793–1815* (2013)

Palin, Michael, *Erebus, The Story of a Ship* (2018)

Platt, Jane, (ed.), *Chancellor Walter Fletcher's Diocesan Book with additional material from Bishop Percy's parish notebooks* (2015)

Sacks, Janet, *Victorian Country Life* (2012)

Towill, Sydney, *Church and State in Diocese of Carlisle, A Spiritual and Temporal History 1559–1900* (2000)

Towill, Sydney, *Georgian and Victorian Carlisle* (1996)

Trevelyan, G.M., English Social History (1944)

Uglow, Jenny, *In These Times* (2004)

White, Stephen, *Solway Steam* (1984)

Williamson, W.A., *Local Etymology, or Names and Places in the British Isles* (1849)

Poetry

Crabbe, George, 'Letter 4, Religious Sects', from *The Borough* (1810)

Hardy, Thomas, 'Heredity', from *Moments of Vision* (1917)

Online Articles

Barrigan, Alice, North Yorkshire History, northyorkshirehistory.blogspot.uk (2014)

Hodgson, Barrie Bell, josephbellengineer.wordpress.com
Mayer, Nancy, www.regencyresearcher.com
Mitchinson, Petra, Carlisle Journal 1845 – The GRAHAM Poisoning Cases (2014)
Oxford Archaelogy North, 2011, Knockupworth Farm, Burgh by Sands, Cumbria Archaeological evaluation report.
Shannon, Bill, John Ainslie's plan of Solway Moss – Recording a lost landscape. British Library's Picturing Places (2016)
various (regarding World War I), www.freewebs.com/7borderandyeo/5thterrier1.htm
Woolnough, Guy, Blood Sports in Victorian Cumbria – Journal of Victorian Culture online, Keele University (2014)

Online Sources

British Newspaper Archive
CASCAT – the Cumbria Archive Service Catalogue
Family Search (records of births, marriages and deaths)
Find My Past (census records, records of births, marriages and deaths)
General Register Office (birth, marriage and death certificates)

Research carried out in person at:

Cumbria Archive Centre, Lady Gillford's House, Carlisle (parish registers, wills, deeds and other documents)

Acknowledgements

I am indebted to the following for the many ways in which they have assisted me in writing this book:

My cousin, Ann Thomlinson, for helping me with the research and for her hospitality on my visits to Carlisle.

My wife, Margaret, for understanding my obsession with family history and helping to compile the index.

My daughter, Katherine, and my son, James, for their interest and encouragement; also James, for finding additional information, advising on the manuscript and helping me find Mary Beck's grave; and Katherine, for visiting Knockupworth and putting me in touch with Michael Graham.

My cousin, Iris Currie, for supplying me with family papers.

Matthew Whitfield, for expert historical advice, especially with regard to dating buildings.

Petra Mitchinson, for her transcripts of the Grinsdale murder trial reports, on which Chapter 14 is based, and for putting me in touch with Bridget Casson.

Bridget Casson, for her transcripts of memorial inscriptions, for other pieces of information and for putting me in touch with Liz Johnson.

Liz Johnson, for information about the Beck family and for allowing me to use family photographs.

Michael Graham, for information about the family of his grandfather, W.S. Graham.

Alice Barrigan, whose North Yorkshire History blog provided me with some details about the family that I might otherwise have missed.

David Thomlinson, for background information about the technicalities of Rugby Union.

Robert Currie, for giving me some different perspectives on the family history.

Kevin McEwen for his interest and advice.

The helpful staff of the Cumbria Archive Centre in Carlisle.

Stephen White of Carlisle Library.

The team at Carnegie Scotforth for their help, creativity and professionalism in producing the book.

List of Illustrations

16. Family group outside Knockupworth Hall; left to right, William, Mary Sewell, John, Jane, Robert

17. John Graham (1864–1948)

18. R.H. Graham (1865–1922)

19. Richard Graham (1867–1935)

20. W.S. Graham (1870–1920)

21. Inscription inside poetry anthology presented to R.H. Graham

22. John Graham (on right) with bank employee outside Aspatria branch

23. Isabella Holmes/Graham

24. Knockupworth Farmhouse; Isabella Holmes and son Edward on right

25. Harvest at Knockupworth; R.H. Graham on far right; Isabella Holmes and son Edward, third from left.

26. Cyril and Jack Graham

27. Cyril Graham

28. Richard and Robert Graham

29. John Graham with shorthorn bull

30. Phyllis and Dick Graham

Index